AND
REPLENISH
THE EARTH

HARPER & ROW, Publishers

HARPER & ROW, Publishers

New York   Evanston   San Francisco   London

AND
REPLENISH
THE EARTH
the evolution, consequences,
and prevention of overpopulation

MICHAEL L. ROSENZWEIG

University of New Mexico

Cover illustration: Marion Seawell, 3491 Sacramento
St., San Francisco. Copyright
1971. All rights reserved.

Sponsoring Editor: Joseph Ingram
Project Editor: Holly Detgen
Designer: Frances Torbert Tilley
Production Supervisor: Robert A. Pirrung

And Replenish the Earth: The Evolution, Consequences, and Prevention of Overpopulation

Library of Congress Cataloging in Publication Data
Rosenzweig, Michael L.
  And replenish the earth.

  Bibliography: p.
  1. Population. 2. Evolution. I. Title.
[DNLM: 1. Evolution. 2. Population growth. HB851
R816a 1974]
HB871.R68   301.32   73-13304
ISBN 0-06-045589-6

48,632

To the women of my family, especially to my mother Phyllis Fine Rosenzweig, of blessed memory. May my daughters transport the burden of our fitness into the future with as much joy, success, and goodness as the generations of their mothers have shown in getting it this far.

Whoever is wise should know these things;
Who is prudent should understand them
For the pathways of the Lord are right
and the righteous shall walk in them.
But transgressors shall stumble therein.

Hosea xiv: 10

Well-fed men are capable of understanding
a great deal. . . .

Mowat

contents

preface xi

▯ some principles of population ecology

1   the limited universe   3
2   natural limits to population growth   9
3   the robust balance of nature   22
4   the momentum of population growth   36

▯▯ the human condition: a résumé

5   symptoms of overpopulation in humanity   43
6   prepare to live in China   63
7   the roots of human population growth   68

▯▯▯ goals

8   on optimal population density: a new freedom   79
9   animalistic do-nothingism   82

ix

evolution

10 evolution has occurred   91
11 the theory of evolution by natural selection   126
12 genetics for readers of this book   135
13 testing Darwin's theory: are deductions and assumptions
real?   145
14 the role of mutation in evolution   178
15 adaptation: main product of evolution   200
16 group selection and the evolution of survival   218
17 the evolution of diversity   233

 methods of population control

18 a method that won't work and another that shouldn't
be allowed to   265
19 two practical, maximally moral programs   271

bibliography   281

answers to problems   293

index   295

preface

The well-intentioned ecological doomsday warnings of some of my colleagues have certainly gotten people's attention. But attention is not action. Even if doomsday were indicated, which it is not, it would be wiser to lie and say things aren't that bad. People tend to put doomsday out of their minds.

Since doomsday is not likely anyhow, it is unquestionably our duty and this book's function to tell the whole, simple truth: Overpopulation and ecological insanity are not likely to produce the total extinction of man. Instead, their result will be treatable calamity: massive increases in famine and disease coupled with destruction of our way of life and its replacement by a sparse, bleak, marginal existence in which disease and deprivation will culminate in a permanently higher death rate—especially among infants and children. Surely most people will agree that is worth avoiding.

Although veracity, strict and simple, is a chief goal of this book, it is not enough, because real students (however old) are unhappy at being told "just the facts." These are the critical minds of our civilization. They are uncomfortable unless they understand the reasoning behind the conclusions. And they are always ready to attack and improve a weak argument. Since such people are the only hope for a rational, civilized future, I have written this book for them.

Almost one hundred years ago, Charles S. Peirce, in his article "On the Fixation of Belief" (*Popular Science Monthly*, 1877), pointed out that the world contains more than one kind of truth and that people decide what is true in more than one way. He preferred the scientific method for arriving at one class of truths: measurable, testable truths. Most thinking people agree with him.

While scientific truth is not moral truth, it does help us in making moral decisions. We often use science to predict the material consequences of this or that act. Then we can evaluate the consequences on a nonscientific, moral basis.

Perhaps we should use science this way more often. I think so. But we cannot if, when educating ourselves, we only pay lip service to the scientific method of attaining scientific truth. The most difficult responsibility of any scientific educator is to help people achieve a working knowledge of this method. It is my belief that a textbook should further this goal by presenting detailed summaries of the evidence that has led science to its current knowledge.

Certainly a book's bibliography should be an important adjunct in presenting evidence. To accomplish this, I have included in the Bibliography books of general interest (which are starred) and references to many *Scientific American* articles readily available as offprints. Furthermore, the bulk of the Bibliography is composed of the highly detailed and specialized references which are in fact the sources of this book. The reader should know and be aware that this book is an eclectic summary of the highly individualistic, creative investigations of a veritable army of scientist-thinkers. The most serious student will want to refer to them directly. In the Bibliography, I have tried to make it as easy as possible for that student to track his quarry.

Perhaps my desire to show at least some of the reasoning involved in each conclusion has resulted in the omission of your favorite topic. If so, it is not that I thought it unimportant. It is simply that I chose to develop a smaller number of topics at greater length. Only then can we approximate scientific evidence and argumentation in the brief space allotted to me and the brief time allotted to you.

Evolution itself is almost the perfect topic for illustrating the scientific process. Of course, like any science, it contains mostly half-solved and unsolved problems; I have not tried to avoid them. In addition, not only does evolution depend on empirical observation and experimentation, but also, its history is replete with important theories. It demonstrates the usefulness of theory and the process of theorizing to a degree equaled by no other biological science. Furthermore, its tenets and rational conclusions have stirred up irrational opposition in a manner that clearly juxtaposes these two ways of assessing reality.

The reason evolution has created such controversy is far from trivial. Evolution, unlike any other science save cosmology, is at the heart of the way in which man views himself and his world. For this reason, if for no other, every student deserves a firm grounding in evolutionary science. There is just a chance, albeit a slim one, that knowledge of evolution is one of the ingredients that help make minds humble in confrontation with nature and peaceful, tolerant, and brotherly in dealing with other men. We shall need both attitudes if civilization is to survive the next several generations.

Despite the overwhelming importance of the foregoing two motives for teaching evolution to all sorts of college students early in their careers, neither is as important as the following. In order to deal with the biological problems of the world (especially overpopulation), men will have to know what to expect of evolution. That is the primary reason for the very large section on evolution in this book. Because the evolutionary knowledge required to deal with future problems is knowledge of processes rather than history, I have dwelt heavily on evolutionary mechanics while neglecting fossil history. There is also some justification for this rather cavalier treatment of the marvelous job of paleontology in the fact that many superb books and articles are available to guide students in learning by themselves what I have of necessity omitted (see, for example, Colbert's *Age of Reptiles* or Romer's *Vertebrate Story*). On the other hand, this book is one of the very first attempts at dealing with evolutionary mechanics in a critical manner while using no more mathematics than ninth-grade algebra.

By the way, please don't skip the algebra. Granted it must be read slowly, pencil in hand, working through every step. But it is worth it, because the opportunity to use algebra is an opportunity all too rare in biological curricula. Besides, in the algebra lies much of the evidence that evolution *ought* to occur.

To a very great extent, this book is the result of my eagerness to play the role of tail to lions (in the sense of Pirke Avot iv:20). Little if any is new; most is the result of my association with my teachers. Among them, Elwyn Simons and Ward Goodenough deserve my special gratitude for introducing me to the fossil record. The late S. L. Blank tried heroically (as was his wont) for five stimulating years to acquaint me with the art of biblical interpretation.

On November 1, 1972, my chief teacher died at age 42. Robert MacArthur was a giant intellect, a true lion; and he was sincerely mourned by a much larger group of scientists than his students. He revolutionized ecology by showing how intimate is the relationship between ecology and evolution. As I read over this text, there is almost nothing in it that I did not learn—at least in principle—at his feet.

Many others must share credit for helping me directly with this book. Harold Blum saved me from some pages I had naively written. K. E. F. Watt, Steven Fretwell, and Barbara Smigel read Section IV and offered valuable advice. Sister Mary de Porres Owens had worthwhile and encouraging things to say about the mathematical chapters. Earl Luby noticed that I had written Chapter 11 backwards and helped as much as humanly possible to unmuddle the organization. Robert D. Allen deserves my thanks for administering the emetic that drew this book from me. Finally, Alvin Abbott and Sterling Swift of Harper & Row contributed important ideas that played a large part in determining what is included between these covers.

Some large sections of this book were written "on location" at Cranberry

Lake Biological Station of the State University of New York and at the Mile-Hi, Ramsey Canyon, Arizona. Thanks for these retreats of sanity and solitude to Donald McNaught, director of Cranberry Lake, and to Carroll and Joan Peabody, owners of the Mile-Hi.

Another institution, the University of New Mexico's Biology Department, has been most supportive. Thanks to its chairman, Paul Silverman, this book's debut has probably been sped by a whole year. Mary Montano diligently struggled to obtain the final typescript.

I have appreciated the audiences over the years who have listened patiently to me. Their probing questions greatly influenced the style and content of this book. Their rational response gave me the courage and optimism to write it.

If this book contributes sufficiently to the education of its readership so that it helps to lead to an ecologically rational society, it will be thanking another person, my father, Dr. Max Rosenzweig. He was intensely disappointed by my abrupt decision to reject a medical education for an ecological one. Remember, that was in 1961 when ecology was only a Greek word which most people didn't understand even after it was translated for them. I feel sure he must have thought that I was committing the most profligate waste of a human life—not to mention the instantaneous dissipation of all the money he had spent on my education. Perhaps he will never be truly happy with my choice. However, it should be somewhat palliative for him to realize that if this book contributes even a tiny bit to the construction of a society where effective population control is practiced, it will have contributed to the saving of countless more lives than ever I could have as a physician.

At this point—the last gasp of the preface—most authors finally thank their spouses for suffering in silence during the labor pains involved in whelping a book. Indeed, a monster I have often been—sometimes by neglectfulness, sometimes by short temperedness. However, I do not thank my wife, Carole, for suffering in silence (she doesn't anyhow); instead, I apologize to her. What I do thank her for is help. Substantial, crucial help. She actively participated in the creation of this book and her critical reactions were quite influential at every stage.

But I have not neglected her entirely. We have three marvelous children. Yes, three, of whom she is the natural mother and I the natural father. You might as well hear that from me as from Jack Anderson. Do we feel guilty? No. And our lack of guilt feelings does not come because we are latter-day converts to the cause of a stable population size. We know of *and believed* in the principles in this book even before we conceived our first child.

Now, here I am putting in my two cents after our family is complete at three children. Trying to deprive everyone else of the pleasure of a third child. But remember, I am a father. And what I hope will happen is likely to affect my children. Do not accuse me of having no feeling for them.

Before you criticize me, read the book. Then, fire away. I will surely deserve the largest fraction of the brickbats directed at me. But, please, do not allow your rejection of my character or writing style to interfere with your objective appraisal of the ideas contained in the book. After all, virtually none is mine.

M.L.R.

some principles of population ecology

Nature . . . has the patience to endure insult, yet always wins in the end. . . . It does not command; but all eventually obey.

Lao Tzu, LXXIII

1 the limited universe

THE MYTH OF PRODUCTION

One of the cherished myths of American civilization is that nothing is impossible. This attitude is based on our experience with the marvels that scientists and technologists have worked in the past century. We fly. We escape the Earth's gravitational field and land on the moon. We cure scarlet fever and tuberculosis. We perform heart transplants and talk about engineering our inheritance. Thanks to our internal combustion engines, we speed hundreds of miles on pleasure trips that our forefathers in their horse-drawn vehicles undertook only when paid or forced. Refrigeration brings us fresh fruit and vegetables quickly and safely from faraway places—even in the dead of winter—and keeps it safe in our climatized homes. Our clothing is made of synthetic fabric with special labor-saving qualities. Science pampers us, cures us, entertains us, and amazes us. It seems foolish to say that anything is beyond its capacity.

If, however, you should ask a scientist if he thinks anything is impossible, he would answer, "Of course. Certainly."

"What?" you would ask, definitely surprised by his lack of hesitation and his uncharacteristic decisiveness. "Well," he would continue, "there are certain basic principles of physics which set upper limits to the possible. For example, Einstein showed us that matter cannot travel faster than the speed of light in a vacuum (186,300 miles per second). And then there are some important rules called the laws of thermodynamics. The first one says that the universe has a constant amount of matter and energy. A corollary of this is that no one can hope to create new matter and energy (or destroy old). The second law of thermodynamics says that if it takes a certain amount of energy to do a job, more than that amount will have to be spent to do it! In other words, energy is always wasted; never is it used 100% efficiently."

By now you might suspect your leg was being pulled for having asked so stupid a question. You would interrupt. "Wait. Let's go back to that first law of thermodynamics. You say that energy cannot be created. Yet our electric company is even now building a plant to produce new electrical power for 100,000 families."

The scientist would not laugh at your having caught him in his little joke. Instead, maintaining his serious tone, he would shift to a lower gear and continue his explanation. But now he would realize that his words were slashing away at the fabric of your secure, naive outlook on life.

"No one 'produces' electricity or any other form of energy. 'Produce' is a misnomer. What an electric company does is take existing energy in the form of coal or a rushing river and convert it to electrical energy. Occasionally it may take uranium and break down its atoms to release the energy stored there; that is atomic energy. But it never really produces anything new. It merely transforms what already exists into a different form, a form more useful and convenient for humans. This is a general rule: Technology creates nothing of substance. It can only transform existing resources into things that people perceive as better. It is the processes and knowledge of **transformation** that have improved with the industrial and atomic revolutions."

ENERGY AND LIFE

The impossibilities of physics have biological implications which are crucial for this book and for human society. The most important is that every population must eventually stop growing. Otherwise it would come to need more energy than the universe's total supply.

What does energy have to do with living things? Like everything else, living things get something only as a trade for something else. When they grow, when they move, when they reproduce, they are required to spend energy in trade.

Energy is measured in various units. The one that people usually use to express their own energetic requirements is called the calorie. A small calorie is the amount of heat energy required to raise the temperature of 1 gram of distilled water from $15°$ centigrade to $16°$ centigrade at standard atmospheric pressure. The dietary calorie or kilocalorie (which we usually just call Calorie) is actually 1000 of these small calories.

In order just to live each day we must each spend a certain minimum number of calories; more are necessary the more active we are. It is not wrong to think of *buying* each day of our lives with the energy obtained from our food. Running up a caloric bill and delaying its payment is generally called starvation. But the body sends no warning letters; it immediately begins to repossess. It breaks down the tissues, which cost energy to build and which contain large amounts of energy stored in complex chemical molecules. First goes fat. Then muscle itself yields its energy reserves. Ultimately the bad debtor is punished with death.

Primitive civilized man paid his caloric debts solely with coin of the sun. The sun's radiant energy is collected by plants through a process called photosynthesis. The large, energy-rich molecules of plants are then eaten by other forms of life for their energy content. Man refined this process slightly by allowing his favorite plants and animals free use of the fields and pastures which he controlled. There they grew and could be harvested efficiently.

Even man's tools were fashioned in fires of wood, fires whose energy comes from the photosynthetic activity of trees. So also did man heat his home. And what transported him? His draft animals got their energy from eating the plants, which "fed" on the sunlight streaming down on them. Moreover, the wind that powered his sailing ships derives its motion from heat of the sun.

ENERGY AND CIVILIZATION

Modern industrial man has not abandoned the use of the sun. We have not yet found a way to convert our bodies to the use of coal or oil or electricity, and only plants and animals can now synthesize the fuels we can consume. But we have decreased our reliance on solar coin by learning to use the energy stored in the fossil fuels: coal, oil, and gas. These fuels operate machinery which does many of the jobs formerly done with solar energy. By heating our homes, we need to spend less solar energy in warming our bodies. By using tractors and other machines, we decrease the animal (and human) labors necessary to grow our food, move us about, and do our work. The American of today needs considerably less food for himself than did his grandfather. And feeding a horse is, for most Americans, a luxury, not a necessity. Today we feed our automobiles, vacuum cleaners, furnaces, and dishwashers instead of ourselves and our horses.

The U.S. Bureau of Mines publishes figures reporting the use of nonfood energy in America. Compare the figures for 1968 with those projected for the year 2000 (quoted in Mills, Johnson, and Perry). Figures are in quadrillions of British Thermal Units (a BTU is 0.25222 kilocalories).

Year	Coal	Gas and oil	Atomic	Water
1968	13.4	46.7	0.13	2.4
2000	26.2	93.3	5.1	38.1

Notice that we will require a vast increase in all nonfood energy. The highest proportional increase is projected in nuclear energy, after that, in energy from hydroelectric power plants. But the biggest actual increases are needed in the fossil fuels, which will remain our mainstays.

The fact that fossil fuels are so desperately needed by modern man is chilling. Anyone who has ever burned a tank of gasoline is aware that the gasoline does not reappear as a form of rain. It is gone forever. Fossil fuels are all like that; they aren't merely used; they are consumed. Most were formed in a restricted geological era called the Carboniferous, over 200 million years ago (see Chapter 10). That was an age in which, for some reason, the energy of plants was not fully utilized by their consumers. Dead plants were buried in the Earth's crust and gradually changed to coal and oil. There they lay—an untapped, fossilized bank account—waiting for man to invent keys to their vaults and find ways to spend them.

Like the single tankful of gasoline and like any true bank account, these fossil fuels are limited. Eventually we shall have used them entirely, since no deposits are currently being made. (Even if we could make deposits, we'd have to obtain the energy to deposit from some other source. None is now abundant enough.) How long will our fossil fuels last, then? The most consistent guess is several centuries. But most of what is left is coal. Many believe that oil and gas will be gone much sooner, in only decades (Watt). It is likely that recent gasoline and heating oil shortages are only mild harbingers of much worse.

Since we now depend on fossil fuels for life itself, we cannot shrug off their eventual loss. Just to support a human population the size that the world *now* has, requires some nonfood energy. We have already over-produced to the point where we cannot live on our energetic income but are dependent on capital. Scientists are hard at work trying to control the H-bomb reaction (nuclear fusion) so that the ocean's almost limitless supply of heavy water (deuterium water) can be used to give us the energy we already know we will need. Our grandchildren or great-grandchildren have already been saddled with heavy energetic debts which we can only *hope* they will be able to pay. It seems irresponsible to increase that debt further by enlarging our population.

WASTE: INEVITABLE

The second law of thermodynamics teaches us an equally important lesson about the real limits of energy. Recall that the second law is that some energy is always wasted in any process in which it is used. A good illustration of this is the ecological food chain: Plants fix solar energy; herbivores consume plant energy; carnivores consume herbivore energy. At each transfer much of the energy is wasted.

One of the best examples of this process was worked out 30 years ago by Raymond Lindemann. Lindemann studied the life of Cedar Bog Lake in Minnesota. There, the important plants are pondweeds and floating algae; the herbivores are fly larvae, pond snails, and small animals called rotifers; and the important carnivores are other fly larvae, minnows, and leeches. Kozlovsky revised Lindemann's data according to modern standards and discovered that herbivores got only 14% of the plant energy and carnivores got only 18.4% of the herbivore energy. The carnivores thus got only 2.6% as much energy as the plants because of the principle of waste. Recently other workers have obtained somewhat different results for food chains. Lindemann efficiencies in the Black Sea ranged up to 71% (although that figure is extraordinary and most Lindemann efficiencies in Black Sea groups are about 20%), according to Petipa, Pavlova, and Mironov. But an efficiency of 71% does not violate the second law, which insists only that efficiency be less than 100%. High as it is, 71% still means 29% waste.

The important lesson is that energy flows through the food chain and is dissipated. Even though there is no loss of total energy (first law), there is loss of energy available and useful for paying life's costs. This special energy is called free energy. The second law can be stated: In any energy transfer some free energy is lost. This makes energy a unique resource. Other resources, such as water and minerals, can be recycled; energy cannot. We must be satisfied with our energy income and learn to live within our means.

Many have noted (see Giddings and Monroe) that the Earth's human population is not likely to be limited by energy if we can learn to use heavy water. Perhaps. There certainly are other limited resources. But energetic limitation is the only sure limitation. It can not be evaded. The reader must dismiss from his mind the myth that all things are possible, and energetic limitation provides an ironclad reason for doing so.

STRUGGLING WITH EARTHLY LIMITS

An engineer (Fremlin) suggests that we may one day increase our supply of solar energy by hanging mirrors on space satellites to reflect more sunshine to our Earth's surface. But since both sunshine and warm bodies bring with them a large amount of heat, he calculates another kind of limit that will be reached: the limit imposed by the need to air-condition our entire planet. The devices he dreams up to get rid of our heat are truly science fiction: Ultimately he has the Earth surrounded entirely by a thin metal radiator to dissipate the heat into space. When the human population of the Earth grows to 20 million times its present size, the radiator is forced to operate at temperatures near that of the sun's surface, and the human population stops growing. Fremlin does not discuss how we are to see the sun through the radiator.

The only other alternative to being satisfied with our Earth's energy income is to leave the Earth. "Colonize the planets," say those who would like to believe that space travel is much the same as the voyage of the *Mayflower*. It is not.

Firstly, we now know of no planet with a hospitable environment. People would be better off on Antarctica than on Mars. There probably are hospitable planets in our galaxy, but the nearest one is at *least* light years away. (A light year is about 6,000,000,000,000 miles, the distance a photon of light can travel through a vacuum in one year.) Since a manned spacecraft has to accelerate and decelerate, even with an incredibly advanced space technology, it is highly unlikely that those who leave the Earth would spend less than 50 or 100 years in reaching the nearest of these planets (wherever it is). And while enroute, there could be no question of anything but a *strictly controlled policy of birth limitation* (Hardin, 1959). What a shame if the voyagers would arrive at their new home only to find it already peopled.

Secondly, the Earth's population is now growing at the rate of almost 100 million per year. Can you imagine what it would cost to export (deport is a better word) 100 million people a year? Garrett Hardin has calculated that the gross national product of the United States for a whole year would pay for exporting only one day's growth in human population! And he assumes a vastly more sophisticated and less expensive space technology than is now available.

Thirdly, even ignoring the monetary costs, there are energy costs. At the velocity he needs to escape the Earth's gravity, a 140 pound human has 63,000 kilocalories of kinetic energy. And each 140 pounds of his spacecraft has the same amount of kinetic energy. This only gets him off the Earth; it does not supply him with food for his journey or build his spacecraft in the first place, let alone fuel it for the trip. Not only would we be exporting precious energy with our deportees and their ships, we would lose forever the recyclable resources (metals and other minerals) which they would need for their ships and supplies. Every exiled spaceship would really mean that the Earth could actually support fewer people!

Finally, what if we should choose this means to maintain a stable Earthly population? We would still have a stable population. Our growth would be deported. Suppose we deported 1% of our population each year. This would allow each mother to bear about two and one-third children in her lifetime instead of two. And she would have to kiss the one-third goodbye anyway as it boarded the next ship out! What a cost for that extra third: A huge space industry recruiting 100 million people a year (or 20 million, or one billion, or whatever) to spend their lives in the confines of starships searching the universe for empty, hospitable planets. If they *should* find some, what do they (and we back on Earth) do when those planets too are filled with people? We may be unique as a species, but even within us burns the energy-requiring fire of life. The human population cannot possibly grow forever.

natural limits to population growth

Although energy is the ultimate limit for all populations, in practice many populations are limited by other resources. Nature's limits are imposed on populations by forcing individuals to live marginal existences. The individuals suffer personal shortage and catastrophe, and the population's growth ceases.

The collection of limits includes shortages of food, space, and water; the presence of aggressive competitors and predators; the production of harmful chemicals; and the physiological response to the simple stress of living in a dense population. In this chapter we shall examine a small amount of the research that ecologists have performed on these natural limits. In a later chapter we shall examine the human condition and see whether there is any indication that our present population is up against such limits.

LIMIT: NUTRITION

To avoid death and maintain the health required for successful reproduction, a living being requires not only energy, but also special vitamins, minerals, and protein building blocks called amino acids. Evidence of an experimental nature has shown that many populations are limited by lack of enough food to supply adequate nutrition.

Reynoldson worked on a small pond containing a population of flatworms. After careful study, he decided to add extra food to the pond in the form of chopped earthworms. The flatworms ate regularly, and their adult population stayed very high. Adults began to breed more vigorously too: There was a fourfold increase in fed adults' fecundity compared to unfed flatworms.

9

Eisenberg also studied the effect of supplemental food on a pond population. But his object was a vegetarian snail called *Lymnaea elodes*. Eisenberg constructed cages around the margin of a pond to enclose natural populations of the snail. He treated the populations in various ways. In this chapter we shall compare his control populations to two populations which received extra food. (We shall discuss his experiments further in the next chapter.)

The extra food was 20 ounces of frozen spinach per week for six weeks from 19 June to 30 July of one year. The snails ate all the spinach. Its effect was to increase the growth rate of the population immensely. Since the young snails take one year to mature, the effect in the following table is seen only in numbers of eggs and young.

Average number	Control cages (4)	Fed cages (2)
Adults in spring	984	1224
Eggs (per 10 minute search; 10 July)	435	9382
Young (per sample)		
20 July	29.5	255
27 July	10.7	129.5

The few extra adults that happened to be in the fed pens did not account for the tremendous increase in eggs and young (see the next chapter for the data that demonstrate this). The spinach was responsible. Eisenberg notes that there seemed to be plenty of natural food in all cages. Yet, the snails preferred the spinach. Apparently the shortage is not simply calories but the specially nutritious substances in which spinach abounds.

Work with the red grouse in Scotland provides quite a convincing demonstration that a natural population can be limited by food quality and nutrients rather than gross caloric values. Red grouse are vegetarian birds that eat the shoots of the common shrub, heather, *Calluna vulgaris*, which covers moors in Britain and Europe. Two adjacent moors in Scotland both have heather. But they have very different soils. One has a poor soil derived from an acidic granite. The other's soil is rich in nitrogen, phosphorus, and other nutrients, such as cobalt. The heather on the richer moor is itself richer in nutrients and supports twice as dense a grouse population.

Two adjacent 16 hectare (35 acre) plots were established in the poor moor. One of these was kept as a control and did not change much if at all. The other was subjected to various attempts to increase its richness with fertilizer (Wynne-Edwards, 1968). Miller showed that not phosphorus but nitrogen fertilization increased the birds' preference for heather.

In May 1965, the experimental moor was treated with 105 kilograms of nitrogen per hectare (105 pounds per acre). At first the grouse responded with a large increase in fecundity. After two years the population on the fertilized plot had increased to about the same density as on the rich moor. After three years the nitrogen added in 1965 had apparently been used, and the grouse fecundity on the two plots was again the same (Miller, Watson, and Jenkins).

	Fertilized plot		Control plot	
Spring	Grouse/km²	Young per adult	Grouse/km²	Young per adult
1966	44	1.8	44	0.6
1967	112	0.9	44	.0
1968	81	.0	38	.0

These experiments make it clear that not the number of Calories but the amount of nutrient limits the grouse population size. Nitrogen is important because it is needed to build amino acids, and these in turn are used to form all proteins.

Other instances of nutrient limitation are known or suspected. One of the most consequential concerns lakes. When sewage is pumped into a lake the algae—especially the blue-green algae—experience tremendous growth in population (Hasler). The lake becomes a slimy, turgid, stinking mess, and many of the more interesting animals and plants are lost. This process is euphemistically known as eutrophication. Often it appears that eutrophication is produced by the addition of phosphorus (although some lakes appear to be nitrogen limited). Phosphorus is a crucial constituent of living material; among other things, it is a major part of the nucleic acids, which are the bearers of hereditary information and the blueprints for the synthesis of proteins.

Lemming populations in Alaska also appear to be phosphorus limited. Perhaps you have already read about lemmings. They are large arctic versions of the meadow mouse. Every few years they seem to undergo an increase in population followed by a decline. In Scandinavia, when they decline, lemmings sometimes undertake mass migrations. There are reports of whole populations plunging to their deaths off cliffs and into oceans. Such lemmings are apparently phosphorus-starved. We shall return to them in the chapter on group selection and the evolution of survival.

LIMIT: WATER

Durward Allen recounts an interesting tale of wildlife management. Quail need to drink water every day in the summer. But in California, summer is the dry season. Hence, the arid lands of California used to have no quail at all. To remedy this deficiency of water, shafts sloping underground to 650 gallon watering troughs were installed. They were named after their inventor, and called Glading's Gallinaceous Guzzlers. Each guzzler has a concrete apron to catch rainwater during the winter and funnel it below. Birds can march right down and drink their fill. Because the trough is underground, water losses by evaporation are minimal. The guzzlers contain water right through the dry summer.

Where no quail once lived, large coveys of as many as 200 are now common. More than 2600 square miles of California have each received their guzzler. This has produced a new quail population of several hundred thousand. We do not now know what limits the quail population, but as sure as it once was water, it isn't water any more.

LIMIT: SPACE AND TERRITORY

In the rocky intertidal zone between the dry beach and the constantly wet ocean, barnacles in some places literally carpet the rocks. Young barnacle larvae have no space on which to settle. The barnacle population ceases growth simply for lack of space (Connell, 1961).

Individuals of certain species actively prevent others of their species from sharing their homesites. This behavior is called territoriality. Some investigators feel that many populations are limited in nature by lack of more territories. As you shall see, both instances of territoriality and instances of territory shortages are known.

Bustard observed in Australia that the nocturnal arboreal gecko (a lizard) lives during the day in between the bark and the bole of tree stumps. Each stump holds one male and two or three females (average: 2.2 ♀ ♀). Bustard guessed that these geckos are territorial and that their population is kept low because of the shortage of food.

To test his first hypothesis, he designed an artificial tree stump of celluloid and linoleum. An inner core of linoleum turned inside out provided geckos with a grip. Next, a layer of celluloid (separated from the linoleum by wood strips) provided an enclosed space through which observations could be made. The celluloid was enclosed in another layer of linoleum to provide darkness. This layer could be removed quickly to look at the geckos.

Bustard put a pair of geckos into a cage with an escape hatch, lots of cockroaches to eat, and one artificial stump. After one week he added another male. Despite the presence of superabundant food, the new male was ejected the first night in six of eight experiments. In a seventh, it took two nights and in the other experiment, the new male ejected the established resident during the first night. In all cases only one male remained. After the extra male was ejected new females were added one by one until three had been "asked to leave." The first new female was accepted by all but one of the eight pairs. The average number of females in "completed harems" was 2.5, very close to the 2.2 females observed in nature. The next step surely is to put out artificial stumps in nature and see if the gecko population increases. To my knowledge, this has yet to be done for geckos. But it has been done many times for those birds which require a hole in a tree for their nest site.

One such experiment was done in southern Finland by Haartman. There, pied flycatchers are rare because of the scarcity of holes in trees. Constructing and erecting appropriate nest boxes provides the birds with excellent nest sites, and their population responds accordingly. The following censuses show what happened in one experiment. The nest boxes were put up between the 1961 and 1962 breeding seasons.

| | Number of pied flycatchers | |
	1961	1962
Spruce forest	6	104
Pine forest	0	170

Haartman studied one woodland for 30 years and showed that the increase in bird population lasted as long as the nest boxes.

Another long and careful experiment with nest boxes was reported by Kluijver from Holland. Kluijver worked with a small bird called the great tit, *Parus major*. The close relatives of these birds in America are known as titmice and chickadees. Not only did Kluijver show that nest boxes increased the tit population, he also showed that blocking their holes decreased it. Of 40 pairs of great tits, only seven remained after the nest boxes were blocked.

When territories do not involve discrete objects like stumps or holes in trees, it is quite difficult to experiment with them. After all, one cannot double the area of a portion of the face of the Earth the way one can double the number of nesting sites. That is one of the main points of this book. Nevertheless, it can be shown that many territories are in short supply since many birds lack territories. Homeless birds are discovered by removing territory owners and showing that their territories are quickly reoccupied by new birds.

The first experiment of this type was done in 1949 by Stewart and Aldrich. These men were trying to determine if birds ate enough spruce budworms to control this serious insect pest. They hoped to find natural control agents for it so as to avoid application of chemical insecticides to the valuable spruce forests. Their method was to shoot the birds and analyze bird stomach contents. To maximize the information gained from such a sacrifice of bird life, they decided to shoot birds in one small woodland (instead of over a wider area) and see if the empty territories would be reoccupied by homeless birds.

They worked in a 40 acre experimental area and maintained a 30 acre control area 1.25 miles away. When they began, there were 148 adult males of various species. From 15 June to 8 July they shot 420 adult birds—more than had originally lived in the forest—and many territories still had residents, new males occupying territories "in the same places that were occupied by their predecessors." In the first nine days of their removal experiment, they managed to reduce the population to 28 males by shooting 142 birds. But in the second two weeks, birds were moving in as fast as they were being shot. No further reduction in the census took place.

Moreover, in 1950, Hensley and Cope repeated the same experiment in the same place. When they censused, they actually found **more** birds (154 adult males) than had lived there before the shoot of 1949. They destroyed 528 birds from 14 June to 10 July, 1950, and they weren't even able to make as large a dent in the resident population as Stewart and Aldrich had the previous year. This showed that in 1950, territories were in even more demand than they had been in 1949 and that territories, not shooting, were what was influencing the population. Since those early experiments, many other investigators have confirmed that territories are indeed in short supply.

LIMIT: TOXINS

Individuals of some species of plants produce special poisons or toxic waste products. When they get too numerous, the plants kill each other off. Such poisons may have evolved as a kind of territorial defense for plants. The plant needs to preserve a supply of soil for its nutrient and water supply. It must keep out not only others of its own species, but others of other species.

Wilson and Rice studied the action of sunflowers in inhibiting the growth and germination of other plants which are normally found nearby. In one experiment (Table 2-1) they tested sunflower leaves for toxic properties. They took a realistic amount of decaying sunflower leaves and spread it on pots of soil. Seeds of various species were sown in those pots and were allowed to germinate and to grow into seedlings. Then, the seedlings were dried and weighed. Controls, without sunflower leaves in the pots, were also tried. (In Table 2-1, the average germination ratio is the percentage of seeds that germinated in the test pots divided by the percentage that germi-

TABLE 2-1 EFFECT OF SUNFLOWER LEAVES ON GROWTH AND GERMINATION

Seeds tested	Was growth stunted? Average dry weight of seedlings (mg)		Was germination prevented? Average germination ratio test/control
	control	test	
Sunflower			
(Helianthus annuus)	40	21.5	0.46
Horseweed			
(Conyza canadensis)	43	17.5	0.79
Crabgrass			
(Digitaria sanguinalis)	111.5	13.5	1.015
Jimmyweed			
(Haplopappus ciliatus)	19.5	9	0.675
Wire grass			
(Aristida oligantha)	17	22	0.995

Source: Wilson and Rice.

nated in the control pots; thus, a ratio significantly less than 1.00 indicates inhibition by sunflower leaves.)

As you can see from the dry weights of seedlings, sunflower leaves are not very good for any plant's growth; every plant but *Aristida* was severely stunted. Crabgrass practically didn't grow at all. Equally important was the effect of sunflower leaves on a seed's chance to germinate. Although the two grass species were unaffected, all three other species of seeds showed some significant depression of their vitality. Most depressed was the sunflower itself. A sunflower seed had more than twice as high a chance of germinating if it was sown in a control pot instead of a pot with sunflower leaves.

I don't think you will be too surprised when you hear about the natural history of these plants. They are all part of a process called ecological succession. In succession, one set of plants grows lustily but, even so, is soon replaced by another. One set succeeds another.

In this case, sunflower, horseweed, crabgrass, and jimmyweed are a part of one set. After it has grown for a year or so, the crabgrass disappears. After two or three years the whole set is replaced by an almost pure stand of wiregrass. Clearly, the toxins produced by sunflower go a long way toward explaining this particular succession. Crabgrass goes first because it is the most stunted. The others soon follow because only wiregrass does really well in a field in which sunflowers have flourished.

Instances of such toxic production are many. The self-destruction of the sunflower is just one example. Most antibiotics are such toxins derived from fungi; fungi probably use them to fend off competition from bacteria. Limitation of populations by toxins is known in trees, shrubs, and herbs from widely differing climates. A recent survey of plants in a Pacific-northwestern forest showed that toxins are the rule, not the exception (del Moral). Chemists have actually purified and analyzed various of the poisons involved. Strange as it may seem, population limitation by outright poisoning may not be a curiosity, but a commonplace.

LIMIT: COMPETITION BETWEEN SPECIES

In the previous section on toxins, sunflower was shown to inhibit the growth not only of others of its own species but also those of several other species. This was an example of competition between species. Such competition always results in a population lower than otherwise possible. It is even possible for a population to be eliminated entirely by competition, even though its members are physiologically capable of flourishing.

Some of the best studies of competition have been made in the rocky intertidal zone. Remember the barnacles discussed in the section on spatial limitation? Actually, in Scotland, there are two species, *Balanus balanoides* and *Chthamalus stellatus*. Normally, *Balanus* barnacles occupy the wetter parts of the intertidal zone and *Chthamalus* the higher, drier part. The

Chthamalus zone is under water only at the highest tides near the time of the new moon and the full moon, and then only for a short part of the day.

Connell (1961) showed that the *Chthamalus* barnacles had developed special resistance to dessication and that the *Balanus* were simply unable to survive the dryness of the high zone. But why were the *Chthamalus* barnacles not also found in the wetter zones? Their larvae do try to settle there. Connell showed that if a person cleared a wet-zone rock and allowed only members of *Chthamalus* to settle, they did very well. It appeared likely that the *Balanus* were somehow excluding the *Chthamalus*.

In fact, that is exactly what happens. Connell set up experiments so that he could observe the gradual process of exclusion. The *Balanus* do it by growing faster than the *Chthamalus*. They either smother the *Chthamalus* or else literally pry them off their rocky homesites.

Competition is probably an extremely important limit to populations in nature. But it is also man's usual mechanism for exterminating or rarifying a wild species. No one shoots buffalo in Illinois nowadays—there aren't any. Their land has been usurped by farmers and cattlemen; the buffalo have nowhere to roam. White-tailed deer nearly disappeared in the northeast toward the end of the last century—not because they were being killed (far more are killed today), but because their habitat had been lumbered to the point of total destruction. We needed (and were better able to exploit) the deer's resources. The decline of the deer and extinction of the eastern elk resulted, too, in the loss of wolves (who never ate one single American) and the near-loss of the puma (who is known to have eaten two). The real estate boom in Florida threatens similarly the everglades habitat. And that, without firing a single shot, will mean doomsday for alligator and puma, heron and kite, poisonous water mocassin and benign white-tailed deer. Few things but sewer rats, cockroaches, and starlings thrive on an abundance of mankind.

Stimson provides us with a good way to conclude our discussion of competition. He has studied a group of Pacific marine molluscs called limpets. Limpets are grazing animals related to snails, but with uncoiled shells resembling coolie hats. The six species that Stimson studied graze on the film of algae that grow on rocks. But one species, the owl limpet, *Lottia gigantea*, always seems to be associated with a visible thick patch of algae about 1 foot square. The other five, various species of the genus *Acmaea*, often graze over areas where the algal film is too thin to be seen with the unaided human eye.

Lottia gigantea is the largest species of the limpets in this association. Its shell is from 1 to 3 inches long. Many things about the natural history of the *Lottia* limpets and their patches of algae suggested to Stimson that these patches are really *Lottia* territories and that the *Lottia* defend them simply by pushing their weight around. For example, the size of the algal patch around a *Lottia* limpet is in direct proportion to the food it requires; the bigger the *Lottia*, the bigger its "farm." Moreover, Stimson showed that each *Lottia* lives on its "farm" for at least the duration of his study (four years), and that it visits every corner of its patch every three or four days.

To test his hypothesis about *Lottia* territoriality, Stimson executed several simple experiments. These were designed to answer an additional question: Does the algal patch grow naturally and merely get taken over by an appropriate-sized *Lottia*? Or are the patches actually produced somehow by the activity of the *Lottia*? Stimson first measured the population densities of *Acmaea* limpets within the *Lottia* "farms" and outside them. He found these densities very dissimilar. Areas of 930 cm² outside "farms" had 18 to 21 *Acmaea*. Similar areas within "farms" held only three or four.

Next, he removed the *Lottia* limpets from their "farms" and placed them on nearby "bare" rocks. Within two weeks the algal film on their old patch disappeared. Within three weeks an appropriate-sized patch of algae had formed on their new homesite. *Acmaea* densities plummeted on their new homesites and rose rapidly on their old ones, so that after three or four weeks, there was no way of telling that the *Lottia* limpets had been moved. Clearly, the *Acmaea* populations are being depressed on *Lottia* "farms" by some sort of competition, and the algal growth is somehow enhanced by the presence of *Lottia*.

Stimson showed that the enhancement of algal growth was due merely to their protection from *Acmaea*. He protected rocks from *all* grazers and produced as thick a growth of algae as any *Lottia* limpet could. Hence, these *Lottia* were not producing any special fertilizers or growth substances. They were just acting like any good farmer and keeping the crows out of the cornfield.

Although it is not really necessary, I cannot resist telling you about the ways in which *Lottia* polices its farm. A *Lottia*, upon meeting another limpet (of whatever species, including its own), literally rears back and then lunges forward with a great heave, shoving squarely into the intruder. The trespasser loses its grip on the rock and is washed away by the next wave. If the limpet is large, it is merely shoved and shoved and shoved until it is thrust right off the territory. *Lottia* also gets rid of its sedentary competitors for space, the barnacles and anemones. These are shoved off, eaten off, rasped off, or crushed off; but they are cleared off somehow. Finally, the *Lottia* deals with the large predatory marine snails that have the misfortune to be caught on a farm. Such a snail moves by extending its soft foot out from under its shell and then dragging the rest of its body along. When the *Lottia* gets within range, it raises the forward edge of its coolie hat shell and clamps it down quickly on the tender foot of the snail. The snail of course reacts by withdrawing its foot and losing its grip.

This is why I chose the limpet story to conclude this section: It exemplifies the true complexity of real population limitation. We have seen both territoriality and competition at work here in limiting the *Acmaea* limpets and the barnacles and anemones. What limits the *Lottia*? We still do not know. They appear capable of farming the whole area, but they don't, and we don't know what is holding them back. We have also glimpsed yet another form of population limitation: exploitation. The algae that are grazed by *Acmaea* are kept to a much lower population than is otherwise possible.

LIMIT: EXPLOITATION

When one species, for its own benefit, utilizes another and depresses that other species' fecundity or increases its mortality, we say the first species exploits the second. Such exploitation could take place because the exploiter or predator is an herbivore or carnivore and eats its victim or a part of it. But the exploiter may also be a disease or a parasite. Other, less obvious ways also exist for one species to exploit a second one.

The evidence that exploitation limits population size in nature is not often as good as that which Stimson got for *Acmaea* and algae. Most evidence comes either from equivocal work or from work on controlling the populations of various pests of agricultural crops. In the chapter on the current human condition and again in the chapter on group selection and the evolution of survival, we study two such pests: mites that destroy vineyards; and rabbits in Australia that reduce the grass available for sheep. The mites were controlled by predatory mites, the rabbits by a viral disease.

The most famous equivocal study was done by no less than Theodore Roosevelt, 26th president of the United States. Because of that and because it is so famous, it must be mentioned. Roosevelt liked to hunt mule deer *(Odocoileus hemionus)* on the Kaibab plateau, the land mass that forms the north rim of the Grand Canyon. In order to improve hunting, he ordered government workers to destroy all the native vertebrate predators (except man) on the Kaibab. Wolves were completely exterminated; pumas, bobcats, and coyotes were severely reduced. The deer herd increased (from about 4000) and eventually settled at a density that is perhaps twice what had obtained when Roosevelt ordered the experiment begun.

It would at first appear that the data demonstrate that mule deer are limited at least in part by exploitation. But the data are not at all accurate (Caughley). And, furthermore, immediately before the predatory "control" began, 200,000 head of sheep were taken off the Kaibab. Were the mule deer really predator limited? Or competitor limited? Or both?

One case of predators limiting their victims was clearly demonstrated by Joseph Connell. Connell (1970) worked in the rocky intertidal habitats of San Juan Island, Washington, with barnacles very closely related to those he had studied in Scotland.

The barnacles of the species *Balanus glandulosa* usually occupy a narrow band comprising only the upper 18 inches of the intertidal zone. Clearly, this restriction is not by choice because barnacles settle all over the zone and in a few places do very well all over it.

A predatory snail of the genus *Thais* is responsible for restricting the population of barnacles. The snail can drill a hole through the barnacle's shell and eat the barnacles. Connell showed that this exploitation keeps the barnacle population far below the size which it could reach. He built stain-

Fig. 2-1 A protected barnacle colony. Notice the sharp rectangular outline of the colony where its cage was. Only a few young barnacles survive outside the cage. (From J. H. Connell, *Ecological Monographs* 40:49–78. Reprinted by permission of the publisher and author. Copyright 1970, Duke University Press, Durham, N.C.)

less steel, wire-cloth cages to protect barnacles from *Thais* snails in the lower zone. Figure 2-1 is the most eloquent demonstration of exploitation limitation imaginable. It shows the protected spot with the cage lifted off, three years after the cage was first installed. Notice how tightly the barnacles are crowded into the space under the cage. They have used every available protected square centimeter. This results in the population's edge forming a sharp outline of the cage itself. Outside the cage there are few barnacles indeed. And they are all fairly young. None are destined to get much older either as they will soon find themselves in *Thais* snails' digestive tracts.

Again we have seen a mixture of limits on a population. In the upper zone, *Balanus glandulosa* barnacles are space limited. But where there are *Thais* snails, they are exploiter limited. It is interesting that in Scotland, *Thais* snails are also present. But there they do not appear to play much of a role in limiting *Balanus* populations. Space does that. The reason for the differences between Scotland and Washington remains obscure.

LIMIT: CANNIBALISM

Here is one of the real curiosities in population limitation. It is of minor significance to all but a few species, and it probably never plays much of a role in limiting any vertebrate population. But perhaps you will be interested to learn of it just the same.

The animals that exhibit strong cannibalism are flour beetles of several species. No one knows what their natural environment is (or was), but they are commonly found in flour bins and flour storage warehouses all over the world. A record of their having lived with the civilization of ancient Egypt has been preserved. Their food, their home, their very world is flour.

Flour beetles have four life stages. First they are eggs, then larvae, then pupae, last adults. The pupal stage is the one in which occur the major developmental processes than transform larvae into adults. Pupae, like eggs, are helpless. Oh, they can wriggle a little, but they can't exactly run away. Larvae are voracious cannibals. They eat eggs, other small larvae, and occasionally even pupae. But they are outdone by the rapacious adults. The adults eat virtually every single pupa. This is quite effective at keeping the population very low. Consequently, the beetles never eat themselves out of house and home. You shouldn't think that flour beetles are provident. They simply need a high-protein, wet meal whenever they find it.

That cannibalism is indeed minimizing the population of flour beetles is quite readily and convincingly demonstrated. Park, Leslie, and Mertz discovered a strain of the beetle *Tribolium confusum*, strain bI, which is not very cannibalistic. This strain reaches much higher populations than all others and is the only strain which severely reduces the flour supply that is its home and larder.

LIMIT: STRESS

In the past several decades, science has become aware of another item on nature's menu of limiting factors. It was first discovered by Hans Selye in humans and called stress syndrome. Since then, it has been found in many other mammals when they are at unusually high densities. Somehow the stress of multiple contacts with hostile neighbors causes a large variety of unpalatable, pathological symptoms in mammalian behavior and physiology.

No one yet fully understands the stress syndrome, nor have all its symptoms been described. But it is a potential nightmare. Faced with a superabundant supply of food, water, and shelter, populations increase to a certain point and then mysteriously stop. In one experiment, enough of life's essentials to support 5000 separately caged rats supported instead a population of only 160. At this population size, the rats became extremely aggressive. Besides fighting constantly, they aborted or mistreated their young. Most commonly, mothers ate their own newborn. Their milk supply failed; they lost interest in copulation. Peter Crowcroft's book, *Mice All Over*, is an extremely well-written account of his and Fred Rowe's long study of the stress syndrome in house mice, where much the same occurs as in rats.

Indeed, symptoms of stress have been seen in rats, mice (several species), axis deer, and woodchucks. Recently it has been noted that high blood pressure is another symptom in rats. Endocrine disturbance and imbalance appear to be an integral part of the syndrome. Heart disease is another likely symptom, as is mental illness. Population regulation by stress syndrome appears to be an unpleasant situation at best.

On the other hand, worse than that (for me at least) is the prospect that stress is only a temporary limit to population growth. There is a high probability that species can adjust to greater and greater population densities by natural selection. This would be accomplished because the more lethargic, less high-strung individuals would not be as heavily stressed at any given population density. These would reproduce better and their kind would soon be representative of the population. If this argument is a bit obscure now, return to it after you have read the chapter on natural selection.

Meanwhile, let me ask you if you cherish the prospect of human beings becoming a species of ant or sheep. Is your ideal person the one who can put up with any insult because he lacks any self-respect? Who is capable of ignoring others because there are just so many of them that he *must* in order to live his own life? Do you see why I worry about the consequences of adjusting to stress? If not, let me remind you that the population not limited by stress *is* limited by something(s?) else. When other limits are reached, we shall not have choice living conditions either. I'd rather be a man suffering limitation than an ant suffering limitation.

Kessler has actually done the experiment of allowing house mice to evolve adaptations against stress. First, he began with laboratory mice instead of wild mice. Laboratory mice and generations of their ancestors have long been held captive in crowded conditions, and it is well known that they are rather tame and docile compared to wild varieties. Kessler put his mice in pens of only 13 square feet and let them grow and evolve. He obtained populations of 800 to 1000 mice per pen. That is 60 to 80 per square foot—much higher than any density previously reported. (For example, in their laboratory pens, Southwick reported densities of less than one mouse per square foot, and Crowcroft and Rowe reported densities as high as 25 per square foot.) Moreover, Kessler reports that as time went on his mouse population had shown increased growth rates. Presumably they were continuing their evolution toward the status of a disorganized beehive.

3 the robust balance of nature

Wonder, not doubt, is the root of knowledge.

Abraham Joshua Heschel

Perhaps each spring you notice that your front lawn is not overrun by birds. On the other hand, you can be sure *some* avian representative will show up. One should not take the presence of birds for granted, because the bird population is dynamic. Every year, old birds die and are replaced by young ones. Perhaps one year they will all die? Or perhaps for a few years none will die and our world will reek of birds.

But this simply does not occur. Birds don't disappear entirely and they don't plague us either. With all the variation and transition in their populations, their numbers seem to be held within reasonable upper and lower bounds. Scientists like to call a dynamic situation that holds itself within limits, a steady state. Most people refer to the steady state in the populations of wild species as "the balance of nature."

EXAMPLES OF STEADY STATES

So that you can appreciate the dynamic nature of this balance, I have brought together some examples from the literature of population biology. Appropriately enough, in a book about the population problem, the first example, Fig. 3-1, depicts the population of white storks in Oldenburg, Germany (an area of 5,416 square kilometers) for an extended period of 35 years. Notice that the population is far from constant. It rises and

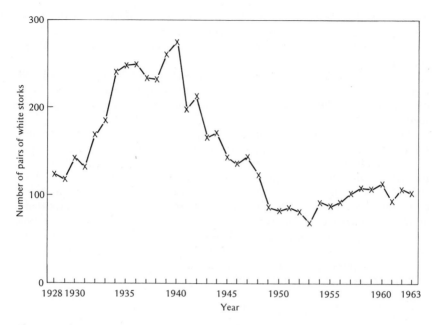

Fig. 3-1   The population of white storks in Oldenburg, Germany. (Data from Lack, 1966.)

falls in jagged pattern. Yet storks neither disappear nor overrun the region.

Gashwiler has conducted a 12-year study of both plant and animal populations in a virgin forest whose dominant trees are Douglas fir and western hemlock. From his data, I have selected six convenient examples in order to show you a few more steady states. The plants (Fig. 3-2) were censused in a 390,000 square foot area (a bit less than nine acres); their population is reported as square feet of forest floor covered. The mammals (Fig. 3-3) are simply reported in animals per acre during the fall of the year.

None of these censuses is in any sense regular or constant. Yet they do tend to stay within limits. Later in the chapter, the data for reindeer on St. George Island, Alaska, will exhibit the same tendency. And in Chapter 7, so will the data for the human population of Japan from 1720 to 1850.

BALANCING BIRTHS AND DEATHS

The fact that many species tend to maintain their populations without much increase or decrease is remarkable. In order to do that, their "births" must equal their deaths. (If you don't mind the liberty, I shall speak of plants and bugs and all manner of life as having "births" although there are more formal terms.) If births equal deaths, then on the average, each hen stork and each mother chipmunk raise two of her kind to sexual maturity. And each plant, despite the tremendous proliferation of its seeds, can expect only one of its seeds to germinate and survive to flower. What accounts for such seeming magic? Is there a scientific explanation? There is and it is surprisingly simple.

Births require resources. Space, nutrients, calories, and water are all required to produce young. But resources are limited. Therefore, the more adults there are, the smaller their average share of the resources and the fewer young each can produce.

Similarly, life requires resources. The larger the population, the smaller each individual's share of resources and the greater its chance of getting a really inadequate share and dying. Moreover, the more individuals in a population, the greater the production of toxins, if there are any; this, too, should increase the death rate. Last, the more individuals the greater a target they become for exploiters. Predators are often attracted to unusually abundant sources of food; wolves, for example, do not eat mice unless mice are superabundant. And a dense population carries an epidemic better than a sparse one—more individuals get sick (see, for example, the data for influenza and Israeli schoolchildren in Chapter 5). All this tends to increase the death rate from exploitation.

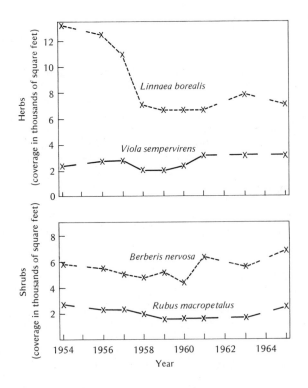

Fig. 3-2 Censuses of four plant species in a virgin forest. The top two are herbs: twinflower and a violet. The bottom two are shrubs: a barberry and a member of the raspberry-blackberry genus. (Data from Gashwiler.)

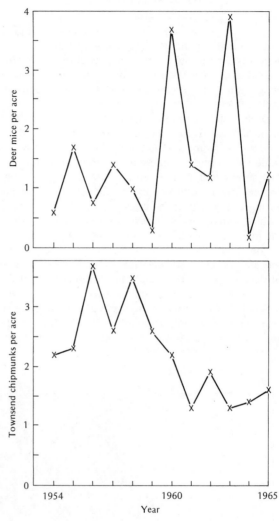

Fig. 3-3 Censuses of two mammal species in a virgin forest. (Data from Gashwiler.)

All in all, at higher populations there is a higher death rate and a lower birth rate. These general relationships are graphed in Fig. 3-4. Eventually, at a large enough population, the birth rate and death rate lines cross. At still higher populations, deaths exceed births. At lower populations, births exceed deaths. Hence, the population always tends toward the size where the lines cross. At that point births equal deaths and the population remains the same.

A LOCAL POPULATION
OF SONGBIRDS

One case where birth rates, death rates (including emigration), and population change has been measured in nature is a population of great tits. The population of this songbird in the 26 hectare tract in England known as Marley Wood has been studied by several scientists over the last generation, including Gibb and Perrins. Much of their work appears in Lack, 1964.

During the time they have been studied, the breeding population of great tits has varied from 14 to 172. Thus, the data come from large, medium, and small populations. Figure 3-5 shows how nicely the real birds exhibit the patterns predicted by the conceptualization of Fig. 3-4. The top part shows that parent birds lay fewer eggs in higher density populations. The middle part shows the relationship of population to deaths per bird during the year (this includes egg deaths too). Except for one year (the one with 51 pairs), this relationship is also like the conceptualization of Fig. 3-4: the higher the population, the higher the mortality.

The lower graph depicts the overall change in the tit population. This too, fits our conceptualization, since higher populations have a high chance of declining; lower populations a high chance of increasing. Again however, one exceptional year stands out as having had very high increase despite the fact that there was a high population of tits (51 pairs). This is the same year that had the low mortality in the middle graph. Such accidents happen and they are typical of natural populations. Perhaps there was a particularly

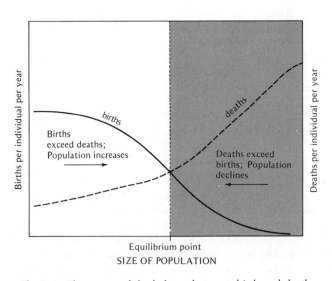

Fig. 3-4 The nature of the balance between birth and death.

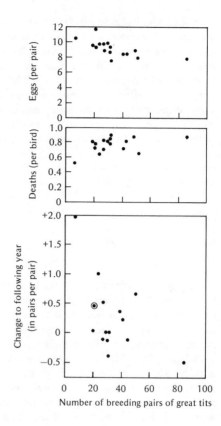

Fig. 3-5 The effect of population size on reproduction and mortality in a songbird. (Data from Lack, 1964.)

Number of breeding pairs of great tits

mild winter. Or perhaps an insect outbreak or an unusually plentiful seed crop made life easier that year for birds.

In any case, great tits have not taken over Mother England. The 51 pair population did become an 86 pair population the next year. But the 86 pair population suffered a 50% decline. Thus, two years later there were only 43 breeding pairs of great tits in Marley Wood. On the average, over the long term each pair of great tits can expect about two of its eggs to hatch, live, and grow into adulthood. Two. No more; no less.

WEEDS GET IN
EACH OTHER'S WAY, TOO

Palmblad wanted to study the same phenomenon in various plants. But he chose to bring his subjects into the laboratory, where, under carefully controlled conditions, they would not be subject to random environments. Of course, this meant they would yield their information more quickly. But one never can be sure (without checking nature) whether the laboratory conditions are at all realistic.

Palmblad tested various weeds by sowing them in plastic flower pots. The pots were 6 inches in diameter and the seeds were sown at densities of up to only 200 per pot. This is high, but not unrealistic. Besides, as you shall see, the effects of density are obvious at much lower seed populations.

Although many species were tested, I have selected only one particularly clear example for presentation, horseweed, *Conyza canadensis,* an annual of the sunflower family which is native to North America.

Population Seeds per pot	Mortality Biological death (%)	Natality Seeds produced per seed sown
1	0	55,596
5	13	11,925
50	49	817
100	58	353
200	64	192

Biological deaths, the figures in the middle column, represent not only those seeds that failed to germinate, but also those that actually died after germinating and, further, even a few that lived but had insufficient resources to flower. We can easily agree that mortality and natality in *Conyza* are strongly dependent on population size.

Actually, Palmblad's figures are likely to be rather good estimates of natality. They may be a bit high because of the protection he afforded his plants. But they are not so high as to cause concern. Thus, if you are sharply critical, you will have wondered why *Conyza* is *not* taking over the world. After all, if each seed produces 192 other seeds even when there are 200 plants in a little 6 inch flower pot, how can births match deaths? Death will always trail behind that kind of fecundity.

The answer is that Palmblad has not attempted to measure all mortality. He has only tried to measure that part which is affected by population density. In nature most seeds die before they ever reach conditions approximating the moist, fertile soil of a greenhouse flower pot. Mortality *in nature* has no trouble keeping up with natality. Consequently, *Conyza* neither disappears nor overruns us.

STEADY STATES ARE ROBUST

An important property of steady states is that they are self-maintaining. In the case of population size, high population leads to population decrease; low population, to population increase. In other words, if the accidents of nature should produce a large deviation from the equilibrium population, the forces of abundance and limitation cause the population to return to equilibrium.

That is why nature's balance is spoken of as being robust. It can stand a lot of perturbation. If we went in and decimated a population of birds, it would bounce back. If instead, we added quite a few, it would still bounce back—back to equilibrium.

The balance of nature can be compared to a ball bearing in the bottom of an otherwise empty ice-cream cone. The force of gravity and the sides of the cone are like the opportunities and constraints of nature. The ball bearing is the population. And the bottom of the cone is the equilibrium point. (See Fig. 3-6.) Imagine holding the cone while being jostled on a subway train. The jostling of course represents nature's accidents. Still, one should have no trouble keeping the ball bearing near the bottom of the cone most of the time.

Not all equilibria are robust. Some are indeed delicate. An example of a delicate balance can be imagined by inverting the cone and balancing the ball bearing on its tip. We shall need a good juggler to maintain *that* balance. Even **he** isn't likely to succeed if he must ride the subway while performing his act. In the chapter on Testing Darwin's Theory, you will encounter a biological situation which leads to a delicate balance.

Let us look at two experiments where investigators have actually challenged nature's balance. In each, animals were either added to or removed from a natural situation. But in both experiments the animal populations quickly responded and obliterated the perturbation entirely.

You have already been introduced to the first experiment. It is Eisenberg's. Remember that he built cages to enclose natural populations of pond snails? We have already examined his control pens and fed pens. Now we shall look at two other treatments performed in the spring just before reproduction. From four pens (which we shall call reduced pens), Eisenberg tried to remove about four-fifths of the adult snails. To four others (which we shall call increased pens), he tried to add enough adult snails so that the populations were about five times the size of controls. Then he measured the fecundity of the populations by censusing the production of eggs and young.

Fig. 3-6
Two equilibria.   Stable   Unstable

some principles of population ecology

Average number	Reduced pens	Control pens	Increased pens
Adults in spring	306	984	4110
Eggs per 10-minute search 10 July	347	435	287
Young snails per sample			
7 July	32	24	18
20 July	31	30	25
27 July	9	7	5
Sept., Oct.	11	11	8

Notice that Eisenberg didn't quite achieve his fivefold scaling of adult numbers. Control pens' populations were only about 3.2 times the size of those in reduced pens. And populations of increased pens were only about 4.2 times as large as those of controls. Still those numbers represent quite large differences in adult numbers. Now comes the important conclusion. Despite the large differences in adults, there was very little difference in the number of young they produced. By September and October, there really was no difference between reduced and control pens, and the depression of numbers on increased pens was minor. Since it is these young that will constitute next year's adult population, it is clear that the snail system has been able to restore itself to equilibrium following large perturbations in each direction.

Another experiment of this sort was performed by Dethier and MacArthur. They had no replicate populations, but they followed their single population for a long time. Their test organism was the checkerspot butterfly, *Melitaea harrisii*, in Maine. Checkerspots feed on a wildflower, *Aster umbellatus*, which is found in isolated patches of field within generally forested country. Patches of this sort are gradually replaced by forest, and this patch was being replaced during the study. This explains the general, natural decline of butterflies which Dethier and MacArthur recorded between 1959 and 1961.

The checkerspot becomes adult in July and reproduces. Females lay eggs in large masses of about 200 eggs and then die. The eggs hatch, feed on asters, overwinter, feed more as spring larvae, and then pupate. The pupae become adults in July, thus completing the cycle.

The experiment was to gather 19,800 young larvae from three nearby fields of *Aster* and introduce them into the experimental field. The data are in Table 3-1.

Notice that the large number of autumn larvae present after the introduction did not appear to suffer any extra winter mortality; 80 survived. However, only 22 of these made it to adulthood; that is 27.5%. In 1961 and 1959, survival through pupation was 27.3% and 55.8%. Thus, this aspect of survival also appeared little affected by the excess butterflies. What *was* affected was fecundity. There was almost no breeding in 1962 and only

TABLE 3-1   EFFECT OF ADDING AUTUMN LARVAE TO A
BUTTERFLY POPULATION

Year (July to July)	Adults	Egg masses per adult (natality)	Autumn larvae	Spring larvae	Overwinter survival (1 — mortality)
1956–1957	24	2.3	11,400	—	—
1957–1958	—	—	14,200	34	1/418
1958–1959	—	—	—	34	—
1959–1960	19	2.3	8,600	29	1/261
1960–1961	—	—	8,000	22	1/364
1961–1962	6	0.66	800 +19,800		
			20,600	80	1/257
1962–1963	22	0.09	400	—	—
1963–1964	6	3.0	1,800	—	—

Source: Dethier and MacArthur.

400 autumn larvae were produced in the field. For the first time, egg masses appeared on the side of the road leading out of the patch. This suggests that the females, finding overcrowded conditions, were emigrating.

In any event, the population quickly recovered from its perturbation. By autumn of 1962, there were only 400 larvae instead of the 20,600 of 1961. By spring of 1963, the adult population had dropped back to six. Moreover, the three fields from which they had removed the 19,800 larvae had also recovered their normal numbers. (This doesn't show in the data above, but it is reported in the original paper.)

Although the population size of many natural species is robustly balanced by the abundance of the species' resources, even a robust balance has a limited ability to resist constant, serious insults. Tackled by the 250 pound right guard of a professional football team, the straphanger carrying the ice-cream cone on the subway is going to lose the ball bearing altogether. All too often, the impact of civilization on a natural species has been like that of the gang tackle of a whole football team. The ice-cream cone is pulverized and the ball bearing vanishes into oblivion. As a final irony, the shock of the encounter is so violent that the guardian of the ball bearing does not always remember to mourn its passing.

RHYTHMIC CENSUSES

Not all populations on the Earth are at a steady state. Some rise and fall rather regularly either with the seasons or with some rhythmicity other than an annual one. The lynx, *Felis canadensis,* has exhibited such oscillations for over 200 years since records were begun by the Hudson's Bay Company in 1735. The company's records were kept in terms of the lynx pelts they obtained every year. These are fairly good

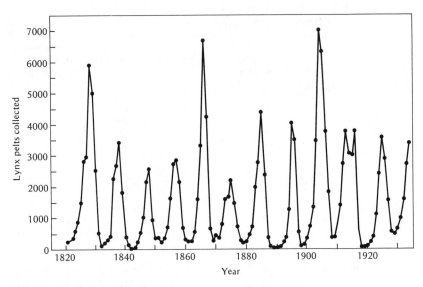

Fig. 3-7 Lynx censuses for the Mackenzie River district of northwest Canada. (Data from Elton and Nicholson.)

indexes of lynx abundance because the company purchased its goods from Indians who insisted on selling in one single lot to the fur trader, *all* species of fur they had trapped. Thus, the records are rather insensitive to the dictates of fashion. As long as HBC wanted any furs, it had to buy whatever lynx pelts were offered. Figure 3-7 depicts part of this record (1821 to 1934, inclusive). This portion was the business of the large Mackenzie River District, which included parts of the Yukon, and the Northwest Territories of Canada. It was compiled by Elton and Nicholson. To this day no one is really certain what causes the lynx fluctuations, although many believe the lynx are tied in some complex way to fluctuations of their chief food, the snowshoe hare (Gilpin).

Even in the face of such violent changes, neither lynx nor insects nor any other fluctuating species becomes extinct very often. Neither does any overrun its habitat and destroy it. Even such fluctuating species seem to have their bounds. That implies they too live in a situation where births occur about as fast as deaths over the long term. It's just that the average of two offspring per couple has much less meaning for the individual lynx couple than it does for the individual tit couple.

POPULATION EXPLOSIONS

Anyone who has seen a chart of human population size which covers the past several hundred years knows that nothing remotely resembling its explosive rise has yet appeared in this book. Does anything like that ever happen in nature? If so, why? And what is the fate of the natural population which explodes? Indeed natural populations can and do explode. When a relatively small population finds itself in an environment in which there is great abundance, that is exactly what happens.

An easy way to study explosive population growth is to examine a population that has been introduced to a different place. For example, in 1880, 435 striped bass were brought from eastern North America to San Francisco Bay and released. Nothing like this fish then lived in the bay. Twenty years later, just the commercial catch of striped bass from the bay was 1,234,000 pounds (Slobodkin). That certainly implies a vast population explosion.

In a more scientific fashion, Einarsen monitored the population of ring-necked pheasants newly introduced to Destruction Island, Washington. In 1937, 2♂ and 4♀ pheasants were brought to the island and released. Figure 3-8 records the spring censuses. Unfortunately for science, the island was commandeered by the U.S. Army after 1942 and the population could not be followed any longer.

A population explosion that *was* followed for a long time is the reindeer population of St. Paul Island, Alaska. In fact, that of St. George Island was also enumerated for the same 40-year time span. These two islands are the Pribilofs and they are only 41 miles apart.

In 1911, 4 bucks and 21 does were brought to St. Paul and 3 bucks and 12 does were brought to St. George. The reindeer on St. Paul experienced a great population explosion from 1925 to 1938. Then the bottom fell out. The population irrupted. Large numbers of reindeer starved to death, apparently for lack of their winter food, which is lichens. Figure 3-9 depicts the history of the St. Paul herd (Scheffer).

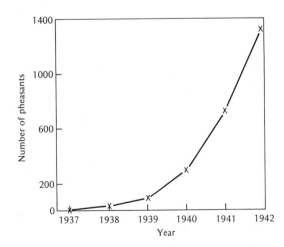

Fig. 3-8 Spring censuses of ring-necked pheasants on Destruction Island, Washington. (Data from Einarsen.)

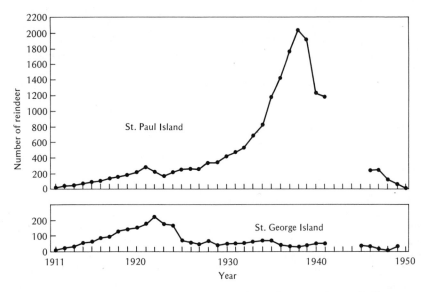

Fig. 3-9 Reindeer censuses on the Pribilof Islands, Alaska. (Data from Scheffer.)

Klein reports that a similar eruption and irruption befell the reindeer introduced to St. Matthew Island, Alaska, but the data are scantier. On 20 August, 1944, 24 does and 5 bucks were released on St. Matthew.

Year	Reindeer population
1944	29
1957	1350
1963	6000
1966	42

As on St. Paul, the reindeer apparently died because the lichens were almost gone.

I have been holding back on St. George's reindeer herd because it is so different. Until about 1925 its census was very nearly the same as that of the St. Paul herd. Then something happened. No one knows what or why. The St. Paul herd exploded and the St. George herd settled gently back to a steady state.

Woodgerd records another case where an introduced herbivorous mammal reached a steady state. In 1939, two yearling bighorn sheep were released on an island of 4 square miles in Flathead Lake, Montana. In 1947 there were six and an additional seven were introduced. Figure 3-10 records available censuses from 1947 until 1962.

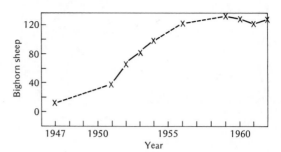

Fig. 3-10 Bighorn sheep censuses on an island in Flathead Lake, Montana. (Data from Woodgerd.)

We still do not know how to tell whether a population will increase gently to its steady state or whether, before it gets there, it is destined to rise to numbers which are unrealistically large and then irrupt violently. But we do know that no population explodes indefinitely. When a population grows to the point that its resources are scarce, deaths overtake births and the population stops growing.

4 the momentum of population growth

Deal with what will become big while it is yet small.

Lao Tzu, LXIII

AGE STRUCTURE

Suppose we wanted to stop our population from growing. How long would it take? Besides the obvious jobs that need to be done in the field of education and in the distribution of necessary medical services, is there anything in the basic nature of population structure that would slow us down? Indeed there is, and it is so important it is worth emphasizing in its own chapter. It is called *age structure*.

Most plants and animals have various stages of individual life. We call these stages "ages," and we note that different ages have different reproductive potentials. The pond snails do not reproduce until they are a year old. The flour beetles and checkerspot butterflies are eggs, then larvae, pupae, and finally reproductive adults. People are no different; humans have embryonic, immature, mature, and post-reproductive ages.

If one should census a population according to age, it would be possible to construct a diagram listing the proportion of the individuals that are any given range of ages. Perhaps 30% would be 0 to 15 years old; 25% from 16 to 30; 20% from 31 to 45, and the rest, 46 and over. That would be one way of reporting a population's age structure.

Age structures reflect the speed at which a population is growing. A rapidly growing population has a high proportion of young. Declining populations have low proportions of young. Most standard texts on

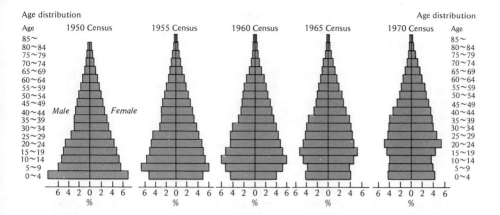

Age distribution

Fig. 4-1 The age structure of the Japanese people at five-year intervals. Notice how the rapidly growing population of 1950 exhibits a triangular-shaped distribution with a broad base. As the population slows its growth, the base shrinks and the sides of the triangle get steeper. (From *Statistical survey of Japan's economy, 1970* and *Statistical survey of Japan's economy, 1971*, Economic Affairs Bureau, Ministry of Foreign Affairs, Japan.)

demography or population biology show a general formula called the steady state age distribution, which describes the age structure of a population growing at any given rate.

A most graphic example of the way age structure is related to the growth rate of a population comes from the demographic history of Japan. Japan was growing rapidly after World War II and her proportion of youngsters was very high. After abortion was legalized, this situation changed. Japan's growth slowed markedly. For a while the average Japanese woman was not even having two children.

These changes are clearly reflected in the age structure changes of the past generation. Figure 4-1 shows Japanese age structure at various intervals. The initial census (1950) records the age structure of a typical growing human population. But birth rates dropped and by 1955 the decline in the 0 to 4 proportion is evident. Of course 0- to 4-year-olds alive in 1950 were in the 5–9 year group in 1955. That is why there is a bulge in that age group in 1955.

By 1970, those who were 0 to 4 in 1950 were 20–24. They still accounted for a bulge in the age structure. But mostly, the age structure had gotten over their influence. It had begun to straighten out and become indicative of a population growing at a very low rate.

THE SOURCE OF MOMENTUM

Japan's age structures teach a very important lesson. Population size and composition respond very, very slowly to even the most radical changes. Even though her women were actually underreproducing during some of the years between 1950 and 1970, her population never stopped growing. Births always exceeded deaths. How could this have been?

The answer lies in the age structure. Where does a population recruit its 70-year-olds? From the 69-year-olds, of course. And they were born long before 1950. Only those now in the first quarter of their lives have been affected by changing attitudes in postwar Japan. This results in a growing population's having a considerable momentum.

Suppose a growing population decided to stop. In 40 years, its 50-year-olds would have to be recruited from present 10-year-olds, and so forth. Since the 10- and 20-year-olds were born when the population was growing, in 40 years the number of 50- and 60-year-olds would grow from the addition of current 10- and 20-year-olds. The decision to stabilize the population would (at first) influence only the very young ages. As these get older, they would sweep the decision up through the age structure just the way Japanese newborns after 1950 are doing. Not until those first newborn die will population growth then cease. Subsequent newborns would naturally continue to bear the imprint of the population's decision to stop growing.

You should be able to agree that the momentum of population growth will cause a delay of about one human lifetime in the successful braking of human population growth. One lifetime is roughly 70 years. Therefore, in dealing with population questions the short-term view is virtually worthless. It takes decades for our decisions to come to fruition, so we must try to see decades into the future in order to do the best job. Unfortunately, as you will see in the next chapter, we have not been doing such a good job. It no longer takes much of a prophet to make reasonable statements about human population problems now and for the next 50 years.

THE CONSEQUENCES OF MOMENTUM

How serious is the momentum of growth? Granting that even after a population decides to stop growing, it will continue to grow for a long time, the important question is, "By how much will it have grown when it does stop?" Nathan Keyfitz has developed a formula to answer this question. Not surprisingly, the faster a population is now growing, the more it will continue to grow after it decides to stop. The following table records the final size of the populations of various countries should they decide to quit growing now, or should they delay that decision for 15 years. In the table, the numbers are the factors by which populations (of the year in parenthesis next to the nation) must be multiplied to arrive at final populations. Thus, the United States, in 1967 at about 200 million, would have a final population of 200 million times 1.16, or 232 million, if it had decided in 1967 to halt its growth.

The higher U.S. multiplier of 1966s population indicates that in 1966 the U.S. population was growing much faster than in 1967.

Country	Multiplier if decision now	Multiplier if decision in 15 years
Chile (1965)	1.49	2.12
Columbia (1965)	1.59	2.45
Ecuador (1965)	1.69	2.79
Italy (1966)	1.13	1.23
Peru (1963)	1.53	2.31
U.S.A. (1966)	1.25	1.45
U.S.A. (1967)	1.16	1.29

According to Keyfitz, a "typical underdeveloped country" is going to be 1.6 times as large if it "stops" growing now and 2.5 times as large if it waits 15 years to stop. Taking the multiple 1.5 as a representation of about what the whole world's multiple would be if it managed to reach a decision today, we discover that even should the world stop growing there will be about 1.75 billion more mouths to feed and backs to clothe when the steady state is achieved. One and three-fourths billion more people; that is not just a sophisticated correction!

the human condition: a résumé

Man: An animal so lost in rapturous contemplation of what he thinks he is as to overlook what he indubitably ought to be. His chief occupation is extermination of other animals and his own species, which, however, multiplies with such insistent rapidity as to infest the whole habitable Earth and Canada.

Ambrose Bierce

5 symptoms of overpopulation in humanity

Woe unto them that join house to house, that lay field to field, till there be no room.

Isaiah v:8

Have some parts of the world reached or, like the reindeer on St. Paul Island, exceeded their steady state number of human beings? If so, signs of marginal life, of poor nutrition, stress syndrome, plague, toxins, or space shortage should be evident.

Many books have been written which review the plight of humanity with more authority and more detail than I could. In this book, I shall be content with an outline. Thus, you, the reader, can best fit facts that first appear isolated into their broad and terrifying pattern.

SYMPTOMS:
STARVATION AND NUTRIENT SHORTAGES

Starvation has been with mankind for ages. Famines are recorded in the Bible. At first, men were totally dependent on hunting and gathering; a bad game year meant empty bellies. Mowat records the tragic decline of the Eskimo and Chippewayans of Canada—hunting peoples—after their game, the caribou, declined in abundance. However, when man became agricultural, grain storage ameliorated his condition. Food supplies became regularized, and only the worst of droughts brought trouble. Starvation was probably minimal. Certainly there was no widespread endemic famine of the sort that current history is recording.

Dumont and Rosier estimate that, in our time, 10 to 20 million people die of starvation every year. Today, at least half the world's people are hungry. They get fewer calories than an American man would need if he did nothing but sleep the whole day. The American food situation is extraordinarily rich and very different from that of most of the world's people. With less than 6% of the world's population, the United States eats about 35% of the world's food. Meanwhile, all over the world, farmers toil just to subsist. India, Egypt, the Dominican Republic, despite heroic efforts, are dangerously close to the brink of mass famine.

In addition to a shortage of calories, many people suffer from shortages of nutrients, especially protein. One of mankind's greatest modern scourges is protein-calorie malnutrition, or PCM, which afflicts millions of people from soon after birth to about age 4.

PCM yields a complex number of symptoms. Affected individuals are always stunted, and their muscles are thin and wasted. Their bodies do not have enough protein to grow and so resorb it from the muscles they acquired while nursing. PCM is called protein-*calorie* malnutrition because if a person gets enough protein but not enough calories, the body utilizes the protein as energy to meet the daily cost of staying alive. Thus, the person simply wastes the special nutritional values that would have come with the protein. (Humans, like most animals, must eat certain essential protein parts—various amino acids—because they cannot be synthesized by the human body. Using them for calories requires they be destroyed.)

The two severest forms of PCM are called kwashiorkor and marasmus. Kwashiorkor is a Ghan word (Ghan is the native language of Ghana) meaning "sickness when deposed from the breast by another child." The significance of the change in diet was long ago recognized by the several African societies that named this disorder similarly. Mother's milk contains just the right proteins; what a baby gets afterward often does not. A baby with kwashiorkor is swollen from water seeping into his tissues through weakened blood vessels; he has a poor appetite and is generally miserable. Marasmus (a Greek word indicating "wasting away") is severe atrophy of the muscles caused by the malnourished body feeding upon itself. Marasmatic children weigh only 60% or less of their expected weights. Combinations of kwashiorkor and marasmus are common.

PCM can occur in more mild forms, but even when mild, its symptoms are terrible. By far the most debilitating is a loss of intelligence. Joaquin Cravioto and his colleagues have studied this symptom of PCM in Latin America and Africa. Because PCM causes stunting, they use the weight of a child as an index of the malnutrition from which it is suffering. They calculate the expected weight for the child's age and sex and emerge with the percentage of expected weight for each child.

Figure 5-1 depicts one study performed in rural Mexico. Children were from 30 to 72 months old when examined and lived in an area of widespread PCM. Notice the generally low IQ scores obtained by these children. An IQ near 100 should have been the average in the culture-free intelli-

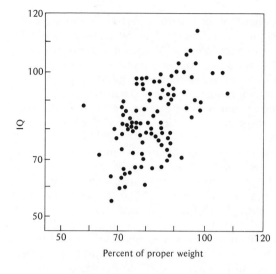

IQ

Percent of proper weight

Fig. 5-1 The intelligence of preschoolchildren depends on adequate nutrition. (From Cravioto and Robles.)

gence tests that were administered. More important is the relationship of IQ to percent of proper weight. The lower the percent of proper weight, the more the child had suffered from PCM, the lower the IQ. Intense PCM had caused some actual mental retardation, because an individual with an IQ below 70 cannot function well in society.

Cravioto repeated his investigations on school-age children. In one test only 20% of normal weight schoolchildren had IQs of 70 or less, but 56% of children weighing 51–70% of what they should weigh had scores of 70 or less. Data were as follows for 299 children:

Weight (% of normal)	Average IQ
51–70	69
71–90	81
91–110	88

In a later study, Cravioto observed the entire primary school population of a rural Guatemalan village. Children, ages 6-11, had been exposed to much PCM in their first 4 years of life. As a control, an upper-class urban school population was studied. For those latter fortunate children, height should be closely related to parental height and *not* related to nutrition. Cravioto also gathered information on the socioeconomic status and parental education of the children. Then he administered various culture-free tests of sensory perception and of integrative abilities important in learning to read and write. Results were shocking.

In the perception tests, the taller quarter of the children did much better than the shorter quarter, *but only in the rural village.* Height had no relationship whatsoever to intelligence in the well-fed city children.

In a test to integrate a pattern of dots with a rhythm, there were 10 possible correct answers. By age 12, 42% of the tallest quarter were able to score 8 or better; 30% had perfect scores of 10. But the shortest quarter could rarely do well; only 9% got 8 or better and **none** were perfect.

In other words, PCM—even in mild and moderate form—not only produces individuals so dim that they cannot manage modern society, but also it virtually eliminates all signs of superior intelligence. Tell that to the next person who anticipates mourning all the geniuses that will go unborn if we limit our population's size.

Cravioto's conclusions were not the effect of socioeconomic status. And they have been repeated elsewhere. For example, in Yugoslavia, a group of 36 children was examined 7 to 14 years after they had been admitted to a hospital for malnutrition and "cured." None had an IQ over 110 and 17% scored below 70. A control group had 32% with IQ over 110 and only 2% under 70.

One doesn't have to be an infant to have malnutrition rob one of brainpower. Over 20 years ago, adult volunteers subjected themselves to prolonged malnutrition. When they had lost 20 to 30% of their body weights, their intellects were considerably impaired. (Proper nutrition returned them to mental health.) Mowat has expressed it most powerfully: "Men with starved bodies have starved minds."

Is it fair or realistic to expect a nation of mentally unfulfilled victims of malnutrition to cope with the twentieth century? Is it fair to ask them to mechanize their farms, industrialize their society, build new cities, learn to use the pill? They probably don't even know where their bootstraps are.

Not only is PCM an unsightly, debilitating disease, it kills, either directly or by making its victims more prone to recurrent infection. Measles is a fatal disease—if you have PCM. So is diarrhea. PCM simply allows one to catch it so often, there is no time to recuperate (Kevany). Consider Kevany's data from a rural Guatemalan area:

Cases of acute diarrhea per year in 100 people aged 1–4 years

General population	Mild PCM	Moderate PCM	Severe PCM
98.8	164.1	252.5	274.5

How important is malnutrition around the world? There is no really good set of statistics. But let me show you some random figures that I gleaned from a few hours work in the library of the University of New Mexico. Remember as you read them that the number of infants dying in their first year of life in a country like the United States is only about 20/1000 births.

The Philippines. A survey compared the diet of residents in Luzon and the Visnaya Islands with what was needed to keep the people healthy. Table 5-1 shows the data. Is it any wonder that the five leading causes of death in the Philippines are either caused by malnutrition or exacerbated to the point of lethality by it. The five are pneumonia, TB, gastrointestinal inflammation, bronchitis and beriberi. What a quaint list of things for an American to die of! Infant mortality in the first year of life in the Philippines is 61.5/1000. In 1960, it was 68/1000.

TABLE 5-1   DAILY PER CAPITA NUTRIENT INTAKE IN LUZON
            AND THE VISNAYAS

Nutrient	Average intake	Recommended minimum intake	Fulfilled percent of requirement
Calories (g)	1672	2193	76
Protein (g)	46.6	54.4	86
Calcium (g)	0.35	1.00	35
Iron (mg)	10	8	125
Vitamin A (IU)	1900	3772	50
Vitamin B$_1$ (mg)	0.80	1.19	67
Vitamin B$_2$ (mg)	0.52	1.36	38
Vitamin C (mg)	70	70	100
Niacin (mg)	14	12	117

Source: Intengan.

India. Two hundred fifty of every thousand people in India die before reaching 4 years of age (10 times the U.S. rate, according to Berg). In the words of Eichenwald and Fry, "Malnutrition in early life is directly or indirectly responsible for more deaths among children than all other causes combined." Today 76% of those who live past 4 are malnourished. Seventy-six percent. That is 408 million Indians.

Pakistan and Bangladesh. Infant mortality is about 130/1000 (first year) in Pakistan. Turmoil in Bangladesh does not allow an accurate estimate, but there it may well be higher. Malnutrition is basically responsible. Eighty-five percent of preschoolchildren have some degree of PCM; 3% are severely malnourished (Rahman).

Turkey. Estimates of infant mortality range from a low of 154 to a high of about 230. In the Ankara children's hospital, 43% of children under 2 seen as *outpatients* were malnourished. Iron and vitamin deficiencies are common. Diarrhea and parasitic diseases are frequent complications, and they are what is usually listed as the cause of death (Baysal).

Iran. Kwashiorkor and marasmus are common. Protein-calorie malnutrition is the major health problem of the small child. "Many infections, notably measles and diarrhea, prove fatal when they develop in a malnourished child" (Heydayat).

Jordan. A carefully selected sample of 2843 children up to age 5 revealed about 8% with PCM. Jordan's infant mortality rate was a moderate 48.4 from 1961 to 1964 (Patwardhan and Darby).

Egypt. During the 5 years 1948 through 1952, one hospital, the Mounira Children's Hospital of Cairo, treated 46,515 children for PCM. Egypt's infant mortality was 118.6 from 1961 to 1964 (Patwardhan and Darby). Another source lists the UAR's 1961 infant mortality as 219 (Bengoa).

Botswana. In the 1940s and 1950s, 20–30% of Botswana's urban schoolchildren were malnourished. But in small communities, where it is still easy to augment the cereal diet with wild fruit, vegetables, and small game, only 3% were affected (Lochrie).

Ethiopia. From weight and height charts it appears that 50% or more of Ethiopian children are affected by malnutrition. Roughly 10% of admissions to children's hospitals are from *advanced* PCM. A survey of 397 children under 5 years in Ijaji found 3.5% with advanced PCM. A survey of 3000 Addis Ababa children found 8% marasmic (Habte).

Swaziland. In 1968, nearly 3000 people were treated for malnutrition including 1000 for kwashiorkor (Dlamini).

Malawi. A survey of 600 children found 30% with overt signs of PCM (Misomali).

Uganda. Kwashiorkor and marasmus are widespread. About 25–30% of preschoolers suffer from malnutrition (Muyanga).

Zambia. Mortality of children before they reach school is at least 300/1000 and may be 500/1000. Examination of primary-school children showed that 25–27% have serious malnutrition and 50–60% are less severely undernourished (Vamoer).

Tanzania. Semiti estimated that the cost to the country of curing PCM including treating everyone, loss of time, and so forth, would be about the same as the entire national budget.

In Latin America the mortality statistics reveal a situation just as bleak. The death rate in the 1–4-year-olds is about 25 times higher than in the United States and Canada. Every year this fact costs 250,000 Latin American children their lives (Horowitz). In Chile in 1960, infant mortality was 119/1000. In Venezuela, in 1961, it was 60. In Mexico it was 74.2/1000 in 1960 and 66.3/1000 in 1964.

BATTLING NUTRITIONAL SHORTAGES
WITH BOTH BRAINS TIED BEHIND OUR BACKS

Often, things that are done to improve matters turn out to be mixed blessings. Much of the attempt to increase food has come from breeding programs designed to discover high-yield grain. These programs have been quite successful. But the old turn-of-the-century varieties had enough protein to prevent PCM. The new varieties don't. Man is advised to consume 15% protein in his diet; he must have 12%. High-yield wheat has only 10%. Hybrid corn has 7%. High-yield rice has only 5–7% protein, whereas traditional varieties have 7–9%. Scotch oats, the growing of which has been uninfluenced by the caloric needs of the world, is about the only common grain left with enough protein to nourish human life, although experimental varieties of Siberian wheat are known to have 22% protein (Borgstrom).

Recently new strains of wheat and rice have been introduced to Asia. This process, termed the Green Revolution, is nothing more than a repetition in the tropics and subtropics of the introduction of new-breed grains into the world's temperate zones. The grains have helped some, but they cannot perform miracles.

The chief distinguishing feature of the new grains is that they can utilize high quantities of artificial fertilizer *if environmental conditions are right*. For example, new rice strains can use up to 120 pounds per acre, three times what previous strains could use. Moreover, they use it to better advantage. One pound of added artificial fertilizer per acre yields 20 added pounds of rice—twice the added yield of the old strains (Brown). These new strains mature in only 120 days, as opposed to 150–180 days for old strains. This gives the farmer time for another crop. The new rice can't stand natural flooding, however, and it is most susceptible to pests and diseases. In most of Asia it is useless.

The new wheat requires fertilizer and irrigation or dependable rainfall, but three-fourths of India's farms are dry. In the Punjab, 80% of the land has been planted in the new wheat. This was done along with a 17-fold increase in irrigation and a 20-fold increase in fertilizer application. Yield has doubled (Ladejinsky).

All that took a great amount of capital. It costs 10,000–12,000 rupees to re-equip one 7–10 acre farm. Where is a man going to get that kind of money if his family is malnourished because he can't buy them food? His credit is worthless. The net effect is that grain production in all of India is up only about 10% owing to the revolution (Ladejinsky).

Worse, the revolution promises great trouble if one year there should be a serious pest or rust or blight. Such years are common in the United States and cost 10–40% of the crop. How can Asia stand that sort of loss even for one year? Yet, I have theoretical evidence that suggests that whenever one increases the extent and density of a species, its pests and disease should evolve to be more virulent, more destructive. If that is so, the Green Revolution may just be a big buildup, with a severe letdown the only sure consequence. Consider what happened to Japan in 1732 (see Chapter 7) when an insect pest destroyed some of the rice crop.

Furthermore, the Green Revolution requires technology: Fuel-eating tractors and artificial fertilizer. Where will that come from? Fossil fuel is not in abundant supply and will be gone in 30 to 300 years. And fertilizer? Look at this table (from Borgstrom) which indicates the way the world's 38.2 million metric tons of fertilizer was divided from 1963 to 1965.

	Consumption of fertilizer (%)	World population (%)
Europe	42.6	13.7
U.S.A.	25.0	5.6
U.S.S.R.	10.1	6.9
Japan	4.8	3.0
Other	17.5	70.6

And that is not the whole picture. In the United States, 25% of the fertilizer was for lawns and gardens. (Should I stop enjoying my garden? How can I get the fertilizer I use to the Indian farmer, who in any case cannot afford the irrigation system to use it?) In South America, where 7% of the world's people live, only 0.8% of the world's fertilizer was used. And most was used in growing coffee, bananas, and cocoa, the plantation crops exported to rich foreigners like us (Borgstrom).

One of the most disgraceful failures of the century involved the construction of the Aswan High Dam on the Nile River in Egypt. As we have seen, Egypt could certainly have used help, but here's what she got instead (Turk, Turk, and Wittes).

The dam was supposed to create a large reservoir making year-round irrigation, and thus year-round agriculture, feasible. Indeed since its construction, yields of cotton, grain, fruit, and vegetables have increased. But at what a cost! The nutrient-laden silt that used to flow down the Nile in the flood season is trapped behind the dam. This silt was a natural fertilizer for both the flooded farmlands and the Nile Delta fishery. Now it must be replaced by costly fertilizers. And what of the once thriving sardine fishery of Egypt, the industry that produced 18,000 tons of sardines per year, the source of critical animal protein to ward off PCM? That industry is dead.

What is more, the fact that the Nile no longer bears the burden of the silt has made it flow faster. This has caused increased erosion. But loss of silt is not the only cost of Aswan. The Nile's floods had rinsed away the salt in the soil. Soil salinity is now rising. Since this makes agriculture impossible (there is evidence it has destroyed at least one or two civilizations—the Hohokam in Arizona and the Babylonian), the salts must be rinsed away at great cost.

The dry period between Nile floods had killed the population of disease-carrying snails. Now there is no dry period, and the snails live along all irrigation canals. They carry a human blood fluke called bilharzia. This parasite invades the human urinary and intestinal tract. Now 80% of those working in the canals have bilharziasis.

The joke of all is that there is actually less water. The dam has allowed much more to evaporate and to seep into the porous rocks underlying it.

Anything else? Yes, but it's only aesthetic and historical. Many of Egypt's fantastically important, totally irreplaceable archaeological treasures are below water now. Who cares?

The tragedy of all this is that it was predicted. Not once, twice. Dasmann reviewed the history of irrigation in Egypt. He predicted the evaporation problem. He noted the increase in disease that had accompanied irrigation in the past. He noted the salinization problem. In retrospect his warning looks weak. But was it right to ignore it entirely? After all, his fundamental message was strong. *Population* is the key to the problem and population density must be limited if the problem is ever to be solved. Tampering with the Nile is just playing a dangerous game.

Even before Dasmann, in 1960, Dr. Abdel Aziz Ahmed, a noted Egyptian hydrologist, issued a clear public warning against the high dam. His statement, which preceded ground breaking for the dam, warned of the silt trapping, erosion, and excess evaporation of water that Aswan would cause (Sterling). He was promptly fired.

Egypt has not been the only country victimized by dim vision. The United States of America has also shared the mixed blessings of unbridled technology. When, after World War II, DDT heralded a new era of insect control, farmers began to apply it indiscriminately in order to increase their crop yields. Suddenly a whole host of new pests began destroying crops. Foremost among these is a group of fruit-eating spider mites. They had been known previously, but never before were they a problem. Vineyards were ravaged.

The problem was that these mites had been formerly controlled by other mites, voracious predators with an appetite only for their cousins. DDT and other insecticides killed these predatory mites, too. This removed the frugivores from efficient predatory control, and increased their population.

Flaherty and Huffaker have entered some vineyards in California and experimented to see if the population of predators can be restored as effective control agents. Nature can indeed accomplish just this but insecticides must be withheld for five years before the job can be done. It is just as if the farmer and his field had to withdraw from a drug habit.

As with the Aswan story, this untoward effect had been predicted. Ecologists in the 1920s and 1930s had noticed that if a general biocide is applied to a system where a predator controls the density of its victims, control would be lost and the victim would increase in density even though it too is killed by the biocide. The trouble is we cannot kill the entire population of anything (although heaven knows we certainly try). We must learn to depend on the help that nature as our ally can give us.

While I am on the subject of grim predictions, let me repeat one of my own. I sincerely hope it is nowhere near as accurate as others have been.

One of the schemes for increasing food production is fertilization of the sea. The vast majority of the ocean is a salt-water desert. Its nutrients fall to the ocean floor where darkness prevents their use by plants. If they could be pumped up, the ocean would be fertile!

Unfortunately the effect of increasing production in a natural system may be to destabilize it. In an unknown percentage of cases, the natural balance that exists between the ocean's food and feeder species would be upset. Both food and feeder species could undergo violent fluctuations in population and even extinction. If we install those behemoth pumps to enrich the sea before we have won a great deal more knowledge about natural systems, we could be in deep trouble. We could cause eutrophication of the oceans as we have caused eutrophication of lakes. Be wary of scientists bearing technological gifts.

SYMPTOM: WATER SHORTAGE

As I wandered through the grisly literature on malnutrition, a macabre comedy kept being reenacted. It seems that proceedings of many of these nutritional conferences fall naturally into a country-by-country report of bad tidings. Often a U.S. agency has sponsored the conference and sent one or more representatives to it. Of course, it wouldn't look good for us to seem perfectly happy in the midst of all the tragic tales, and so when our turn comes, we speak of dental cavities and obesity. After 10 or 20 reports on millions of cases of malnutrition, that certainly does break the monotony.

However, we need not be smug. We are indeed on the verge of a more serious nutritional deficiency. Water itself is being used to the hilt. You semanticists can battle as to whether water is a nutrient, but I'd sure hate to do without it. And I enjoy using it as lavishly as I do.

The southwestern United States has already burgeoned beyond its water supply. Californians take the equivalent of 18 inches of rain per year from their ground-water reserves; only a fraction is returned. Undoubtedly, were it not for the U.S. constitution, Arizona, Nevada and California would have fought many water wars among themselves. (See Fig. 5-2.)

Did you know that the mighty Colorado River, carver of the Grand Canyon, no longer makes it to the Gulf of California? By the time it has reached there, it has been drained of every drop. The once magic wetlands of the Colorado River Delta are desert dry. Evaporation from the Colorado and brine drainage from the irrigated land of California's Imperial Valley produce a very high salinity in the few remaining gallons that reach Mexico. The spray in Mexicali's cotton fields is so salty that plantation machinery must be greased every two hours. One-third of these cotton fields have had to be abandoned (Borgstrom). And that is a large river. Smaller ones like the Tijuana have simply vanished altogether.

Yet, in the midst of the fire, Tucson and San Diego fiddle with their

Fig. 5-2 Water is big news in the arid Southwest. The water debt referred to was 107,200 acre-feet of Rio Grande water. New Mexico promised Texas a share of the Rio Grande's water annually starting in 1939, but was unable to pay only three years later. It took several months of record and near-record rain to pay off the debt.

supplies of the precious liquid. They are nearing the world's record for per capita domestic consumption of water.

Truly we are living high—but I can't say I find it at all unpleasant. George Borgstrom, from whose work I gathered much that I have told you, has estimated that there is enough water income in the world to support only 500 million people living an American-style life. About five billion strict vegetarians could live on that same water. Do you want to *have to* be a vegetarian?

IS THE CART
BEFORE THE HORSE?

Sure we are working on desalinization of salt water. Sure we'll probably learn to recycle dishwater and sewage water. But as the great underground reserve of water in our desert states drops lower and lower, killing an unknown number of plants and animals, will we not learn to demand new technology before we commit ourselves to needing it?

The same may be said for protein production. The problem here has been that meats are best (and cereals one of the worst) sources. But meats are energetically expensive. It is the old second law of thermodynamics at work again: the relay of energy from plant to herbivore loses useful energy. Man gets less from eating the herbivore than from eating the plant directly. Meat is also costly in terms of water. It takes 25 times as much water to produce a pound of meat as it does to produce a pound of rice, the most water demanding of all grain crops.

Shouldn't we demand a cereal that gives us adequate protein before we populate the Earth to the point where only cereal grains are efficient enough to provide us with needed calories? No. We'd rather act like lemmings instead of men. We have used our bottoms and ignored our brains. We are already at the point of having caused much death and misery in the world and more is on the way. Millions now eke unfulfilled, dim existences from a hostile world. And millions more fail. We must continue to hope that technology will help us with higher yields of even more nutritious food. For even were we to achieve a program of zero population growth tomorrow, it would take two generations to stabilize our population.

Hence we are going to need more food if we somehow manage to contain ourselves. In the face of such a threat to human life, isn't it reasonable to demand the technological improvements before we commit ourselves to yet another population increase? Would a bank advance credit to a customer before it was assured of the customer's future income? Why can't we be as careful with life as we are with money?

SYMPTOM: POLLUTION

When you looked at the last chapter, you no doubt wondered if pollution is the human parallel to toxins. In part it is. Now no ecologist is going to admit that DDT or other chlorinated hydrocarbons are not pollutants in any amount. They are and always will be. But most pollutants are not like that.

For example, man did not learn to defecate in 1946. Previous to our high densities, our waste material could be easily purified by natural populations of bacteria. Outhouses, perhaps unpleasant, were not really dangerous (unless you chanced to sit on a black widow's web).

In the late 1950s excessively dense production of sewage caught up with the mushrooming area around Minneapolis-St. Paul. In the suburbs of these twin cities, more than 300,000 people were living with both backyard wells and backyard septic systems. By 1959, half their wells had become polluted from inadequate space for sewage water purification. Crisis is the only adequate word to describe such a situation. There are many hidden costs in high-density life. In this case, modern sewage and water systems had to be purchased. A consortium of the small towns had to be formed and bits of local freedom had to be exchanged for clean drinking water (Fisher).

Sewage, except as it breeds disease, is actually not a poison. It contains perfectly natural (in fact absolutely necessary) nutrients. Much pollution comes from too much of such good things. Some, however, is really toxic. Sulfur dioxide, a by-product of oil burning, has reached such high concentration that it has killed people in major metropolises and in smaller towns like Donora, Pennsylvania, where a locally high concentration developed in the late 1940s. A terrible smog in London in 1952 caused an estimated 4000 deaths in one week.

Another major toxic pollutant in our atmosphere is lead. The concentration of lead in the atmosphere in Los Angeles is as high as 4 μg/m^3. In midtown Manhattan the average lead concentration is 7.5 μg/m^3. In Paris it can be 9 μg/m^3.

Water is considered safe to drink if lead concentration is below 100 μg/l (Thienes and Haley). But the U.S. Public Health Service uses a more stringent criterion and rejects drinking water with only 50 μg/l. Rainwater around the country contains about 36 μg/l. We're getting close.

Furthermore, it is clear that autos are responsible. In case you had not heard, gasoline for autos contains tetraethyl lead. Amounts in rainwater vary with gasoline consumption (Lazrus, Lorange, and Lodge). In cities where gasoline consumption is high, samples of rainwater (and air) have correspondingly high levels of lead.

A study of the lead isotopes in air pollution revealed that they emanate from those in gasoline, not those available as natural pollutants (Chow and Earl).

What is all this lead doing? It is making its way into our bodies, there to do unknown harm. Plumbism, or lead poisoning, is an ancient condition. But that makes it no less painful or debilitating. It has many symptoms including such things as loss of hair, anemia, sterility, and loss of muscle tone (Chisolm). One symptom is almost always present: encephalopathy. Freely translated that means brain damage. The encephalopathy can be minor fatigue and dullness, or it can involve convulsions and coma. Plumbism can also kill.

People with plumbism exhibit blood levels of lead ranging from 100 to 600 μg/100 g blood. The traditional danger level is considered reached at 70 μg lead/100 g blood. But recent very careful studies have shown that levels of only 20–40 μg interfere with the efficient functioning of human enzymes. And a study of children indicates that their toxic threshold level of lead is only 36–50 μg.

A glance at Table 5-2 will show you that modern Americans are too close to these danger levels. People whose jobs take them into particularly intimate contact with the internal combustion engine have the highest levels of all. But downtown megalopolitans need not be ashamed. They have achieved about one-third the dangerous level.

Furthermore, the figures of Table 5-2 are only averages. There is a pretty broad spread around those averages. Thus, even though the suburban Philadelphian averaged 13 μg, some had levels of 32. And even though the downtown Philadelphian had levels which averaged 24 μg, many had levels over 35 and some had levels of 60. A sample group of Manchester, England,

TABLE 5-2   AVERAGE LEVELS OF LEAD IN THE BLOOD OF
U.S. MALES IN VARIOUS HABITATS AND OCCUPATIONS
COMPARED TO THE ESTIMATED LEVELS OF LEAD
IN THE AIR THEY BREATHE

Habitat-occupation	μg lead per 100 g blood	μg lead per m³ air
Rural Californians (mountains)	12	0.12
Rural Americans	16	0.5
Suburban Philadelphians	13	1.0
Urban Americans	21	1.0
Los Angeles aircraft workers	19	1.9
Cincinnati police (all)	25	2.1
Pasadena city employees	19	2.2
Downtown Philadelphians	24	2.4
Cincinnati traffic police	30	3.8
Cincinnati auto test-lane inspectors	31	4.2
Los Angeles traffic police	21	5.2
Cincinnati garage workers	31	5.5
Boston auto-tunnel employees	30	6.3

Source: Goldsmith and Hexter.

children had blood levels averaging 31 μg, and 17% exceeded 50 (Bryce-Smith).

The level of lead in the atmosphere (and in our blood) is steadily increasing. In downtown San Diego, an area *not* experiencing much growth in traffic, levels of lead in air have been growing at about 5% per year (Chow and Earl). The U.S. Environmental Protection Agency compared atmospheric lead levels in 1968–1969 with those of 1961–1962. Philadelphia had increased by 2 to 36%. Cincinnati was up by 13 to 33%. And Los Angeles had increased by 33 to 64% (Craig).

Who knows what damage lead is already doing to our minds and lives? At the end of this chapter I shall review evidence that even "subdangerous" levels of lead may be severely debilitating.

No one, I hope, believes that we should ignore such pollution. No one, I hope, believes we can only attack it by limiting our population. No. We must clean up our air and water right away. But we must also recognize that to keep it clean requires that we set a limit to the insertion of filth. If the air can stand just so much gasoline being burned, then more people means either less gas per person or too much pollution.

The second law of thermodynamics applies here too. We can never transfer 100% of all pollutants to safe form. Life will always result in toxins. Too much life will always result in pollution.

You will hear a lot about pollution increases not being caused by population. Skeptics say that most increases are caused by each individual polluting more. Indeed not all increases in pollution are due to population growth. When we switch to disposable bottles and cans, we do get more pollution from the same number of people. When each individual uses more electricity, more coal must be burned for him.

But often we can trace much of the rise in pollution per person to population growth. For example, each individual today spends more time and produces more pollutants in transit. Does he do this because he likes to drive or because he is more likely to own a car? In part perhaps. But in part, he does it because a larger population *forces* him to. As population rises there is a natural increase in the distance between home and work, home and shopping, home and medical services. All this occurs because a larger population takes up more area. In fact the average distance of a round trip in a city is directly proportional to the square root of the area of the city (Watt).

Such increases are reflected both in gasoline consumption and in the amount of land that is gobbled up for roads. A population of one million commuters requires 12 times as much roadway area **per person** as does one of 10 thousand commuters (Watt).

Another example comes from England. There it was discovered that when many people all burn fuel to heat their homes, they make such a concentration of smoke that the sun's warming rays cannot penetrate to help heat the homes. Each man must burn even more fuel to compensate for it (Watt). The British have switched to smokeless fuels.

One last example should be mentioned. When land is plentiful, it doesn't pay the farmer to use much pesticide. He can grow enough food without it to meet the demands of his consumers. As I shall soon point out, land is no longer plentiful. So it now pays the farmer to spray his crops with various polluting pesticides—organophosphates, chlorinated hydrocarbons, and so forth. All are expensive, but worth the price when land becomes scarce and food becomes expensive.

In summary, every man has always produced waste products. But as men live in greater densities, these products become disease-fostering or poisonous or both. And as men live in greater densities, each is forced to produce more potential pollutants. We must soon clean up our air and water, before we wind up controlling our population with the toxins we pour into them. But to keep them clean we must eventually stop our population's growth.

SYMPTOM: STRESS SYNDROME

Stress syndrome, which we have much to learn about, may be even more degrading in Western civilization than pollution. Aggression and high blood pressure plague our society. Are they caused or aggravated by high density? Baby beating (even to death) has become commonplace. Who will love a baby if its mother doesn't? Is baby battering a product of overpopulation? It certainly is chillingly similar to the bestiality we see in stressed mice and rats.

Who knows how much of the rise in crimes of violence, in riots, in drug use and other irrational behavior is caused by population stresses?

Certainly you can't tell a ghetto black to go farm his own food supply. Utter dependence on a technology that deserts you and your family must lead to terrible frustration when there isn't enough land or resources to subsist on.

Kenneth Watt has shown that there is a chilling correlation between the population of a city and the annual amount of money each citizen is taxed for police protection.

City size (people)	Per capita cost of police ($)
10,000–25,000	5
25,000–50,000	6
50,000–100,000	7
100,000–250,000	9
640,000 (San Diego)	14
1,610,000 (Detroit)	27
3,575,000 (Chicago)	29
8,085,000 (New York)	38

Populations of the four named cities are 1964 estimates; police costs as of 1967; unnamed cities from the 1960 census.

Of course it cannot be argued that the crime rate is controlled only by population size. There are many other complicating influences on it. But assuming the police are not hired for fun, but to serve a purpose, it seems certain that the crime rate tends to be much higher in communities of larger populations.

A further, rather unpleasant thought occurs to me. Having lived in places ranging from the smallest in Watt's sample to almost the largest, I can say that I was best protected from crime and felt most at ease where I only had to spend five dollars a year. The safest streets are those that don't need police. Having to live with unsafe streets undoubtedly contributes to the already stressful environment of the city.

No one knows how much if any of the high mental-disease rate in the developed West is traceable to too many westerners at one time. The discoverer of the stress syndrome feels also that much fatal heart disease is traceable to stress. He finds that half the victims of lethal heart attacks have had no blood clots. These people have died suddenly and apparently without cause. Stress is implicated because the hormones that are affected by it are responsible for maintaining the vital sodium-potassium balance of the heart muscle.

SYMPTOM: WORLD-WIDE EPIDEMICS

Unlike the other symptoms of overpopulation, epidemic out-breaks of infectious diseases have not yet increased. One can take little comfort in this. Plagues are the only method of population control that can be expected to strike all of a sudden. The only warning we could hope for has already been received: We are dense and mobile enough to support a lightening epidemic. The oft-repeated flu epidemics are proof of that. They have also proved that an epidemic can spread faster than immunizations can be manufactured to combat it.

Endemic disease has increased owing to population, however. And it has increased even more than we might like to think. We shall examine this problem in the discussion of how symptoms interact to amplify each other.

SYMPTOM: SPACE SHORTAGE

We are swiftly running out of space. The Japanese and San Franciscans are happily dumping trash into their respective bays to create more. If there is so much empty land, why do that? Why don't *you* go live in the middle of the parched Mojave? Or how about a frozen arctic island? I can get a cheap one for you.

Clever people point out that people live in high density by choice. All America, they say, lives on only about 5% of her land. That is a half-truth. Drive across the country someday. See how much land is both useful and unused. Precious little. That New Yorker may not know it but he uses 5 or 6 acres to produce his food, a bit more for his minerals, and still more for his wood supply (Borgstrom). We still maintain a few acres out of production, but not for long. The lumbermen are already working on producing paper out of sewage: the timber harvest is nearly at maximum. And even with our high farm yields, we'll not be producing a food surplus for much more than the next ten years. It seems the clever people have forgotten that not all land is equally good for all uses.

This is such a serious problem, it is worth examining in some detail. Let us begin with paper pulp consumption.

In 1963–1964 the United States, with less than 6% of the world's people, used 38.4% of its paper pulp (Borgstrom). And the world paper-pulp production was near a maximum. Most of the world (62.8% of its people) made do with only 4.9% of its paper pulp. What will happen to our standard of living when the rest of the world demands its fair share?

Worse, even though we have more forest per person than almost any other country, we are no longer self-sufficient in that regard. In 1968 there were about 3 acres of forest per American. But each American used the forest products of 5 acres. Most of the rest came from Canada.

The story is not much better in agriculture. In the middle 1960s, a North American used about 2.6 acres of farmland and 3.2 acres of pasture land to grow his food (Borgstrom). About 0.4 acres of farmland produce were exported.

In round figures then, we Americans required about 6 acres for food and 5 acres for wood; 11 acres per person in all. Since there are now 210 million of us, we require about 2.3 billion acres of useful land.

How much can we get from our own nation? All 50 states have 2,352,405,120 acres; in round figures, 2.35 billion acres. Looks like we just make it, doesn't it? Wrong. Of that acreage, much is wasteland: deserts, rocky steep, and arctic permafrost. All in all, we have approximately an acre and a half of wasteland per person. That comes to about 300 million acres. The remaining 2.05 billion acres is just not enough to support us in the style to which we have accustomed ourselves. What do you think can happen when we have 300 million people who want 3.3 billion acres and have only 2.05 billion?

Japan is even less well off than we are. It has been estimated she would need four or five times as much productive land as she has in order to meet her needs. About 85% of Japan is mountainous and almost useless for habitation. Her people actually live at the highest density in the world, 1333 per square kilometer (about 4000 per square mile). Minoru Muramatsu (an authority on population growth and public health) has said: "In terms of space, Japan already has too many people. If you live in Tokyo, all you can find is a place to eat and a place to earn money. There is no green, no trees. I don't feel that people are living a very human life." (This passage is quoted in Boffey).

The whole world is really using virtually all its land. During the years from 1882 to 1952, 80% of the remaining unused, but usable land was converted to human use (Borgstrom). Now only *at most* 4% and probably less than 3% of the Earth's useful land remains unexploited frontier.

One often unmentioned result of the land shortage will be the death of the small-owner, single-family dwelling. As prime building lots get scarcer, as timber supplies become increasingly insufficient, as other resources develop inflated prices to reflect their relative scarcity, the single home will become increasingly unaffordable. America, like Europe before her, will move into smaller quarters. One-room and two-room apartments for whole families will become sought-after luxuries. Is this preferable to our present life-styles? Not to me it isn't. We can avoid it. All we need do is decide we want to.

THE AMPLIFICATION OF SYMPTOMS
BECAUSE OF INTERACTIONS

Symptoms of overpopulation are not independent. They unite and interact to form a full-blown syndrome. Poorly fed people are more susceptible to disease and pollution. So are poorly housed people. People who live in small quarters lack the privacy required to palliate their stress. Protein-calorie malnutrition causes even poorer nutrition as populations suffering from it decline in intelligence and thus technology.

The interaction of the symptoms of overpopulation is so often ignored and so intense that it should be illustrated. Turn back to the beginning of this chapter. Look at the death rates. That gives you a rough idea of the magnitude of the problem. Remember that people with malnutrition got diarrhea far more often—and eventually died of it in many cases. Remember that malnourished people found measles a fatal disease.

An old but disastrous case of the interaction of famine and disease concerns the people of the Pueblo de las Humanas whose language, Piro, and customs are long extinct. This pueblo was in the very center of New Mexico on the Chupadera Mesa. In 1598 it housed about 1000–2000 people. Archaeologists of the twentieth century have shown that the pueblo area was first settled about the year 800. But the community was destined not to survive the seventeenth century.

Catholic missionary activity began in the pueblo in 1626. The records of the mission provide us with our knowledge of the fate of the village. In the three years from 1659 to 1662, the Pueblo was so robust that the inhabitants could afford to build a magnificent, large church and associated buildings. Its walls are thick, hand-quarried stone. It had beautifully carved, massive beams and, presumably, all the other trappings and refinements of an important mission. Certainly this was no indication of the imminent death of the whole society.

Drought struck in 1666. Famine followed. Four hundred and fifty died in 1668 alone. Hard times also befell the surrounding Apaches, a more primitive people who earned their living hunting game and raiding the pueblo. As their game suffered, they turned more and more to pirating the little remaining food stocks of their pueblo victims. Then, in 1671, the people of the pueblo, weakened by lack of food and water, suffered a devastating plague. Sometime between 1672 and 1675 the few remaining inhabitants abandoned their homes entirely. Now all that remains of Pueblo de las Humanas is a haunting ruin preserved by the U.S. National Park Service as Gran Quivira National Monument and a few totally decultured Indians of mixed ancestry living near El Paso, Texas. Let us hope that the history of the Pueblo de las Humanas does not become the tale in miniature of all human civilization.

Here is another case. These data, taken from Israeli schoolchildren, show the relationship of space to one's susceptibility to influenza (Watt).

Number of people per room	Percentage getting influenza
0.0–1.0	39.9
1.1–2.0	44.3
2.1–3.0	52.4
3.1–4.0	58.9
4.1–5.0	67.3

Wanting lots of "breathing room" is not just a luxury, after all.

Science is beginning to discover that mild to moderate contamination of the body with toxic pollutants is not benign. In one set of experiments Friend and Trainer inflicted various amounts of biocides on young ducks and examined their resistance to duck hepatitis virus, DHV. For example, they administered a polychlorinated biphenyl (PCB) to ducks from age 10 days to 20 days. PCB is one of the most abundant pollutants in the chlorinated hydrocarbon group (DDT is the most abundant). At age 25 days the ducks were challenged with the virus. Of 58 which had received PCB, 28 died (48%). Even where a low dose of PCB was given, 7 of 20 died (35%). In controls not given PCB, only 3 of 21 (14%) succumbed.

Using DDT and dieldrin, Friend and Trainer have repeated their work. With dieldrin, DHV mortality was from 19 to 59%. With DDT, DHV mortality was 19 to 40%. Only 6% of the controls were killed by the virus. It seems quite clear that chlorinated hydrocarbons *even in doses that don't kill*, weaken resistance to critical infection.

Perhaps you object to having to worry about ducks. However, we can't do experiments like that on people. But we can work on mammals. Maybe you won't mind worrying about rodents?

Hemphill, Kaeberle, and Buck are one group of investigators examining the way lead lowers rodent resistance to bacterial infection. They gave mice either no lead nitrate, 100 μg lead nitrate, or 250 μg lead nitrate every day for 30 days. These doses are absolutely inconsequential—not only did mice not die, none appeared the least bit debilitated or abnormal. However, when they were all challenged with a bacterial infection of *Salmonella typhimurium*, *all* mice which had received 250/μg/day died within 3 days. After 16 days, when the dying stopped, 60% of those which had received 100 μg of lead per day were dead. But only 30% of the control mice had been killed. Even though lead was not administered in sufficient quantities to cause any outward sign of harm, it interacted with the bacterium and doubled and tripled the death rate. Now you can understand why I am so unwilling to allow to pass unmarked the fact that our blood levels of lead are at "only" 25 to 40% of lethal concentrations.

CAN WE IGNORE THE WHOLE SYNDROME OF OVERPOPULATION?

One might take exception to my presentation of any of the foregoing symptoms. Lead isn't necessary in gasoline; get it out. Low-protein cereals should be supplemented with high-protein beans. Save space by building upward. Farm the oceans. Recycle water, aluminum, paper, nickel, tin, etc., etc., etc.

Don't you see that these are *all* necessary? And that they are all last-minute holding actions? They will help for a while, but when we are using our resources efficiently and our population grows again to the point where there is not enough to go around, what do we do? As you can see by the land inventory, that really won't take very long at all. What do we do when it happens?

If there were only one symptom of overpopulation, we might guess that it was just a coincidence. But when the whole syndrome is upon us, can we still risk the hope that we aren't near our limit? We do not predict overpopulation; **we are observing it.**

There are many things we can and should be doing. But to anyone with respect for human life, it is clear that the one thing we should not be doing is permitting our population to continue to grow. We must insist on technology before increase. Unfortunately that is the reverse of our present course.

6 prepare to live in China

The ideal state is a small, intimate community where all the necessities of life are present in abundance.

Lao Tzu, LXXX

Père David was a Catholic missionary in China during the last century. Were it not for him, the Père David deer would now be extinct. When he came to Peking, the last of the species, totally unknown to Europeans, were secreted in the huge garden which lay behind the walls of the Emperor's palace. Poaching was a capital offense.

Somehow, magically, Père David talked a small part of the herd to Europe. When revolution hit China a few years later, the palace was stormed and the palace deer roasted. The European herd became the last remnant.

What had happened to Père David's deer? People were too much for it. It required the vast natural forests that once were common in China. But people needed this land for farms. Too bad for Père David's deer. And for who knows what else that wasn't saved.

The Chinese have led civilization for thousands of years. I don't think things have changed. China is not underdeveloped; she is overdeveloped. After all, who was first in art and literature? Where was civil service born? Gunpowder and rockets? Pasta and delicate cooking? Whose culture influenced whose (until the last miserable hundred years)? Whose agronomists bred the weeping willow? Who taught us to use cotton? Whose pharmacopeia first included such important medicaments as ephedrine, arsenic, calomel, alum, camphor, talc, cinnabar, iodine, and opiates? In all of these things as in countless others, we are beholden to China.

In the things that are important, China still leads. India, too, whose people were cultured and comfortable until the mid-eighteenth century, is overdeveloped. But she has not yet begun to adjust. China has.

Already 24 centuries ago, an emperor of China was concerned about the overpopulation of his country. However, until the Communist revolution, famine and despair stalked China. People starved to death in the streets of Shanghai while a few others lived in plenty.

The trouble was that China was producing just barely enough for everyone's minimum needs. Under the usual relaxed conditions of food distribution, when the average amount of food produced is not much higher than the average amount required, some are bound to receive less, some allowed more than the minimum. And so some die, while others live in plenty.

A similar situation troubles most of the world today. In the words of President Johnson's Science Advisory Committee in its report, *The World Food Problem:* "The world's . . . nutritional problem arises from the *uneven distribution* of the food supply among countries, within countries, and among families with different levels of income. Global . . . surveys . . . suggest that there is no . . . shortage of food in terms of quantity (calories) or quality (protein) at the moment."

It takes intense planning and effort to ensure that everyone receives just about the average amount of food. And it takes a stringent, rigid, totalitarian system of distribution. This is the fundamental significance and cause of the rigidity of Chinese Communism. Faced with starvation as the alternative, it is no wonder that Mao and his system were welcomed and supported by his people. He and his regime have saved untold millions of Chinese lives. In this country, that honor is usually reserved to the physician. Do we not revere him? It is thus that the Chinese nation worships Mao.

An American I once met had spent some years in a Chinese prison in the early 1950s. He had been working in China when the Korean War erupted. When China entered, being American was sufficient grounds for detention. He was imprisoned with Chinese, rather than in a POW camp.

Each week his small group met to discuss a prearranged topic. The topic was supposed to have come from Mao himself. Topics were always formulated and discussions always led so that the conclusion was the same in every discussion group in the land. And everyone in China belonged to a discussion group.

Often these discussions were about women and sex. Revolutions, you see, are very puritanical (Brinton). Women were encouraged to wear plain clothes, to work hard, to forego prostitution. They were also exhorted to delay marriage (child brides had been a Chinese custom; before the revolution, people usually married at 15 or 16 years of age). And when they did marry, they were practically ordered at these sessions to have only three or four children. More was grounds for social ostracism—a cruel punishment indeed in a land where travel is prohibitively expensive and one's own village people are the only things left to see and do. All this began to happen in the early 1950s when America was still gloating over its post-war baby boom.

The first official sign of the revolution in attitudes occurred with the marriage law of 1950. This prevents women below 18 and men below 20 from marrying. Although it remains on the books, this law has since been superseded by what the Chinese call a "movement." The "movement," as you will soon read, is far more stringent.

In August, 1953, the revolution began to become overt and official. The Chinese cabinet ordered its Minister of Health "to assist the public in the prevention of births" (Sauvy, p. 234). By the time of the eighth Communist Party Congress (Sept. 1956), Chou En-Lai could declare: "For the protection of women and children, for the upbringing and education of the rising generation, and for the health and prosperity of the nation, we are in favor of some adequate regulation of reproduction. We are entrusting the Ministry of Health with the job of activating a positive program for the prevention of births" (Sauvy, p. 236).

Notice that there is no specific mention of overpopulation in the foregoing or in what is to come. Later we'll examine this point, which is a matter of some interest.

In the period 1956–1957, the campaign to check births intensified. Propaganda urged even later marriages: 20 for women, 25 for men. Stories of unhappy women appeared in the Chinese press; these women were described as mired in family duties and thus prevented from working for society! Stalwart masculine heros published their decisions to delay their weddings. In some cases functionaries simply refused to register marriages if the partners were younger than the newly prescribed minima (Meijer). By March 1957 both sterilization and abortion had become legal (Sauvy, p. 234).

Then in 1958, with the advent of the so-called Great Leap Forward, the government temporarily abandoned its goals. They were soon reaffirmed after the famines of 1959–1962.

"Rather than relying on publicity and voluntary compliance, social coercion was applied through close surveillance and threats of loss of status and privileges" (Piotrow). Marriage is frowned on if the man is below 30, the woman, 25. Students may not marry until they have completed their studies. Government workers who violate the rule are subject to dismissal. "Younger couples might not get rations for themselves or their newborn babies" (Huang). Three years is recommended between marriage and the first birth, and three between that and the second. Two children are the recommended limit and slogans like the following are common: "Two children is just right; three is too many; and four is a mistake" (Huang). Clothing ration tickets for a third child are often not issued.

On the other hand, abortions are free upon demand to workers (and available virtually free to others). Contraceptives, including progesterone pills, are widely available and research on a "once-a-month" pill is being actively pursued. Vasectomy (male sterilization) after two children "is advocated, is free, and is not popular" (Snow).

Which leads directly to an important question: How successful has this government's program been? Edgar Snow reported in *Life* magazine that Mao was not too happy. He felt that the women of the countryside still had as many children as they required to have a son. (Curiously, although Chinese women want sons, they are about the only society perspicacious enough to desire that the firstborn child be a daughter.)

It is difficult to get more objective data on the success of Mao's campaign against excessive births. Despite its sophistication (or perhaps because of it), China remains the country without statistics. The last census was taken in 1953 and revealed that China had 583 million people. But many have questioned the accuracy of this census. Aird estimated the true population of China in 1953 at 608 million and in 1960 at about 720–725 million. More standard figures based on the official 1953 census are included in the following table from Piotrow (p. 19):

China's population (in millions)

Year	Low estimate	Probable estimate	High estimate
1950	—	552	—
1955	611	615	619
1960	655	676	696
1965	700	728	760
1970	747	815	845
1975	797	—	932
1980	848	—	1027
1985	895	—	1122

Perhaps you might agree with me in questioning the importance of exact numbers when the population of one civilization nears the billion mark. One must hope that China will succeed in stemming its growth.

There is a curiosity in the Chinese program. Chinese, being among the most orthodox communists, simply do not believe in overpopulation. They reject Malthusian "doctrine" on ideological grounds. According to Communist doctrine, imperialism and capitalism cause famine and poor living conditions. Consider this gem from Engels: "The productivity of the land can be infinitely increased by the application of capital, labor and science" (quoted by Meek, p. 58).

But neither Marx nor Engels had the responsibility for 800 million Chinese lives. Real leadership in real China has had to bend Marx and Engels just a little, all the while professing a complete disbelief in that which motivates their wisest acts. Instead of emphasizing their plight, they talk of freedom for women, education for children, good health for all. They never admit why it is that all those things are endangered by excessive reproduction. They never admit that too many Communists have just as small a chance of obtaining adequate food, clothing, and shelter as do too many capitalists.

Be that as it may, one must wish China well as she pioneers in population regulation. One must also wish her *bonne chance,* because China probably does not yet have a practical program of long-term population regulation.

The coercion now practiced may be serious, but having lots of children is more serious. As I shall explain in Chapter 18, the Chinese people should gradually become immune to current government pressures and begin again to produce too many babies. Without a rational program of overt population regulation, even the Chinese will fail. China is doomed to become super-overdeveloped. Then even the most stringent rationing and food distribution, even the most totalitarian control of lives, will not save her people from nature's limits. Chinese will again die of famine and disease, of exposure and want.

We shall see that a practical program of density regulation requires an understanding of modern genetics and of the mechanism of natural selection. Communists have refused to acknowledge either. Unfortunately, Karl Marx wrote that mankind would mystically evolve to lose all his avarice if placed in a true communistic society. But this cannot occur because of the way inheritance and evolution work. One hopes that the Chinese will prove as flexible toward Communist dogma against genetics and natural selection as they have toward the dogma against Malthus. They cannot allow either to interfere with their valiant attempt to secure better lives for themselves.

Meanwhile, let us examine the Chinese model. From it we can see what freedoms even the most intelligent can expect to lose in an overpopulated nation. We shall lose the freedom to travel at will over long distances, the freedom to eat much meat, the freedom to obtain a comfortable house, to wear any but the most primitive cloth, to own more than one pair of shoes, to buy what we like when we like, to enjoy the luxuries of TV, radio, most electric appliances, to own boats and cars, to visit or even have any natural environments. We will demand that our political system regimentalize our lives to minimize any chance of our suffering. And most important, having made all those sacrifices, we shall still lose the freedom to raise our children in health and safety, with an adequate diet, decent clothes, and good education. The newborn will no longer have any reasonable guarantee of reaching a productive, fulfilling adulthood.

What shall we have purchased with all these freedoms? Nothing of permanence. Nothing of value. Merely the next several generations of unchecked increase. When that is over, nature will see to it that we lose that freedom, too. The freedom to raise more than two children to adulthood is only transitory. There is still time to realize this and to preserve all the other freedoms—spiritual, political, and material. These freedoms can indeed be permanent if only we are willing to purchase them by renouncing the temporary one. There is no more precious gift we could give our children and grandchildren.

7 the roots of human population growth

What has caused the incredible boom in human population? Is it the culmination of a gradual increase whose geometric proportions have only recently become evident? Or does it result instead from some really radical change in human ecology?

One's sense of intuition rebels at the complete acceptance of the gradualistic notion. There was no severe population trouble for the first two million years of human existence. Two hundred and perhaps even one hundred years ago, almost all the world was truly underdeveloped. Then in a brief flash of geological time, in an instant of even man's existence as *Homo sapiens,* we are sinking in a sea of humanity. In five or six generations we have lost our elbow room, our privacy, our horizons, our frontiers.

In this case intuition is perfectly reliable. In most places, for most of man's history, population did not increase. Increases have instead been sporadic. They have been preceded by ecological change (often caused by major advances in civilization). There are even cases known in which change brought a decrease in population.

EIGHTEENTH-CENTURY JAPAN

A classical example of a steady-state population was Japan. It is known that at least from 1720 to 1850, Japan did not grow. Her 1721 estimated census was 26 million; in 1852, she estimated her population at 27.2 million. Figure 7-1 depicts the known Japanese censuses during this period. This "is one of the longer and closer approaches to stationary population equilibrium *at a subsistence level* found in *recorded* demographic history" (Bronfenbrenner and Buttrick, p. 169, emphases mine).

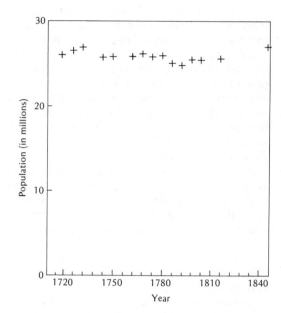

Fig. 7-1 Japanese population in the Tokugawa period. (Data from Droppers.)

What controlled Japanese population size? Disease and famine. From 1690 to 1740 there were eight famines, four very destructive. From 1741 to 1790 there were seven, five destructive. From 1791 to 1840 there were six, only two destructive (Droppers).

Years of particularly destructive famines in Japan

1702	1710	1721	1732	1749	1757	1780	1783	1787	1825	1836

During times of famine, smallpox and measles did their grisly work with aid from dysentery and typhus.

Regional censuses before 1720 indicate that Japanese population grew steadily during the 1600s and probably even during the first decade or two of the 1700s. But the limits of the Japanese archipelago to support human life were eventually reached. The common Japanese suffered the consequences.

The 1732 famine was "caused" when a fly ravaged the rice of western Japan. Three-fourths was destroyed. Over 2.5 million Japanese went on relief, but at least 200,000 died anyway.

Worst of all was the series of famines from 1780 through 1787. Examples of the destruction of both human life and human spirit were rampant and have been preserved by contemporary Japanese authors.

One town of 800 homes declined to 30. A traveler met a man who bragged he could live without eating humans because he had a rich uncle.

Dogs and rats fetched exorbitant prices over the meat counters, but a rare work of art couldn't even be traded for a single cup of rice. Stealing and looting became accepted practice (Droppers).

Since people who died of starvation were not very nutritious (their muscles having wasted away), those doomed were killed outright and pickled. A story is told of a farmer who counted the loss of his wife and son to starvation. He pleaded with a neighbor to kill his other son, since he too was doomed to die. There being no food, the neighbor agreed after first extracting the promise of half the boy's body. The neighbor killed the son and was in turn killed by the farmer "in revenge." The farmer of course pickled both (Droppers).

In the face of such degradation, the Japanese retaliated by practicing contraception, prostitution, and *mabiki* (Bronfenbrenner and Buttrick). *Mabiki* means "thinning out," a not too delicate, but brutally realistic agricultural euphemism for outright infanticide. A farmer looked at his crops, counted his children, and did what he had to do to preserve those to whom he was already committed. As we have seen in this century, the alternative is for most or all the older children to die or be stunted by PCM. Unhappily, that also would have been the likely fate of the infant had his life been spared.

Japanese population is now about 105 million. This increase occurred after the Japanese finally allowed themselves contact with Western civilization. They learned to trade for food grown elsewhere. So *mabiki* became temporarily unnecessary and was abandoned.

In the last quarter of a century, as the Japanese teetered artfully atop one of the most precarious ecological promontories in the world, they have had to reinstitute *mabiki*. But today it is possible to perform it sooner, call it abortion, and render it infinitely less traumatic to everyone concerned. Biologically, abortion is accomplishing the same function as *mabiki* in much the same way. To those with respect for human life, there is only the hope that abortion can be minimized. The Japanese are showing that concern.

EXAMPLES OF OTHER
NONGROWING HUMAN POPULATIONS

Few ages have been more disastrous to civilization than the sixth century A.D., when the triple scourge of war, pestilence, and famine, afflicted the subjects of Justinian; and his reign is disgraced by a visible decrease of the human species, which has never been repaired in some of the fairest countries of the globe (Gibbon).

There are many European communities known whose populations have remained constant for nearly the last thousand years. These areas are literally carpeted with people. Occasionally wars or plagues have created small, fleeting vacuua (Langer). Often these communities have exported their surplus. Unwanted masses went to the Americas, to South Africa. Emma Lazarus' lines are well-chosen: "Give me your tired, your poor, your huddled masses yearning to breathe free, the wretched refuse of your teeming shore. Send these, the homeless, tempest-tossed to me." Too bad we have run short of golden doors. There is no more market for surplus people. And occasional wars and plagues are unacceptably devastating. Consequently, in the past three decades, Europe has begun to grow rapidly.

Permanent or nearly permanent decline from ecological change is known in several arid regions. The Bible records a census for what is now Israel and Jordan during Solomon's reign. Starting from its figures of adult Israelite men, one can estimate that the region supported about five million (Huntington, p. 263). In the last century, its population was about 500,000 and steady. This difference, a whole order of magnitude, may be larger than the truth, but there definitely had been a decline. Ancient farms, carefully terraced for arboriculture, lay unused. Forests were gone. Cities, once alive, had become archaeological treasures. Recently, the introduction of modern techniques of agriculture and afforestation have supported a large population increase. The area now supports about as many as it did in Solomon's time.

In Arizona, another arid-zone civilization, the Hohokam was once a large and complex Indian nation. A relic of its past can be seen at Casa Grande National Monument. Dilapidated structures on the monument are typical of dozens of similar Hohokam towns. Despite their former splendor, they have decayed and disappeared. Even assuming Hohokam houses held only one person, these people were overwhelmingly more abundant than their descendants, the Pima.

The Pima live along the Salt River near Phoenix. They have had a bad time from the wretched refuse (Webb). But the white man did not destroy their ancestors, the Hohokam. He found the Pima already restricted to the Salt River valley.

Archaeologists tell us that the Hohokam were dependent on earthen irrigation ditches. They fed themselves in Arizona's hot, dry center by channeling water to their fields. But the water carried with it a normal quantity of salt, and as the water evaporated or was used by the food plants, the salt remained behind in the soil. It formed an impenetrable layer because the area is underlain with an impervious clay. The land became alkaline and waterlogged. Excavated Hohokam granaries show signs of having been elevated again and again—presumably to keep their contents dry (Shetrone). But there was no way the Hohokam could maintain the fertility of their fields in the face of the environmental changes which they themselves had unwittingly wrought. Faced with declining resources, their population crashed and its remnant retreated to the Salt River valley.

A better known case of population decline is recorded in the history of Ireland. In the seventeenth century, Ireland had about 2 million people. Then the potato was introduced from the Americas to her farmers. Her population quadrupled (Boulding).

In the 1840s, Ireland's potato crop was decimated by a merciless competitor—potato blight. Millions of Irish—some one-third of the population—starved to death. Another third left, most to come to America. In the past century, by marrying in their middle and late 30s, the Irish have managed to hold down their population to the several million their island can support. That is of course very nearly the same as the prepotato population some 400 years ago.

Late marriage is not without its human costs. Woman is adapted to having children earlier than age 35 or 40. Certain congenital defects including one that causes mongoloid idiocy are much more common in children whose mothers have passed 35. Yet, no one can condemn the Irish for their experiment. They have avoided a repetition of the far more consequential miseries that were inflicted upon them over 100 years ago.

MIXED BLESSINGS

Since it is apparent that human population has often in the past reached its steady state, we must look for a great ecological change to explain our population explosion. The change is basically twofold and to a small extent threefold. First, modern medicine has eliminated the greatest part of once-dreadful infant mortality rates. Second, agronomists have discovered methods of increasing the yield of food per acre by the use of new strains of plants and animals, by husbandry of the soil, and by combating parasites and pests—our competitors. Third, the Industrial Revolution has provided man with machinery and power, which greatly increases the productive capacity of each farmer. We examine these in reverse order.

The Industrial Revolution is least important. Its main effect has been to allow fewer men to raise food for all. Thus, it has made urban life possible. It has fostered a different life-style, but not a different number of lives. Occasionally it has perhaps allowed land to be worked that could not have been before machinery became motorized.

The agricultural revolution has no doubt raised our steady state. It has most definitely provided us with a greater resource supply. At any substantial density of people, their nutrition will be better. Thus their capacity for birth will be higher. And their stronger resistance to disease will minimize their death rate. In other words, the equality of birth and death occurs at a higher population density.

Yet the increase in agricultural capacity has not been as large as most people seem to think. It has not resulted in a world where even 10 times as many can live, but instead it has perhaps doubled our world's ability to support people. In the United States and Canada, where there has been truly remarkable progress in technology, plant breeding, and crop-pest and disease control, a doubling of wheat yield per acre was achieved in the pivotal years 1934–1965 (Borgstrom, pp. 46, 47). A similar experience was recorded in Australia from 1900–1965 (Borgstrom, p. 55). That's about the best we can hope for in the rest of the world, too. Perhaps more will come, but more cannot be counted on. (See Fig. 7-2.)

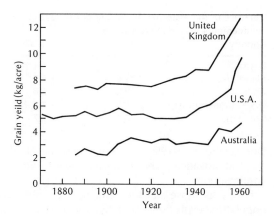

Fig. 7-2 Grain yields in developed countries have about doubled overall as a result of the agricultural revolution. In restricted places for certain grains like corn, the increase has been fourfold or fivefold. In other cases the increase has been much more modest. The differences between countries reflect differences in climate for the most part. (From Miles.)

A great deal of the land that was once too poor to be planted has been artificially fertilized and now supports human life. Borgstrom (p. 26) estimated that about 600 million people (about one of every six people alive today) owe their very existences to land reclaimed with artificial fertilizer. Despite this, he concludes that most of the increase in the world's supply of food comes from greater intrinsically fertile acreage being farmed and from increased planting of more than one crop per year (multicropping). As we have seen, we are almost out of "new" land. And multicropping has only limited additional applicability. Agricultural promises must be kept realistically conservative.

The growth in human population would have occurred with agricultural advancement alone, but it would have been slower if medical progress had not also occurred. Medicine has provided womankind with the extra punch that threatens to knock out our natural environments in our own lifetime.

Previously each woman produced about five live babies on the average. Actually, the rare women who married young (15) and lived to die of old age, averaged about a dozen children. But since many delayed marriage, many were sterile or celibate, and many died in childbirth and of various diseases, the average woman had only five live births (Sauvy). Of those five children, a very large number died in infancy or early childhood. The actual average number of surviving children per woman was thus only 2.4 (Sauvy). My paternal grandmother, when she immigrated to the United States from Poland in the early part of the century, had already lost two of her four sons to a plague. They had been healthy and normal, but they died in a week in which most of the town's children were destroyed. Who can think about birth control in such an environment?

The difference between modern and not-so-ancient mortality statistics is astonishing. Sauvy relates the statistics from various countries from 1937 and 1957 while their women were absorbing some benefits of modern medical technology.

**Decrease in the maternal death rate per thousand
confinements in one 20-year period**

Country	1937	1957
Ceylon	20.5	4.1
Mauritius	11.6	1.6
Chile	9.2	2.8
U.S.A. (nonwhites)	8.9	1.3
Colombia	8.4	3.7

During the mid-1950s, in countries that had already fully implemented medical advances, the maternal death rate was only 0.5 per thousand confinements.

Lovely as those statistics are, they do not account for very much of the population explosion. Actually, the vast and remarkable medical achievement has been in lowering mortality of infants and toddlers. It is these saved little babies that are the source of our mammoth growth. In Western countries today, when care is provided, only 15 to 20 of every thousand live-born die within their first year. Even where care is poor, such as in black urban ghettos, mortality rarely exceeds 40 or 50 per thousand.

Compare that to the mortality statistics in Latin America, Turkey, Uganda, the Philippines. The infant mortality rate is ten times as high in those countries (see Chapter 5) as it should be.

TABLE 7-1   INFANT MORTALITY RATES

Country	1940	1950	1960	1964
Sweden	39.2	21.0	16.6	14.2
Netherlands	39.1	25.2	17.9	14.8
Finland	88.3	43.5	21.0	16.9
Denmark	50.2	30.7	21.5	18.7
Switzerland	46.2	31.2	21.1	19.0
New Zealand	—	27.6	22.6	19.1
Australia	38.4	24.5	20.2	19.1
France	95.3	52.0	27.4	23.4
United States	47.0	29.2	26.0	24.2
Canada	56.4	41.5	27.3	24.7
West Germany	64.1	55.6	33.8	25.3
Belgium	93.2	53.4	31.2	25.8
U.S.S.R	—	81.0	35.0	30.9
Italy	102.7	63.8	43.9	35.5
Hungary	130.1	85.7	47.6	39.2
Ceylon	148.9	81.6	56.8	52.8
Mexico	125.7	96.2	74.2	66.3
Portugal	126.1	94.1	77.5	69.0

Source: Oiso.

The trend to lower infant mortality rates has been worldwide, however. Table 7-1 from Oiso ought to demonstrate that to anyone's satisfaction. Figure 7-3 shows graphically the decline in Japan's and in England and Wales's infant mortality rates from 1896 to 1969: typically remarkable, very recent, and clearly explosive. The same trend has been evident in later years of life. The following table (adapted from Bengoa) shows how much better Sweden does in maintaining life than several other poorer countries where medical care and food is scarcer. The figures from the UAR may be closest to those of mankind before medical science.

Country (year)	People who die before 1 year (%) (infant mortality/10)	People who die from 1 to 4 years (%)
Sweden (1962)	1.6	0.3
Venezuela (1961)	6.0	1.8
Philippines (1960)	6.8	3.1
Chile (1960)	11.9	3.4
U.A.R. (1961)	21.9	11.6

Is it true that all this decrease has been caused by increasing standards of public health? Yes, because often the decrease in mortality can be traced

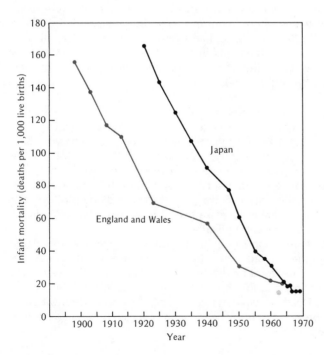

Fig. 7-3 In nations with modern medical care, infant mortality has plummeted.

to the establishment of *one* medical institution. For example, Williams notes that after a children's health service was established in Malta, the infant mortality plummeted. In 1942, it was 280/1000; in 1956 it was 40, and in 1962, 30.

Quite spectacular evidence that western medicine is responsible comes from the Middle East. In the 1920s a wave of Jewish immigration to what is now Israel brought with it an influx of European medical practice. Infant mortality responded rapidly (Sereni and Ashery, p. 79).

In 1924 and 1925, and again in 1933, the following infant mortality rates (per thousand) were measured in Palestine's three religious groups:

	Moslem	Christian Arab	Jew
1924–1925	200	152–162	131–160
1933	157	129	69–82

Meanwhile in Jordan (then Transjordan) the infant mortality rate was still 200 in 1931–1933. And in Iraq during 1931 to 1933, Baghdad lost 273 of every 1000 infants; Batzra, 233; and Mosul, 389 (Sereni and Ashery). In the 1950s, the Iraqi infant mortality rate was still about 300 (Patwardhan and Darby). And we have seen above that in the U.A.R. in 1961 it was 219 (that is, 21.9%).

But there is more. Moslem towns close to Jewish settlements were really the only Palestinian towns whose infant mortality dropped. In 1931, Hebron and Gaza, far from Western medicine, had infant mortalities of 237 and 246. But Acre, near the Jewish settlements in the valley of Jezreel and the city of Haifa, had an infant mortality of only 110, quite similar to that of their Jewish neighbors (Sereni and Ashery).

Can you still doubt the role medicine plays in supporting the population explosion? Suppose medical knowledge saves 20% of all babies. Then every generation has 1 1/4 as many people as it would have otherwise had. In three generations, about a century, there will be 1 1/4 x 1 1/4 x 1 1/4 or about twice as many people as there otherwise could have been.

Such a profound change in our limitation by disease has accelerated the population explosion. Not only can we grow to a higher density, we can do it much faster. The potential increase was already being born. Medicine converted it to reality by preventing deaths.

Often an examination of the causes of a problem, suggests a reasonable solution. Not this time. In fact, this time we can see a solution to be avoided. Do we eliminate good medicine and let babies die? Do we outlaw the practice of agronomy and force people to starve to death? Either would be sheer stupidity. Death is what we are trying to avoid. Deprivation is what we seek to prevent. Neither need be promulgated by men; nature will do that job if we let her.

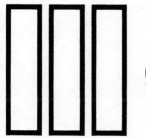

goals

Someday when the world is cemented over, a blade of grass will break through a tiny crack and through that crack freedom will grow again.

Ilya Ehrenburg, *Thor*

8 on optimal population density: a new freedom

In my simplicity I remember wondering why every
gentleman did not become an ornithologist.

Charles Darwin, *Autobiography*

I'll bet the average citizen of the United States doesn't want to live in New York City. I know that most New Yorkers do not choose to live there, do not care to live there, but are forced to. The industrial revolution has pushed men off farms and into unplanned, uninvited megalopolis. They don't like it but they aren't free to do anything about it. We have created a society in which most people are not truly free to select the environment in which they wish to live. I propose that they should enjoy this freedom.

People who think about population size always wonder what the optimum population is of this or that subdivision of the planet Earth. The fact that some like Manhattan and others dread it should suggest that this is a bad question. There is not one optimum population density for all. Each person has his own preference. Further, different population densities are safely supportable at any one place. Each density, however, implies a different sort of environment.

MUTUALLY EXCLUSIVE ASPECTS
OF HUMAN ENVIRONMENTS

A New York State of 5 million souls is certainly feasible. It implies vast tracts of forest and mountain wilderness, clean air and water with little need to expend money to obtain them, small cities with easily manageable trash and traffic problems, a minimum of restraint on business and on individuals.

However, it also implies the loss of many Manhattan-supplied specialty goods and services. It takes a large population to generate enough people interested in the pre-Baroque music of Palestrina to support devoted Palestrina scholars and musicians. Quality maintenance of large public trusts like museums and libraries would cost more per person. A large population is the reason "you can get anything in New York."

Well, almost anything. You can't hardly get in or out. You can't see a wilderness or even a fairly natural beach, forest, or meadow. About the only animals around are people, dogs, cats, people, roaches, rats, people, pigeons, starlings, people, and an occasional pet ocelot. The only plants are aspidistra, monstera, philodendron, and geranium. Fine for some. Not fine for all.

Perhaps New York State could support a population of 50 million. This would imply more human-oriented goods and services, fewer natural, low-pressure environments. Pollution would require a great deal of time, energy, and money to be reduced to tolerable levels. The pressure on the land might reduce the size of the New York State forest preserves. At the very least, they would be less restorative, less refreshing, less free of people and their gadgets. Many New York species might become extinct; wildflowers would become even scarcer than they are now. Land hunger would reduce the size of house lots and increase the proportion of people who live in apartments and other rented dwellings. Home ownership would be for the rich. People would need to be constrained carefully to protect them from each other. "Keep your dogs licensed and leashed; don't drive private cars on this thoroughfare; don't plant or cut trees without city permission; don't buy more than five pounds of meat per month."

I could say more, but it would be pure speculation. No one really knows what constraints need to be imposed by a carefully planned community of any size in any particular environment. What we do know is that many different densities can be comfortably supported in a given place. We know that these different densities will be different in what they offer people and what they force them to do. In general, with a given level of technology and a given knowledge of ecology, higher densities yield more people-oriented goods and services, more behavioral constraints, greater costs of pollution control per person, and less nature.

Since nature imposes a limit to all populations in all environments, we might as well decide what population density we'd like to achieve. Why let nature pilfer our choice? Why let her impose her marginal and unpleasant limits? We should recognize our opportunity and seize it. Perhaps a formal body should be created to study the question of optimal population. If it is, it should exist at both local and federal levels. Its job would be to determine the human condition at each reasonable population density—a job which would require a tremendous research effort—and to inform and educate the people as to these alternative densities and their implications. The local people can decide which alternative they prefer. It is possible that slight downward adjustments would have to be made by the federal body if every community picked a very high density and as a nation we needed to be less dense to be self-sufficient. This is unlikely.

VARIABILITY

It is also important to avoid a tyranny of the majority. The population should be able to be maintained at widely different densities within a small area. The areas devoted to each density could be determined by proportional representation. If 40% of the people of a county wanted to live at a density of 100 per square mile, then 40% of dwelling places should be built in such densities.

Making sure that small areas have widely divergent densities has two great advantages. It minimizes the sacrifices that any group has to make. City people can quickly get to the country. Country people can get to the city. Also it provides families with a real choice, a true freedom of density. Because a man lives near many densities, he does not have to quit his job to take advantage of this freedom.

Exact sizes of areas to be used will vary. In order to get a few really large cities of a million or two, many smaller units could contribute high-density land. In order to preserve the large contiguous areas that are necessary for wilderness, we shall also need to pool the low-density land from many smaller units.

Details large and small remain to be elucidated. Long years of study and research lie ahead. But this is the right course. We must decide what we want or lose our choice. Everyone should be free to be able to live in the density that he enjoys most—the density that for him, maximizes his fulfillment and delivers the richest possible lifetime.

9 animalistic do-nothingism

There is no need to repeat . . . either the ill-founded attacks of churchmen on Darwinism, which have often been recalled, or the ill-founded attacks of Darwinists on the Church, which are usually forgotten. It is enough to say that, while many churchmen . . . showed a lamentable ignorance of the findings and the principles of biology, the same could be said of various Darwinists in relation to theology. Mixed up with the truth, there were ignorant, unjustifiable, absurd and violent assertions on both sides.
D. Lack, *Evolutionary Theory and Christian Belief*

If society ignores nature, as man and all other living things have always done in the past, then man's population will reach a steady state by natural forces. We cannot tell what this steady state will be. Perhaps it will be even smaller than our present population. The brunt of previous chapters has been to show that it will come and how it will come.

However, just because a species is due to be regulated in density is no reason to fear for its existence. When man's population stabilizes, he will almost certainly not be extinct. Quite probably, civilization as we know it will be. But man himself is the world's most adaptable creature. He will be the last to go.

I shall not repeat the unpleasant hand-to-mouth future for *Mankind ignoramus*. However, it is relevant to repeat the fact that as density rises beyond a certain point, so does death. It is not important why a child dies—only tragic that he does. And if we assume haughtily that we can evade God's rules, that we can always overbreed and still maintain a constantly low death rate, then we have assumed an infinitely growing population. In that case, in the light of our superior brainpower, we shall be the first species to deserve its skimpy fate. But will those doomed children deserve theirs? It will be our mistakes that harm them.

Being basically squeamish, I prefer not to permit my world to deteriorate to the point where my grandchildren will be subjected to a higher death rate. But I will admit that this is fundamentally my aesthetic opinion. I have the feeling, however, that I am in the majority—the overwhelming majority.

RELIGION'S RESPONSIBILITY

Because religion is also reluctant to allow innocent children to suffer and die, I am sure that religion will be man's greatest ally in his attempt to regulate his density. The sanctity of human life is one of religion's most important basic principles. In the face of the certainty that man must either control himself or doom his children, I have confidence that the religious will choose life and health and self-control. Saving lives is more important than refraining from a particular method of birth control.

The first four chapters of Genesis are among the Bible's most succinct, most important statements of general ethical principles. Often, however, they are couched in charming allegory and missed if not carefully thought about. One God created the universe and its inhabitants. Whence our impertinence to assume we can freely destroy God's creations? Cain's punishment for slaying Abel is God's indictment of murder. It was His first proclamation of the sanctity of human life. Can we dare ignore it?

The slaughter of our children and our children's children by overpopulation will be just as willful as Abel's murder, because we have the knowledge to prevent it. Moreover, the extermination by men of other species has often been direct. Greedy men battered to death the last great auk. Greedy, cruel men deprived the last American herd of wild bison of water until they were crazed with thirst, and then shot them. Greedy men poach the world's remaining leopards to satisfy our vanity. Greedy men destroy our everglades and its creatures. Where does the Lord sanctify greed, cruelty, and vanity? It is life that is holy.

If not, why was Noah commanded to preserve animal species (Genesis vi:19, 20)? Why are animals included with naive and innocent children as inhabitants for whose sake Nineveh ought to be spared (Jonah iv:11)? And why does Genesis (viii:1) insist that God remembered Noah and *every living thing*?

Get out your Bible! Genesis i:26, 28 reads (in part), ". . . let them [men] have dominion over the fish of the sea, and over the fowl of the air, and over the cattle, and over all the earth . . ." and God said to them, "Be fruitful, and multiply, and replenish the earth, and subdue it: and have dominion over the fish of the sea, and over the fowl of the air, and over every creeping thing that creepeth upon the earth." Read it again. Those words are "dominion," not "destruction" and "subdue," not "destroy."

Moreover, the English version (like any translation) misses some of the overtones of the original. The original doesn't say: "have dominion," it says "וירדו." This Hebrew word carries not a hint of destruction. Instead it has overtones that clearly intend man's use of other life for food. In addition to "have dominion," it can also mean "draw honey" or "draw bread from the oven." In the Noah section, the Bible is even clearer about the intended use of animals as food: ". . . into your hand are they delivered. Every moving thing that liveth shall be for food for you; as the green herb have I given you all" (Genesis ix:2, 3).

When Genesis i:28 says "subjugate" or "subdue the earth," it is again clear in the Hebrew that destruction is not intended. In fact, one of the senses of כבש, the Hebrew word used for "subdue" is "preserve—that is, prevent from rotting: pickle."

And when the Bible repeats these sentiments in Psalms viii:7, it changes Hebrew words and clearly specifies משל, "to rule." Here the beautiful alternate meaning of the verb is "liken" or "compare." Thus, while the primary meaning of verse 7 makes man king of beasts, the poetical overtones find him not above comparison with his subjects. Furthermore, the English translation of the rest of verse 7 is quite insufficient: "All things are under his feet." The problem is that there is a good Hebrew word for "thing," דבר, and it is not used. Instead the Psalmist uses שתת, a root which is difficult. It may deal with drinking; thus "everything which drinks. . . ." It may also mean foundation or support; thus the animal world is viewed as a basis upon which man's very existence depends. This is not ambiguity. Such complexity is characteristic of the Bible's wealth.

The Book of Job points out that although man has license to use nature for his sustenance, man is not the be-all and the end-all of the world. In Job, God points out that many species and many habitats exist despite man's inability to tame and use them. Here is the Bible's pronouncement of the fundamental value of wilderness.

Who hath left a channel for the waterflood, or a way for the lightning of the thunder; to cause it to rain on a land where no man is, on the wilderness wherein there is no man; to satisfy the desolate and waste ground, and to cause the bud of the tender herb to spring forth? . . . Who hath sent out the wild ass free. . . . Whose house I have made the wilderness, and the salt land his dwelling place? He scorneth the tumult of the city, neither heareth he the shoutings of the driver. The range of the mountains is his pasture, and he searcheth after every green thing. . . . Whatsoever is under the whole heaven is Mine. (Job xxxviii:25–27; xxxvix:5–8; xli:3)

Genesis bids us be fruitful and multiply. But in the same sentence we may read "and replenish the Earth." Replenish means refill. It means replace your generation with a successor. Replenish is a fine translation of the original Hebrew, מלא. This word means "fill." Not "overfill."

Finally, the animal world itself is charged with the responsibility to be fruitful; and Noah—the personification of the good man—is held responsible for helping them carry out their responsibility (vii:15–17): "Bring forth with thee every living thing . . . that they may be fruitful and multiply upon the earth." Who but God could have foreseen that man would one day need to have such a commandment? Which but our generation has before needed to keep it? Truly they are devils who cite scripture to justify the rape of God's Earth, to sanctify their lustful, prideful attempt to people the world with their own descendants.

There are those who say we should not interfere with God's natural plan. But what is that plan? And why have we been given minds capable of warning us of our fate? Anyone taking penicillin has tampered with his fate, as has anyone living in a house instead of a tree or cave, or wearing clothes. Even eating actively preserves life. Who bids us ignore threats to the lives of our descendants, he bids us to sin.

ARE THERE ALTERNATIVES?

Many well-meaning people notice the symptoms of over-population and ask that something be done to treat them. Grow more food. Grow more nutritious food. Build more livable cities. Clean the air and water. Develop new sources of energy. These people are not to be ignored.

Unless we mount a massive campaign to treat the symptoms of human overabundance, many more of us will die or live unsatisfying lives than necessary. But we must also recognize the limitations of symptomatic treatment. It can never supply us with infinite resources for an infinite population. And the longer we ignore that fact, the more costly, more dangerous, and less successful our technological treatment becomes. Some feel we have already lost the chance to do any good by symptomatic treatment in many countries (Paddock and Paddock). Perhaps they are right. But this should never stop us from trying. Starving, deprived people must be helped for as long as we have resources to help even one.

CAN FREEDOM BE PRESERVED?
WHAT FREEDOM?

There are those who, owing to their love for freedom, would drift into do-nothingism. Recognizing that density regulation means giving up the freedom to produce any number of children at will, they are cast into a pit of indecision. Perhaps it will help them to realize that the freedom they might give is the most loving, valuable gift they could give; that it is the sole way they can guarantee their children's chance to raise healthy grandchildren in a safe, abundant world. Perhaps it will help to remind them that the freedom they might give is only transitory, any-how—nature would soon take it away. A population that always raises more than two fertile adult children per couple is an infinite population, and infinite populations are impossible. Perhaps it will help to remind them of all the political, economic, travel, nature-pleasure, gustatory, and health freedoms that *can* be made permanent, that are available for trade to the population willing to pay with the *temporary* freedom of population growth. If young men are willing to risk their very lives for the freedom of their countrymen, who will not be willing to sacrifice his excess births for the permanent freedom of his own descendants?

Man is supposed to be better than other species. I wonder whether he is. At any rate, he now has a chance to prove it. Is he truly rational? Can he actually regulate his own population for his own comfort, health, and safety? Can he respect other life forms? If he can, he will be the world's first animal to do it. He will have proved himself uniquely moral, uniquely wise, uniquely respectable.

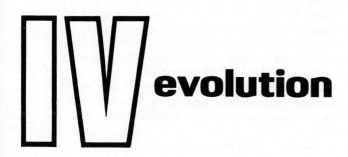

IV evolution

The alternative to doing nothing about the size of our population is not clear. What can we do? In general several proposals have been seriously advanced:

1. Educate people so that they voluntarily produce the appropriate family size.
2. Tax and/or reward families according to the appropriateness of their family size.
3. Sterilize everyone temporarily and issue birth permits and fertility drugs only as needed.
4. Require overtly that each family be limited to two children, but leave the method of birth control and timing of each birth to the family.
5. Allow only those of superior mental capacity and/ or physical health and/or aesthetic sensibilities and/or genetic constitution to reproduce.

Proponents of the last-mentioned solution are generally aware that if enforced it would cause a precipitous decline in population. But let me assure you they have no idea just how precipitous! In fact this "solution" is so heinous to me that I cannot delay telling you it is no solution at all; it has nothing directly to do with population density control. Much later we shall be able to return to it and dismiss it in detail.

Perhaps solutions (2), (3), and (4) are also distasteful to you. They are to most people. However, our planet spins in a real universe and if proposal (1) seems unlikely to work, we will have to select one of the others. Believing in fantasies is only wishful thinking and never will amount to anything else.

Which brings us to the crucial question. How does one evaluate proposals to control population size? Surely at least three types of judgments enter into an evaluation. First there is pragmatism: will it work? If not, there is no sense talking about it. Pragmatism is in fact the only *necessary* yardstick by which to measure a proposal designed to produce a stable population.

However, pragmatism is not the only *desirable* criterion. Both ethical and political considerations will almost certainly enter into any discussion of the value of a proposal which has passed the test of pragmatism. The ethical questions concern matters of religion, abortion, and human life. The political ones center about the question of how much interference in people's private lives is good or avoidable and how important is the individual compared to the state or the society.

Ethical and political questions are certainly not the special province of the scientist. Although my opinions in these areas are of no more (or less) value than yours, toward the end of this book I shall take the liberty of presenting them. At least this will ensure that such considerations are never forgotten. In fact you probably have already noticed that I am not exactly reticent about offering my ethical opinions. This is no reaction to the general beratement of science for its lack of morality (although perhaps that allowed the ethics to get past the reviewers). It is a simple consequence of the fact that I, as an individual, am concerned that science be used to help people achieve their moral standards. Since it may sometimes be easier for the scientist to recognize that certain of his work is likely to have moral consequences, I point out things which have obvious moral implications. Let the reader recognize the numerous moral issues in the text of which its author is unaware because he is too close to the scientific issues.

It is probable that you are reading this book more because Rosenzweig is a scientist and less because he is an opinionated moralist. It is therefore fitting that the overwhelming portion of the book deals with serious scientific topics in a scientific manner and in significant depth. Up to this point the choice of scientific topics has probably seemed quite logical to you. But now I am about to launch into a highly detailed presentation of evolutionary mechanics and that must seem strange. What has evolution to do with overpopulation?

Plenty. Without a firm understanding of evolution, one is simply unable to evaluate the practical prospects of the various proposals. Furthermore, no matter which proposal is selected, it will take knowledge of evolutionary processes to predict how the proposal is likely to change people and their lives. Thus, an evolutionary understanding also provides us with some of the facts we need to make our moral and political evaluations. In order to understand the reason for our collective desire to overpopulate at least the Earth and preferably the whole Universe, we must examine the consequences of the process called natural selection.

It has been my experience that those who have studied evolution have no trouble relating it to population problems, while those who have merely been told about it can never grasp the relationship. Therefore, I encourage you to accompany me on a rigorous journey through the difficult maze that is the science of biological evolution. I trust you will appreciate it a bit for its own sake too; it is, after all, one of the major scientific keys to understanding ourselves and the world in which we live. But even should you find yourself uninterested, I promise you that no one can hope to grapple with the monumental problem of limiting a population's size until he has first mastered the fundamentals of evolutionary thought.

10 evolution has occurred

I rejoice that I have avoided controversies.

Charles Darwin, *Autobiography*

In 1831, Charles Darwin shipped out on H.M.S. *Beagle* to see the world. When he left, he was utterly convinced that each living species had been created as is and had remained as is for all time. He did not believe in evolution—even though his grandfather, Erasmus Darwin, was a famous proponent of evolution and had exposed Charles to the idea.

When, almost five years later, Darwin returned to England, he was just as utterly convinced that evolution is real! What happened on that journey? How had Darwin been led to change his mind? How had he come to believe that the incredible number of species (about two million) with all their marvelous and diverse appearances, behaviors, and physiologies had been produced by some very slow, very mechanical process?

To answer this question, I shall spend this chapter taking you on your own voyage of the *Beagle*. I will not show you exactly what Darwin saw. Instead, you will read some of the most powerful and convincing examples of evolution that evolutionists have discovered in the years since Darwin's *The Origin of Species* was first published. Darwin's experiences were similar, but less complete. Seeing only the things he saw and realizing that evolution is their only reasonable explanation takes Darwin's genius.

WHAT IS EVOLUTION?

Before we embark, we must know what it is we seek. This is no small problem with evolution, because evolution does not happen to individuals. Nobody has ever evolved. Each of us is conceived, develops, and dies.

Evolution is a special kind of change that can occur only to a group of organisms. *Evolution is a change in the inherited phenotypes (the heritable appearance) of members of a population.* Let us define the three technical words in that statement. The *phenotype* of any organism is all of its measurable features: its color, size, biochemical constituents, rates of development, behavior—everything, in fact, that one can tell about the organism from examining it directly. A *population* may be defined as a group of organisms of the same species living in a more or less restricted place. Defining *species* is difficult (see Chapter 17), but you will not go wrong if, like Darwin, you use "similar phenotype" and "same species" interchangeably. Later you will do better. Return to the beginning of the paragraph and reread the definition of evolution.

How is it possible for the population to evolve if its members cannot? Simple. Although the population is composed of individuals, it has different ones at different times. Hence, looking at a population at two widely separated times allows us to tell if it has evolved. If the individuals we observe in the population today do not have the same phenotypes as those we would have seen in earlier generations, and if any of these new phenotypes can be passed along to future generations, then we say that this population has evolved.

FOSSILS:
HOW CAN EVOLUTION BE OBSERVED?

In order to observe evolution, we must compare a population with its ancestral populations. In practice, we usually observe past populations by obtaining samples of their membership, called fossils. Often these samples are small in number. With luck, the observed ancient individuals are more or less typical of their populations. Eventually, as the number of our samples increases, we gain confidence in our ability to describe the ancient population. (See Fig. 10-1.)

Of course, we can never prove that the small part of the phenotype we observe as a fossil is inheritable. We simply assume it is. The alternative is believing that the phenotypic changes we note in the fossil record have been caused by great changes in the environment. The alternative would say, for example, that cows were alive long, long ago but they grew up in an environment which made them look like dinosaurs.

Not too many people take this alternative seriously. They observe that a cow looks like a cow in whatever modern environment it grows up. They believe that it also would have looked cowlike in all past environments.

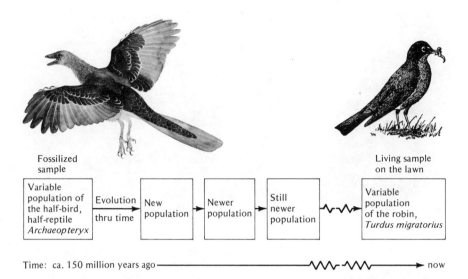

Fossilized
sample

Living sample
on the lawn

| Variable population of the half-bird, half-reptile *Archaeopteryx* | Evolution thru time | New population | Newer population | Still newer population | | Variable population of the robin, *Turdus migratorius* |

Time: ca. 150 million years ago —————————————⌇⌇⌇——→ now

Fig. 10-1 Diagram of the definition of evolution. Evolution is the modification of heredity in a population's membership. Although *Archaeopteryx* (left) may not have been the exact ancestor of modern birds, it must have been fairly close to that ancestor. It retained many reptilian features: teeth, bones in the tail, and digits on the forward edge of the wing. But its feathers are completely birdlike. (*Archaeopteryx* restoration by Maurice Wilson. Courtesy of the Trustees of the British Museum (Natural History). Robin by G. M. Sutton. 1928. *An introduction to the birds of Pennsylvania.*)

Thus, they believe the reason that the dim past yields no cows must be that there weren't any. The evolutionist is convinced that today's herd has descended from some ancient herd that was unlike cows, but gradually came to resemble them.

WHAT IS A FOSSIL?

A fossil is any trace of an organism that was left more than 10,000 years ago (Fig. 10-2). Why 10,000? Because that is about when the last glacial ice sheet retreated toward the poles. That event defines the beginning of the Holocene (or recent era) for geologists.

ARE FOSSILS ACCURATE SAMPLES?

Undoubtedly, the most impressive evidence for believing that fossils are worth studying comes from the occasional discovery of living

Fig. 10-2 Fossils are any traces of ancient life: The shell (a) is a 370-million-year-old brachiopod imprint from the middle Devonian of Pennsylvania. The slab of crinoid columns (b) is 420-million-years-old from the Silurian of Pennsylvania; crinoids are in the starfish phylum. The odd-looking animal (c) is a trilobite of the middle Cambrian age from Utah; trilobites are primitive arthropods (related to spiders, lobsters, and insects). And the fossil Pennsylvanian fern frond (d) is about 300 million years old from Illinois.

forms that are just like previously described fossils. A paleontologist (a student of fossils) finds a new and unusual fossil. No one has ever seen anything like it alive or dead. The paleontologist describes the specimen in print. Time passes, often enough time for the paleontologist to die. Then someone discovers a living representative of this supposedly extinct fossil group! This does not happen often, but when it does, it is overpoweringly convincing.

For example, *Latimeria*, the coelacanth, is a member of an ancient sub-family of fish known for a long time only from fossils. Scientists used to believe that coelacanths of all types became extinct 75 million years ago. But in 1939, a living coelacanth was caught in the deep waters off the Malagasy Republic. (See Fig. 10-3.) Others were soon taken from the population. There they had lived, thousands of feet underwater, unrecorded by scientists. Try to imagine the excitement of the biologists who first saw them. Try to imagine seeing a living dinosaur poking its head out of the nearest manhole!

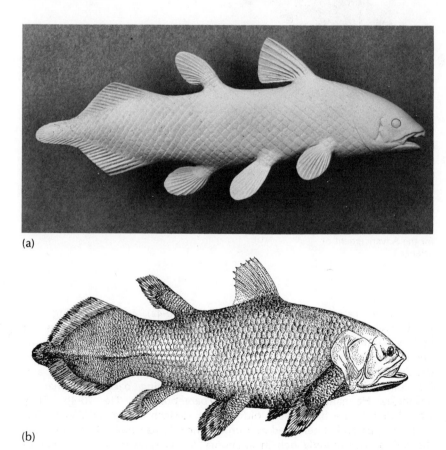

(a)

(b)

Fig. 10-3 A fossil coelacanth, *Diplurus* (a), and its only living close relative, *Latimeria*. (*Latimeria* from J. F. Crow, Ionizing Radiation and Evolution. Copyright © 1959 by Scientific American, Inc. All rights reserved. *Diplurus* courtesy of The American Museum of Natural History.)

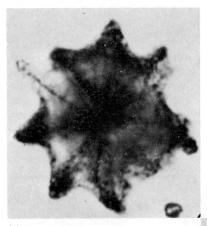

(a)

Fig. 10-4 *Kakabekia umbellata*
(a) and *K. barghoorniana* (b).
(*K.u.* from E. S. Barghoorn.
1965. *Science* 147:563–577, No.
3658. *K.b.* from Siegal et al.
1967. *Science* 156:1231–1234,
No. 3779. Copyright 1965, 1967
by the American Association
for the Advancement of   (b)
Science.)

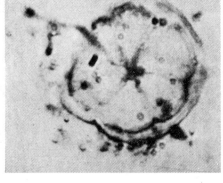

In another case, *Kakabekia umbellata* (Fig. 10-4a), an odd-looking bacterial fossil, was discovered in Canada in rock about 1.9 billion years old by E. S. Barghoorn. This organism lived when we believe the Earth's atmosphere was composed mainly not of oxygen and nitrogen, but of gases deadly to human life: methane and ammonia. A year later, S. M. Siegel and his colleagues announced the discovery of living bacteria similar to *Kakabekia*. He named them *Kakabekia barghoorniana* (Fig. 10-4b). They were living at the base of an old wall of Harlech Castle, in Wales. This wall has apparently been used as a urinal since Roman times. Consequently, the soil is uncommonly rich in ammonia. Siegel showed that in order to live, *K. barghoorniana* actually requires high ammonia concentrations. Thus, not only have we justified our suspicions about the appearance of ancient life, we have also confirmed our suspicions about the environment in which we think it lived—a living fossil in a fossil environment.

DATING FOSSILS

How do we know how old a fossil is? There are a variety of dating methods. But the radioactive-aging method is the best.

We all know that uranium can be radioactive. But do we all know what happens to radioactive substances? They disappear. Well, at least they change—right before your very Geiger counters—into something else. Radioactive uranium, for instance, decays into lead and helium (a stable gas). Radioactive potassium becomes argon (also a stable gas) and ordinary calcium. Radioactive carbon becomes nitrogen. There are many such examples.

Radioactive transformations are often not quick. Some take hours, others years, still others eons. In 4.56 billion years, only half the U^{238} (a uranium isotope[1]) I've got in my hand right now, will have become lead and helium (Fig. 10-5). This number is called a half-life. Each kind of radioactive substance has a half-life. Once we know these half-lives we can use them to determine the age of rocks and the fossils found in the rocks. For instance, when 1.0 g of U^{238} decays to 0.5 g in 4.56 billion years, it produces over 0.4 g of lead (the rest of the weight has become helium and nuclear energy). In another 4.56 billion years, only 0.25 g of the U^{238} will be left, but the lead will have increased to over 0.6 g. To tell any age, all

Time (yrs)	Wt (g)	U^{238}	Pb^{206}	Wt (g)	Ratio: Pb/U
0	1.00			0	0
10^9	0.865			0.116	0.134
2×10^9	0.747			0.219	0.293
3×10^9	0.646			0.306	0.474
4.56×10^9	0.500			0.432	0.864

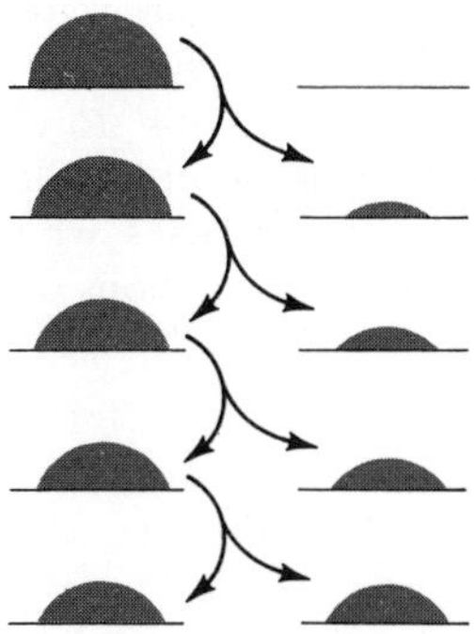

Fig. 10-5 Course of radioactive decay of ^{238}Uranium to ^{206}Lead.

[1] As you probably know, every element has alternate forms, called isotopes. Different isotopes are distinguished by the fact that their atoms contain different numbers of neutrons. Since the atomic mass of an element is approximately the sum of its protons and neutrons, different isotopes of the same element have different atomic masses. They are distinguished by writing their atomic masses (to the closest integer) as a superscript to the right of the symbol for the element. Thus, "C^{14}" is how carbon-14, a radioactive isotope, is written. Other carbon isotopes are stable (not radioactive), for example, C^{12}. When an element has more than one radioactive isotope, each has a characteristic half-life and breaks down in its own characteristic way.

we do is measure the ratio of uranium to lead. Which is older, a rock with 0.2 g of U^{238} and 4 g of lead or one with 0.1 g of U^{238} and 1 g of lead? Remember, the more uranium *compared* to lead, the younger the rock.

U^{238} has too long a half-life to make it useful in dating younger fossils. But U^{235} has a half-life of 713 million years. And potassium, K^{40}, breaks down into argon (A^{40}) with a half-life of 1.3 billion years. These are just right for dating many fossils.

Another useful isotope is C^{14}. It occurs with regular carbon in all living things as a certain small but constant fraction of living tissue. Like all radioactive substances, it is constantly decaying. But as long as an organism lives, its radiocarbon is constantly being replenished as it decays. After death, the C^{14} begins to become a smaller and smaller proportion of the total carbon of the dead tissues. In fact, in 5,570 years it will be only half as common as it was when the organism died. Therefore, comparing the amount of regular carbon to radiocarbon allows us to date the youngest fossils and recent teeth, bones, wood fragments and the charcoal of camp-fires dead for 10,000 years.

In general, the repertoire of radioactive tests now encompasses the ages of life on the earth. Most fossils can be dated this way more precisely than ever before. (See Table 10-1.)

HUMAN EVOLUTION

Because people are so reluctant to admit that evolution has anything to do with them, I will use human examples in this section of the book whenever I can. We begin with the story of man's evolution from an apelike animal to his present form. This story is fairly complete despite the fact that humans and prehumans did not make good fossils very often— because they didn't live in bogs or oceans where remains are preserved owing to the poor environmental conditions for the bacteria of decay.

Fig. 10-6   (By permission of John Hart and Field Enterprises, Inc.)

TABLE 10-1 A SUMMARY OF GEOLOGICAL TIME

Era	Period	Epoch	Years before present[a]	Duration[a]	Brief description
	Precambrian			At least 2 billion years	Fossils rare and primitive. Algae are known from at least 2.5 billion years ago.
Paleozoic			——600 million——		
	Cambrian			100 million years	Marine forms with parts hard enough to fossilize become common. Algal reefs. Annelid worms. Brachiopods and trilobites.
			——500 million——		
	Ordovician			75 million years	Algal reefs continue but corals appear. Echinoderms radiate forming modern groups like starfish. Clams appear. Brachiopods and trilobites remain abundant. First fish.
			——425 million——		
	Silurian			20 million years	Algal reefs become rare and disappear. Coral reefs usurp their position. Land plants and animals appear. Giant sea scorpions and armor-plated fish.
			——405 million——		
	Devonian			50 million years	Coral reefs extensive. Fish radiate and the first bony fish evolve. Brachiopods dominate the ocean. First amphibians and ferns. Primitive, wingless insects.
			——345 million——		

TABLE 10-1 (Continued)

Era	Period	Epoch	Years before present[a]	Duration[a]	Brief description
Paleozoic	Carboniferous	Mississippian	———310 million———	35 million years	Coral reefs diminish. Trilobites nearly extinct. Brachiopods still dominant. Amphibians abundant. Large primitive trees. Major deposits of oil.
		Pennsylvanian	———280 million———	30 million years	Conifers evolve. Reptiles appear. Giant winged insects; spiders. Most coal is deposited from great swampy forests.
	Permian		———230 million———	50 million years	Periods of glaciation and aridity. Trilobites disappear. Reptiles begin their reign over the land. Some strike out on the path toward mammalhood. Appalachians are built.
Mesozoic	Triassic		———180 million———	50 million years	Dinosaurs evolve. First frogs. First primitive mammals.
	Jurassic		———135 million———	45 million years	Dinosaurs flourish. First birds (Archaeopteryx). Nevadan revolution: Birth of Sierra Nevada, Coast, and Cascade ranges.
	Cretaceous		———65 million———	70 million years	Flowering plants appear. Dinosaurs common but disappear near end. First snakes and lizards. At end Rocky Mountains are born. Important oil deposits.

Era	Period	Epoch	Years before present[a]	Duration[a]	Brief description
Cenozoic	Tertiary	Paleocene		7 million years	Placental mammals appear, proliferate, and diversify. Early mammals become extinct.
			——— 58 million		
		Eocene		24 million years	All modern orders of mammals appear, including first bats and whales. Warm, wet climate.
			——— 34 million		
		Oligocene		9 million years	First appearance of many recently extinct mammals like saber teeth, mastodons. First mice, monkeys, apes, rabbits.
			——— 25 million		
		Miocene		13 million years	Climate drier; grasslands expand. Grazing more important. First hominids (*Ramapithecus*), deer, giraffes, foxes.
			——— 12 million		
		Pliocene		9 million years	Cooler, drier climate. Vast grasslands. Great herds of hoofed mammals. Hominids develop into man's immediate ancestor, *Australopithecus*.
			——— 3 million		
		Pleistocene		3 million years	Glaciers cover land. Man evolves.
			——— 0.01 million		
		Holocene			"Civilized" man. Now.

Sources: Richards; Newell, 1963; Simons, 1972.
[a] Years are approximate.

Probably we know so much about human evolution because we are anthropocentric—interested in ourselves. Science has worked much harder at understanding the evolution of people than that of any other species.

MISSING LINKS

Bear in mind that the so-called missing link, the extinct form that was intermediate between man and apes, is no single individual. Instead there are many missing links and they are populations. The populations are links in time—each subsequent population descendant from the last and ancestor of the next. So fossils that we actually observe are samples of missing links. The picture they present of human evolution is so internally consistent, so clear, that we have every reason to believe they are good samples indeed. When you have seen the evidence, I think you will agree that no important links remain missing.

DIFFERENCES
BETWEEN APES AND MEN

Where is the place to begin the description of the evolution of *Homo sapiens*? One could start with the origin of life itself some two billion years ago and work onward. But the entire tale is too voluminous for this slim book, so I have chosen to discuss the relatively brief time of the last 3 to 20 million years, and to focus on the development of our family of species, the Hominidae. Currently, of course, this family is represented by only one living subfamily, the Homininae, one genus, *Homo,* and one species, *Homo sapiens:* us. But in the past, other hominid species and at least two other genera *(Australopithecus* and *Ramapithecus)* and one subfamily (the *Australopithecinae)* have walked the earth.

The hominids evolved from the pongids, or great ape family, and studying this divergence is really studying the major bone of contention between evolutionists and their opponents. Furthermore, this study will provide us with an interesting contrast between a part of man's prehistory which is fairly well known (the last 2 or 3 million years) and another part which is only now beginning to be appreciated: 12 to 15 million years ago.

Just what do we need to account for? What are the differences between mankind and "apekind"? When we know them we can begin our search for missing links, intermediate populations that bridge the gap between the population of men and the populations of apes.

There are few anatomical differences between apes and men. Our brains are much larger and our foreheads are higher. We have shorter jaws and flatter faces from which our noses protrude. The ape's jaws stick out—a condition called *prognathism* ("pro" means in front; "gnath" means jaw). Our teeth are different, too. They are set in our jaws in a gracefully curved arch called a *rounded dental arcade.* The ape's arcade is more rectangular than arched. Apes have large spaces between some of their teeth; human teeth touch each other. Also, our canines, or eyeteeth, are no longer than our other teeth; an ape's are longer, resembling fangs.

Humans are bipedal; we walk. Apes brachiate; they swing along in trees, hanging by their arms. This difference is associated with many others. Because we are bipedal, we differ from apes in having: (1) a broad, cup-shaped pelvis; (2) large, muscular buttocks; (3) a stout heel; (4) long legs; (5) arched feet; (6) a backbone curved into an S-shape; and (7) a foramen magnum (the large hole at the base of the skull through which the spinal cord enters) which points downward instead of backward. There are a few other differences, such as our relative hairlessness and our lack of a baculum (penis bone). Compare humans and apes visually, using Fig. 10-7.

We should expect the fossil history of most of the foregoing differences to be traced successfully, because they are differences in bones and bones fossilize easily. But there are significant differences between us and apes which do not fossilize well: (1) We take longer to reach sexual maturity (about 17 years, as opposed to 10 in chimpanzees and 8 in gibbons); (2) we are left- or right-handed; (3) we associate in large groups and have an intricate means of communicating ideas, symbols, and abstractions to each other; (4) we are aggressive, even warlike (apes are quite peaceable); (5) we are fertile throughout the year (reproduction in all apes is seasonal). However, one nonskeletal difference is eminently "fossilizable." Man makes abundant tools which reflect, because they shape, his complex culture (Fig. 10-8). Another important but much less "fossilizable" cultural attribute is that we make containers—baskets and pots in which to store things (Fig. 10-9). The invention of such receptacles may have been one of the milestones in human evolution. It permitted the gathering of seeds. This in turn fostered the emergence of agricultural man.

There are other differences between apes and men, but there are more similarities than differences. We share most features of anatomy and many biochemical peculiarities. For example, neither apes nor men can synthesize vitamin C, both have vermiform appendices, neither have tails. In a few pages you will learn about the great resemblance in ape and human blood, especially the similarity of blood proteins called albumins.

FOREST APES
OF THE PLIOCENE

Fifteen million years ago there appears to have been neither modern apes nor men. Apelike fossil primates which might be ancestors of both have been found dating from this time back to 30 million years ago. However, these older fossils are skeletal remains, often only a part of the jaw, perhaps only a tooth, rarely nearly complete skeletons. For our discussion, the most interesting of these fossils are the group called dryopithecines (forest apes). (See Fig. 10-10.) These fossils have been found in Africa, India, and Europe. Today their names and the number of species, genera, and families they belonged to are still confused. But clearly the dryopithecines

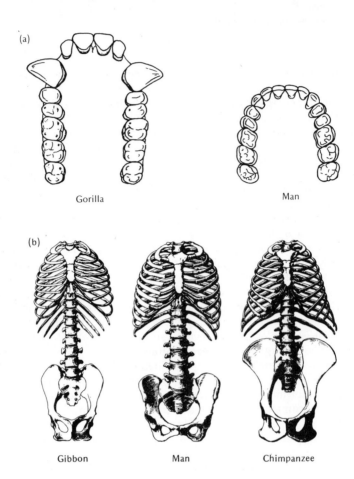

(a)

Gorilla

Man

(b)

Gibbon

Man

Chimpanzee

(c)

Orangutan

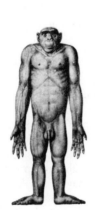

Chimpanzee

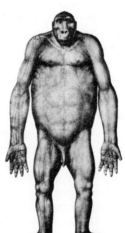

Gorilla

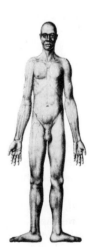

Man

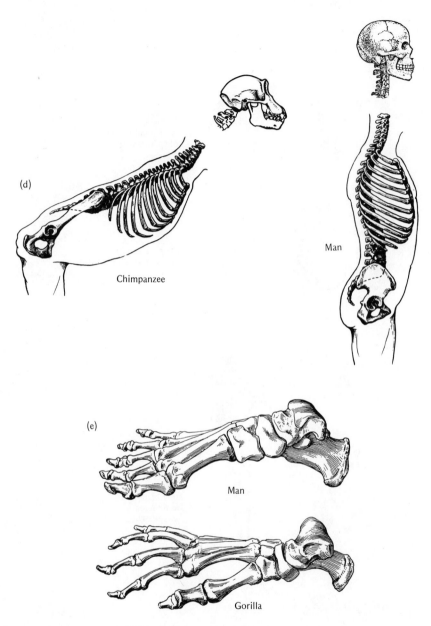

(d)

Chimpanzee

Man

(e)

Man

Gorilla

Fig. 10-7 Anatomical differences between apes and man: (a) upper jaw (By permission of the Trustees of the British Museum (Natural History), (b) pelvis and trunk skeleton (Courtesy of Prof. A. H. Schultz), (c) body proportions (Courtesy of Prof. A. H. Schultz), (d) curvature of spine and pelvis and direction of foramen magnum. (Trunks courtesy of Prof. A. H. Schultz. Chimp skull from Clark. 1959. Human skull from J. Napier. The antiquity of human walking. Copyright © 1967 by Scientific American, Inc. All rights reserved.) (e) foot skeleton. (From Gregory.)

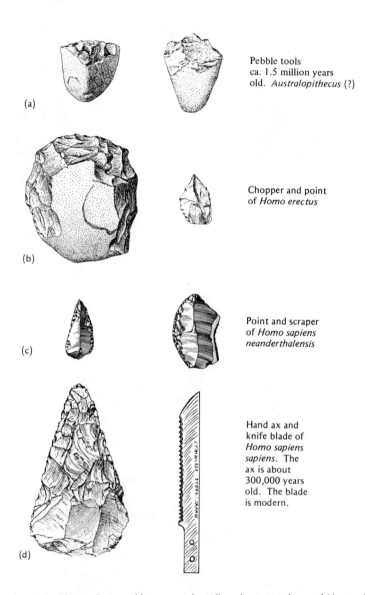

Pebble tools
ca. 1.5 million years
old. *Australopithecus* (?)

(a)

Chopper and point
of *Homo erectus*

(b)

Point and scraper
of *Homo sapiens
neanderthalensis*

(c)

Hand ax and
knife blade of
*Homo sapiens
sapiens*. The
ax is about
300,000 years
old. The blade
is modern.

(d)

Fig. 10-8 The evolution of human tools. (All tools except those of *H.s. sapiens* used by permission of the Trustees of the British Museum (Natural History). Hand ax of *H.s. sapiens* courtesy the Royal Anthropological Institute of Great Britain and Ireland.)

Fig. 10-9 A storage basket of the Pima Indians, Arizona. Baskets such as these were made to hold as much as 50 bushels of wheat. This one holds about 20. Development of collecting baskets and storage baskets for wild grain may have been the evolutionary step that led to agriculture. (Courtesy of Mrs. A. E. Robinson. From *Basketweavers of Arizona.*)

contain good and reasonable candidates for ancestors of apes like the gorilla and the chimpanzee, and are quite closely related to what must have been our ancestors. One, *Aegyptopithecus zeuxis,* is about 30 million years old and is very much what one might expect of the common ancestor of apes and men (Simons, 1967).

Dryopithecines had larger canine teeth than we do, but smaller ones than those of great apes. Indeed, the roots of our canine teeth are larger than they seem to need to be, suggesting that our ancestors had bigger ones (Fig. 10-11). In English, human canine teeth are often called eyeteeth. The fact that our canines have extra-large roots compared to our other teeth prompted the expression: "as difficult as pulling eyeteeth."

Each dryopithecine lower molar (grinding tooth) had five cusps or points arranged in a Y-shape. Although today most human molars have four cusps, many still possess the ancient dryopithecine Y-5 cusp arrangement (Fig. 10-12). In fact, this pattern predominates on first lower molars. All

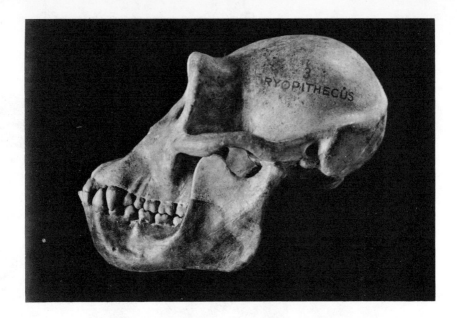

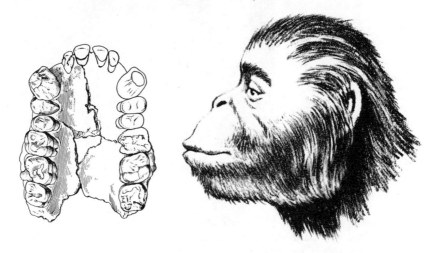

Fig. 10-10 Fossils of *Dryopithecus* and a reconstruction. (Reconstruction from *Life: an introduction to biology* by George Gaylord Simpson and William S. Beck, copyright, 1965, by Harcourt Brace Jovanovich, Inc., and reproduced with their permission. Upper jaw from Gregory and Hellman.)

Fig. 10-11 Modern human teeth showing the overly large root of the canine (eyetooth). (From W. E. L. Clark. *The fossil evidence for human evolution.* © 1955 by The University of Chicago. All rights reserved.)

Fig. 10-12 The *Dryopithecus* Y-5 molar pattern in man and *Dryopithecus*. (From Gregory and Hellman.)

Dryopithecus   Man

first lower molars of Chinese, Mongols, and Australian aboriginals have it and so do most others.

The dryopithecines had a pelvis adapted to a four-footed gait, but lacked the huge ilia (large pelvic bones) of modern chimps and gorillas. Their legs weren't long like ours, but then their arms weren't long like an orangutan's or a chimp's.

Dryopithecine teeth were quite suggestive of the difference between apes and men. Most had apelike teeth (though not as extreme as modern apes). Some are known with slightly rounded dental arcades, very small canines, and other details suggesting mankind. Elwyn Simons has united the manlike forms under the name *Ramapithecus punjabicus* and removed them from the dryopithecine group. These fossils come from Africa and India and probably parts in between. They lived roughly 14 million years ago as determined by potassium-argon dating of the site where the late Lewis Leakey collected one. Though Drs. Leakey and Simons disagreed on the names of some of these fossils, they did agree on the important point: in the late Miocene and early Pliocene times, some 12 to 14 million years ago, animals that showed signs of developing the apelike features we find in modern Pongidae roamed the Old World's warmer regions. Coexisting with them and probably appearing quite similar to anyone but an expert primate anatomist was a group of primates with dental features that are decidedly manlike. Dr. Leakey in fact has formally classified these manlike jawbone fossils into the family of man, Hominidae. Dr. Simons agrees.

The *Ramapithecus* fossil known as the "Calcutta mandible" provides a piece of information which is remarkable. It shows that *Ramapithecus* individuals took a very long time to mature—like man, but unlike pongids. The mandible, or lower jaw, contains all three molars. But these molars show very uneven wear. The first is badly worn; the second only moderately worn; the third hardly worn at all. Similar differential molar wear is known from man and from fossil men (including *Australopithecus*, which is discussed next), but it is never found in apes. Here is the reason according to Simons.

In all men and apes, the third molar (or wisdom tooth) is a sign of maturity. It erupts as skeletal and sexual maturity are attained. In apes, maturity is achieved soon after the first two molars erupt. Thus, the molars erupt in quick succession and there is no time for them to wear differently;

they show about the same amount of wear. In man, the first molar erupts at about the same chronological age as in apes, but the second is a bit delayed and the third waits many years while we complete our long period of immaturity. Hence, a newly mature human has a fresh third molar and a worn first molar. *Ramapithecus,* therefore, exhibits another important human trait, lengthy maturation.

If all this is borne out by later finds, the picture of this part of human evolution would be as follows:

1. Apes evolved from Old World monkeys by gradually losing their tails. Soon they diverged into forms which appear to be (from dental evidence) dryopithecine ancestors *(Aegyptopithecus)* or gibbon ancestors (gibbons are the separate ape family, *Hylobatidae*).

2. Dryopithecines then diverged 15 to 20 million years ago into (a) forms that would later become men *(Ramapithecus)* and (b) forms which would evolve into the modern Pongidae *(Dryopithecus)*.

BIOCHEMICAL SIMILARITIES
OF APES AND MEN

In addition to the fossil evidence that reveals the family tree of apes and men, there is another kind of evidence based on biochemical similarity. This evidence relies on the techniques of the science of immunology to compare the proteins in the blood of apes and men. The best way to understand these techniques is to examine one example, the work of Vincent Sarich. In order to understand it we must recall that some vertebrates (especially mammals and birds) have the ability to make special substances, called antibodies, which attach themselves to substances foreign to the animal producing them. The important thing about these antibodies is that they are highly specific; they work strongly only on the particular chemical they are constructed against. Thus antibodies can yield specific tests for the presence of the compound they are supposed to destroy.

Now suppose Sarich injects a rabbit with the fraction of a gorilla's blood called the albumins. The albumins are proteins foreign to a rabbit and the rabbit proceeds to make antibodies against them. Later, these antibodies are taken from the rabbit's blood and mixed with fresh gorilla albumin. They combine with the gorilla albumins and force them together into heavy clumps. These aggregates drop quickly to the bottom of our test tube, where they are easily seen and measured.

Now we want to find out how similar human and gorilla albumins are. We add the human albumins to the *antigorilla* antibodies. If human albumins are just like a gorilla's, the rabbit's antibodies will be able to clump them just as well. If they are almost the same, then there will be almost as much aggregate at the bottom of the test tube. If they are very different, the antibodies will be nearly powerless and almost no human proteins will fall to the bottom. One can compare any two species this way.

TABLE 10-2   ALBUMIN DISSIMILARITIES

Albumins tested	Antibodies used		
	Anti-*Homo*	Anti-*Pan*	Anti-*Hylobates*
Homo	1.0[a]	1.09	1.29
Gorilla	1.10	1.17	1.31
Pan (chimp)	1.14	1.0	1.40
Pongo (orangutan)	1.22	1.24	1.29
Symphalangus (gibbon)	1.27	1.25	1.07
Hylobates (gibbon)	1.27	1.25	1.0
Macaque[c] (monkey)	2.23	2.0	2.30
Tarsier (primitive primate)	11.3	b	b
Cow	32	b	b
Pig	>36	b	b

Source: Sarich.

[a] A value of 1.0 indicates no dissimilarity. The higher the value, the greater the dissimilarity.

[b] Not reported.

[c] Five other monkey species were also tested and gave similar results.

Sarich used this method to generate fractions called *albumin dissimilarity.* The numerator of his dissimilarity fraction is the amount of aggregate he got when he tested the antibody preparation, for example, chimpanzee albumin mixed with antichimp antibody. The denominator is the amount of aggregate he got when the new albumin was mixed in, for example, human albumin on antichimp antibody. Thus the larger the fraction, the more *dissimilar* the pair of species being tested. (See Table 10-2.)

Sarich's results, summarized in Table 10-2, are startling even to a confirmed evolutionist like me. They appear to put the hominoids into three groups (no surprise), but the three are (1) gibbons (2) orangutans, and (3) men, gorillas, and chimps! In fact, the two very nearly identical genera of gibbons, *Hylobates* and *Symphalangus,* are only a bit more similar to each other than are we to *Pan* and *Gorilla.*

The orangutan is very slightly more similar to man and chimpanzee than it is to gibbons. Hence it appears that the gibbon's precursors were the first to diverge from the hominoid line that would lead to man, and that the orangutan's forebears followed soon after. Only later did the ancestors of man, gorilla, and chimpanzee go their three separate evolutionary ways.

The basic message of Table 10-2 is lost if one looks only at differences. The fundamental fact is that there isn't really much albumin difference among apes and man. Notice that the monkey's dissimilarity is substantial, the tarsier's is large, and those of cow and pig virtually complete. Although we clearly have diverged from our pongid relatives, just as clearly we have not gotten that far away, not at least as regards our anatomy, physiology, and body chemistry.

THE FAMILY
by Mary Oliver

The dark things of the wood
Are coming from their caves,
Flexing muscle.

They browse the orchard,
Nibble the sea of grasses
Around our yellow rooms,

Scarcely looking in
To see what we are doing
And if they still know us.

We hear them, or we think we do:
The muzzle lapping moonlight,
The tooth in the apple.

Put another log on the fire;
Mozart, again, on the turntable.
Still there is a sorrow

With us in the room.
We remember the cave.
In our dreams we go back

Or they come to visit.
They also like music
We eat leaves together.

They are our brothers.
They are the family
We have run away from.[2]

MAN'S IMMEDIATE ANCESTOR:
AUSTRALOPITHECUS

By about two million years ago, probably even three or four
million years ago, the Hominidae not only existed, but had developed most
of the *postcranial* anatomy of the human being (postcranial means "all but
the head"). Even the head had many human characteristics. The teeth were
almost human (except for the large size of the molars), and the jaws,
though large, were smaller than those of *Dryopithecus.*

The original discoverer of these hominids, R. A. Dart, didn't immediately
conceive of the small-brained skull that he found as a true hominid, even
though he recognized the many hominid features of its teeth and jaws
(see Fig. 10-13c), so he named his find *Australopithecus* (southern ape—
"southern" comes from the place in Botswana, Africa, *south* of the equator).

[2] Copyright © 1973, by Minneapolis Star and Tribune Co., Inc. Reprinted from the
February, 1973 issue of *Harper's Magazine* by permission of the author.

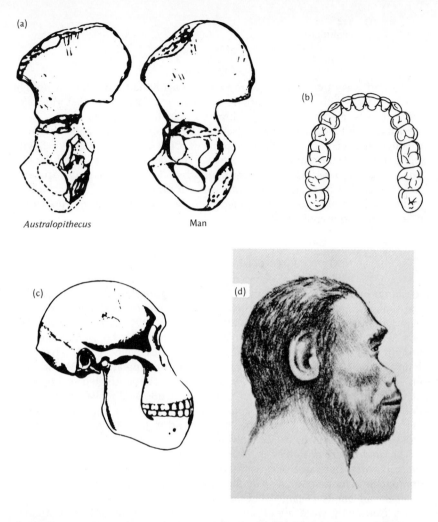

(a)

Australopithecus   Man

(b)

(c)

(d)

Fig. 10-13 Remains and a reconstruction of *Australopithecus*. Notice especially: the modern pelvis, indicating an upright posture (a); the rounded dentition (b); and the small canine (c). (Pelvises from Dart. Dental arcade used by permission of the Trustees of the British Museum (Natural History). Reconstruction from *Life: an introduction to biology* by George Gaylord Simpson and William S. Beck, copyright, 1965, by Harcourt Brace Jovanovich, Inc., and reproduced with their permission. Skull from W. E. L. Clark. *The fossil evidence for human evolution.* © 1955 by the University of Chicago. All rights reserved.)

Indeed, fossils of *Australopithecus africanus* have brain sizes about the same as gorillas. Soon Dart changed his mind and called *Australopithecus* a true hominid. But convincing the rest of the world was most difficult.

In 1936, a decade after Dart's find, Robert B. Broom discovered the pelvic bones of *Australopithecus* (Fig. 10-13a). Except for small details, the familiar human form was evident, proving that *Australopithecus* had walked upright. This was no complete surprise, however, since the foramen magnum of

Dart's find was directed downward, which already had indicated an upright posture. Many other details of the skeletal anatomy show that *Australopithecus* was far more like a mini-brained man than anything else.

In the late 1950s, Louis Leakey's wife, Dr. Mary Leakey, made the most exciting discovery of all: skeletal remains of *Australopithecus* lying with stone tools of the earliest-known type. The remains were dated by the potassium-argon radioactive decay method at 1.75 million years. Students have concluded that: (1) *A. africanus* was a toolmaker,[3] and (2) *A. africanus* gradually changed into a form called *A. habilis* and it, in turn, into *Homo erectus* about one million years ago.

NEXT: *HOMO ERECTUS*

Although the record of change from *Australopithecus africanus* to *Homo erectus* is most complete at Olduvai gorge in Tanzania (thanks to the Leakeys and the Tanzania climate), *Homo erectus* was first discovered by a Dutch physician, Eugene DuBois, in Java in 1891. DuBois had decided Java was the place to look for "the missing link." So he went there and found it! As it later turned out, the species he discovered could have been found in most parts of the tropical and warm-temperate Old World. Still his luck remains amazing. For 40 years other expeditions tried to duplicate his find in Java without success. Originally DuBois' discovery was called *Pithecanthropus erectus* (erect ape-man), but now it is considered *Homo erectus* (erect man). *H. erectus* has been found in Java, China, North Africa, East Africa, and elsewhere (see Howells, 1966).

The anatomical advances in *Homo erectus* are mostly in the skull. The most important of these occurr in the brain size; *H. erectus* had a brain size approaching modern man's. In fact some larger-brained members of *H. erectus* had brains as large as some of today's smaller-brained *H. sapiens*. But a cautionary word about small brains: the most famous small-brained *H. sapiens* was the French author Anatole France, no illiterate, whose cranial capacity was only 1017 c.c. So *H. erectus* was not necessarily a stupid species. Tools that he made are fine and are evidence of extreme dexterity and technical skill. Apparently *H. erectus* also shared other aspects of man's modern behavior: some *H. erectus* skulls have been found neatly opened as if their contents had been eaten in a cannibalistic feast or ritual.

[3] The skull Mary Leakey found was a member of a second species of *Australopithecus*, *A. robustus*. This species was not ancestral to ours. *A. robustus* may or may not have made the tools. With the skull were the two lower leg bones of an *A. africanus*.
Mary Leakey has excavated many tools at Olduvai and it is clear that extensive tool making was practiced by the hominids of almost 2 million years ago. But since both species of *Australopithecus* are found with the tools, it is not clear which one was the tool maker. Perhaps both were? Since *A. africanus* was our direct ancestor and *A. robustus* only a distant cousin, our biases lead us to conclude that *A. robustus* may have made tools, but *A. africanus* surely did—a reasonable conclusion, but not ironclad.

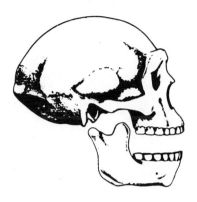 

Fig. 10-14 Remains and a reconstruction of *Homo erectus*. (Skull from Clark, 1955. © 1955 by the University of Chicago. All rights reserved. Reconstruction from *Life: an introduction to biology* by George Gaylord Simpson and William S. Beck, copyright, 1965, by Harcourt Brace Jovanovich, Inc., and reproduced with their permission.)

NEOTENY

Notice in Fig. 10-14 that the larger braincase of *H. erectus* has created a higher forehead. From the picture of the juvenile *Australopithecus africanus* (Fig. 10-15), you can see that youngsters have very high foreheads compared to their parents. Thus, the evolutionary increase in brain size has produced adults which look more and more juvenile. Such an evolutionary change, the maintenance of juvenile characters into adulthood, is called *neoteny*.

Other features of human skulls also have been produced by neoteny: bones are thin and joints do not close until late in life (in the twenties, considered old or at least middle-aged until recently). Also man's brain maintains a juvenile growth rate (that is, fast) far longer than an ape's.

CHANGE IN BRAIN SIZE

The brains of our ancestors got larger gradually (Table 10-3). We now have a virtually complete series of fossil skulls which take us from mini-brained *A. africanus* to *H. sapiens* in tiny steps. Despite the relatively small steps, this brain enlargement is one of the fastest known evolutionary changes in the history of life on Earth. In less than two million years, the average hominid brain volume has more than doubled. As you will soon learn, that slow pace is blinding speed compared to more ordinary rates of evolution.

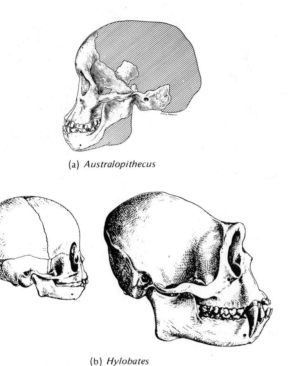

(a) *Australopithecus*

(b) *Hylobates*

Fig. 10-15 Neoteny in the skull. Evolutionary changes in humans have tended to make the adult skull retain juvenile features. Pictured above are the skulls of a juvenile *Australopithecus africanus* (a) and juvenile and adult gibbons (b). Notice the high forehead of the juveniles. Both species have adults with low foreheads (see also Figs. 10-13 and 10-14). (*Australopithecus* from Ashley Montagu. *Introduction to physical anthropology*. 3rd ed. 1960. Courtesy of Charles C Thomas, Publisher, Springfield, Ill. and Dr. Montagu. Gibbons courtesy of Prof. A. H. Schultz and The Amer. J. of Phys. Anthropology.)

Human brain size is not now increasing. Apparently it has not been for about 250,000 years. In fact, *H. sapiens neanderthalensis* (Neanderthal man, a race of our species which flourished during the recent glacial period) had brains whose volume averaged about 100 c.c. more than ours. Perhaps brains are no longer increasing because the already large size of the newborn's head is just barely able to squeeze through its mother's pelvis and be born. (Even today, the maternal pelvis must separate slightly during delivery to allow the baby passage.) This is only a guess though; perhaps we must look for another reason.

TABLE 10-3 HOMINOID CRANIAL CAPACITIES

Hylobatidae and Pongidae	Approximate range (c.c.)	Average (c.c.)
Hylobates	82–125	102
Symphalangus	100–152	125
Pongo	276–540	395
Pan	275–500	375
Gorilla	340–752	497
Hominidae		
Ramapithecus	?	?
Australopithecus	430–600	about 500
Homo erectus	775–1225	978
Homo sapiens neanderthalensis	1300–1600	about 1450
Homo sapiens (today)	1000–1700	1350

Sources: Schultz; Simons, 1972.

NAMES OF FOSSILS

Where do we draw the line between *H. erectus* and *H. sapiens*? We have a complete series with lots of overlaps. In fact a knowledgeable museum artist once fleshed out an *H. erectus* skull and dressed it in opera cape and top hat. It looked perfectly ordinary! Paleontologists draw the line at about 300,000 years ago. But they know that this line is arbitrary. The evolution of human anatomy, behavior, and physiology—of all the measurable features of man, of man's phenotype—has been a gradual process. It continues today. It has involved an unbroken chain of living organisms through time. Each of us has an australopithecine he might call grandpa. Furthermore, the fossil finds indicate that our ancestors were a widespread population. The gradual changes that made them us probably spread over the world a few or even one at a time. There is no reason to believe otherwise. In Chapters 11 and 13 we shall see that this has occurred because (to paraphrase P. B. Medawar), though each of us can find an ancestor in any previous generation, only some members of each previous generation would be able to find descendants in ours.

THE SPEED OF EVOLUTION

The eminent paleontologist George G. Simpson has written a popular account of the evolution of horses (the book is called *Horses*). In it, he describes how horses have changed quite gradually over the past 60 million years (or so) from a speedy dog-sized ancestor called eohippus, or dawn-horse. The fossil record of the horse family is one of the most complete. It is easy to see how, slowly but surely, one species gradually changed into one or more others, and so on to our modern-day thorough-breds, zebras, and burros.

In horse evolution, many changes occurred, and not all of them occurred in all lines. These changes are an interesting story in themselves, but are too voluminous for this book. I will concentrate on only one aspect of one structure—the size of the molar teeth (the grinding, rear teeth). It exempli-fies the extremely slow rates of evolution that are commonly found by paleontologists.

HORSE DIET
AND TOOTH WEAR

Steak may be tough, but what really wears away your teeth are the stems and leaves of plant foods. Think of the poor horse, then. Nothing to eat but rough foods and no dentist to make him dentures when his teeth wear down (Fig. 10-16). A horse with worn teeth is an old horse, ready to die.

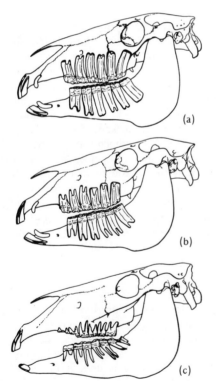

(a)

(b)

(c)

Fig. 10-16 Dental battery of adult horses at different ages: 5 years (a), 8 years (b), and 39 years (c). The teeth gradually wear down down through life; the crowns are almost gone in old animals. The roots get longer. (From Chubb.)

Horses are grazers, which is to say they eat grass. And of all plant foods, grass is one of the hardest on the teeth. Not only do a grass's cell walls contain silica (abrasive particles that make chewing grass a little like chewing glass), but also the grazer frequently scrapes close to the ground in cropping his food. Here he is likely to gather a bit of useless dirt with his meal. Dirt can also be rather hard on the teeth.

Eohippus, the horse's remote ancestor, was not a grazer, but a browser like a deer or giraffe. He ate the stems and foliage of bushy plants—a much softer diet than grass, though it still wears down teeth. This change in the horse's diet occurred in the geological time called the Miocene (which lasted from 25 million to 12 million years ago). However, not all horses became grazers. Some, called *Anchitherium*, stayed browsers and continued to evolve until, as a form called *Hypohippus*, they became extinct some five million years ago in the Pliocene.

CHANGE IN TOOTH SIZE

A larger horse requires larger teeth even if he remains a browser. He has more flesh to feed and so must grind more plant food every day. In the evolutionary line that leads from eohippus to *Hypohippus*, there was just such an increase in size. The molar teeth increased in length and surface to compensate for it. (Some say the size change was made possible by the tooth-size increase, but in either case the teeth of *Hypohippus* were much larger than those of eohippus.) In fact, they had a surface area about nine times as large as eohippus, and were about three times as large in any linear dimension. This change had taken about 50 million years! (See Fig. 10-17.)

Because the fossil record is so good, the stages of evolution from eohippus to *Hypohippus* can be examined to see if this change really went so slowly. Perhaps instead there was no change for long periods, then occasional quick, large ones. According to Simpson, the record reveals that slow almost imperceptible change is really what happened. Following Simpson (1953), we shall use the paracone height as our index of tooth size (the paracone is one of the cusps of the molar).

From eohippus to *Mesohippus*, the paracone grew at an average rate of 2.4% per **million** years. (What good would a bank account do you at that rate of interest?) From *Mesohippus* to *Hypohippus* it grew a bit faster— 4.5% per million. Still nothing to make slow-motion movies of! Such rates are not at all atypical; other parts of the horse's phenotype were changing even more slowly.

Now let's look at the line leading from eohippus to the grazing horses. Here there was also an increase in size. But, more important, when the grazing diet became available, there was an immense need for higher teeth that would be long lasting, so that the horse could live long enough to grow up and raise a family. We might expect this to have caused a faster rate of evolution than in the nongrazers, and it did. But it was all still slow,

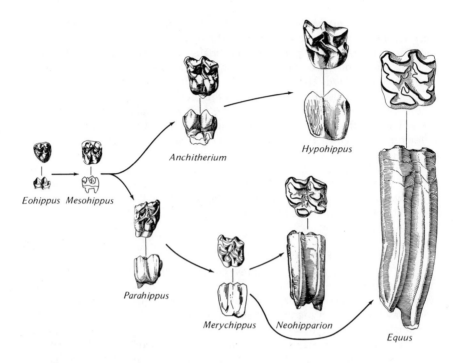

Fig. 10-17 Fossil teeth of ancient horses, drawn to the same scale. The teeth are upper premolars. Both the grinding surface and the side of each tooth are depicted. The fossils are presented in order of age with the oldest on the left. Refer to the text for relationships and dietary information. (From Stirton, Osborn, Wortman.)

very slow. From *Mesohippus* (a browser) to *Merychippus* (a grazer), the paracone grew at 7.9% per million years. After that burst of "speed," it slowed down again, so that from *Merychippus* to *Neohipparion* (a grazing contemporary of *Hypohippus*) it increased at 5.9% per million years.

Despite the great importance of the molar teeth to the horse, evolution proceeded fantastically slowly, building micro-minor change on micro-micro–minor change. And yet these tiny changes have produced a tooth in today's horse that is three times as long as it was in *Merychippus,* the first grazing horse, and about 20 times as long as it was in eohippus 60 million years ago.

SEEING EVOLUTION IN OUR OWN TIMES:
THE MYSTERY OF THE BLACK PEPPERED MOTH

Some people collect moths and butterflies the way others collect stamps and coins. And some moths and butterflies are as rare as a

1909 SVDB Lincoln penny or a Graf zeppelin airmail stamp. Moth collectors are just as willing to pay a price to get their rarities as stamp collectors.

When Darwin was a young man, almost all British peppered moths, *Biston betularia*, were colored a mottled pale-gray and white—they looked peppered. The black form of the peppered moth existed but was rare. We know this because collectors made quite a to-do about them. Today you couldn't get a 1968 dime for one. In the woods about Birmingham, England, they are as common as they were once rare. Evolution has actually occurred before our very eyes! We need no fossils to observe this case of it.

THE EXPLANATION

Biologists noticed that the black form was common in areas to the east of big industrial centers, like Birmingham. Knowing that the winds in England usually blow from west to east, they guessed that the smoke and soot from factories had something to do with the success of the black form.

Sure enough, the British biologist H. B. D. Kettlewell found that in forests in which the blacks were common, trees were black and sooty. Forests that still had lots of the gray and white peppered moths—the old "typical form"—were fresh and clean. The tree trunks in these forests were covered with speckled gray and white lichens (a lichen is a combination of an alga and a fungus that can grow on a soilless surface).

	Forest condition		
	Sooty		Unpolluted
	1953	1955	1955
Black form (%)	89.86	90.52	5.40
Peppered form (%)	10.14	9.48	94.60
Total moths caught	621	559	318

You might have guessed that the black moths were just sooty, but that is wrong. Blackness is due to natural moth pigmentation and is inherited. Also inherited is the typical peppered form. What, then, is the connection between the black moths and the sooty forests?

Kettlewell guessed that these moths, if they were seen, were eaten by birds. He felt that it was reasonable that they were more easily found if they didn't resemble their backgrounds—the tree trunks. A peppered would be relatively safe on a lichen-covered trunk, a black one on a sooty trunk. (See Fig. 10-18.) This is called camouflage, or cryptic coloration. He set out to test this guess.

His test was divided into two parts. In the first, he released moths into the woods of the clean and sooty variety. Then he tried to recapture them using various methods. If he was right, the black ones would have survived better in the sooty woods; there, a greater proportion of them would be recaptured than of the peppered color. The situation would have been just the reverse in clean, lichen-covered woods.

In the second part, he wanted to show that birds were responsible: that they eat these moths and that they have a harder time finding well-camouflaged food.

THE SURVIVAL EXPERIMENT

In his survival studies, Kettlewell raised moths himself. Then he painted a dot under the wing of each moth before he released it. In this way he would know which of his captures were animals he had previously released.

In 11 days, Kettlewell released 799 moths into the lichen woods.

	Blacks	Peppereds
Number released	406	393
Number recaptured	19	54
Recaptured (%)	4.7	13.7

Thus the peppereds had a better chance of survival in the lichen-covered woods. In those 11 days, each peppered moth was about 2.9 times as likely to last as a black one.

In the sooty woods, it was the black form which held the advantage. Here the experiment was done twice. In 1953, in 11 days, 27.5% of the blacks, but only 13% of the peppereds were recaptured. For this period, a black was 2.1 times as likely as a peppered to survive. In 1955 in four days, 52.25% of the blacks, but only 25% of the peppereds were recaptured. The advantage of a black was similar to 1953: a black was 2.1 times as likely as a peppered to survive.

In the next chapter, we shall learn that such inherited differences in survival are intimately connected with a measurement called fitness. Darwin predicted, in fact, that differences like these were just the things to cause evolution by natural selection.

THE BIRD-WATCHING EXPERIMENT

The second part of Kettlewell's experiment is very interesting because it provides a likely explanation of how the differences in survival come about. Dr. N. Tinbergen, a famous student of the behavior of birds, hid in a blind, taking motion pictures of birds being given the chance to eat moths released by Kettlewell. At first, three moths of each type were put on a tree trunk. Then as soon as one form was completely gone, the moths were replenished to equality. Thus, the birds always had at least one moth of each type on the tree trunk before them.

In Birmingham, the blacks were seen much less often by the birds. For example, redstarts ate 43 peppered but only 15 blacks in two days. In the

(a)

(b)

Fig. 10-18 Both forms of peppered (peppered and black) moths on both types of background. Can you find the peppered form on the lichen-covered tree trunk (a)? (From the experiments of Dr. H. B. D. Kettlewell. University of Oxford.)

clean woods, the opposite was true. The spotted flycatcher ate 81 blacks and 9 peppereds; the nuthatch: 40 blacks, 11 peppereds; and together, three other bird species ate 43 blacks, but only 6 peppereds. It is clear from the films that the birds had trouble seeing the peppered moths against a peppered background of lichens, and the black ones against a black background of soot.

OTHER CASES
OF MODERN EVOLUTION

For the first time in the history of biology, a change in the average appearance of a member of a natural species, an evolution, was observed. The pollution of woodland with soot that had come about after the Industrial Revolution had resulted in the members of a species changing color to match their new environment. As you might expect, there are many kinds of moths. Kettlewell estimates about 100 different kinds have evolved blackness in sooty environments.

Though I have gone into great detail about moths, there are other cases of observed evolution known to science. Our radical interference with nature has caused many of them. One is the development of resistance to DDT in mosquito populations. Another is the development of tolerance to antibiotics by *Streptococcus* and other disease-causing bacteria. There are others. Sure, no one has seen a fish population turn into an alligator population. Although this has actually happened, what we have learned from the fossil record of the horse's tooth should have taught us that such a thing is not likely to have been seen in the 100–200 years we've been looking. Evolution occurs in slow, almost imperceptible steps. But, as Homer Smith put it, in tens and hundreds of millions of years, these steps can and have added up to the difference between fish and philosopher.

Since men have discovered in detail the history of many evolutions by obtaining fossils and dating them, and since they have actually been able to observe evolution in progress, why should so many still refuse to accept the fact that evolution has occurred?

Some say it is because evolutionary theory is a direct attack on religion. But it isn't. I see no reason why a man cannot believe in God, participate in a religion, and also accept the evidence of his senses about the way in which the world of life evolved. In fact, many scientists do just that.

Why should God bother with revealing to us the scientific story of Creation when He has equipped us both to discover it ourselves and to enjoy immensely the work of discovering it? Instead, perhaps He has given us a scientifically inaccurate account in order to emphasize that it's not the science that's important here—it's the ethics. Is not the major function of religion to guide us toward moral lives, something science is and always will be powerless to do? By forcing rational men to ignore Genesis' superficial scientific meaning, knowledge of evolution forces men to seek the true, deep meaning of the story of Creation. I believe God's basic message in the Creation story of Genesis is: Act as if this were the way I created the world. In our discussion of the moral implications of doing nothing about population control, we have already needed to draw on some of the ethical lessons of Genesis. I'm sure a careful rereading of Genesis will now suggest many others to you.

No, I think the real reason many people will not come to grips with the reality of evolution is not ignorance, not religious conviction, but a sense of false pride. People like to feel superior to other life forms. They are too proud to be related to monkeys—however remotely.

Unfortunately, the ability to "progress" that we once prided ourselves on has led us to the brink of the destruction of civilization by atomic war or population explosion or environmental despoilation. Today, many people are less confident about man's real superiority over monkeys and apes. Certainly no other animal threatens to destroy its own environment. Honestly, not only am I proud to be related to monkeys, but this sometimes makes me wonder whether I'd rather be one. If I were, I think I'd insist, despite all evidence to the contrary, that I was no distant relation of any human being.

Seriously, the evidence for evolution is too brutally overpowering to ignore. Let us therefore agree to pursue a second question, the one which will bring us the information we must have to deal with population control: "What causes biological evolution?"

11 the theory of evolution by natural selection

Science consists in grouping facts so that general . . . conclusions may be drawn from them.

Charles Darwin, *Autobiography*

NATURAL SELECTION

Darwin returned from his voyage in 1836, having experienced two things which changed his life forever. He had unearthed a large number of the fossilized bones of many extinct South American vertebrates and he had been to the Galapagos Islands where he observed that many extraordinary species unknown elsewhere were living in places and finding their food in the fashion of other species found in mainland areas (see Chapter 17). These two experiences led him to build the rest of his career upon the conviction that evolution is real.

But what makes evolution happen? It took Darwin until 1839 to answer that question. Darwin called his answer "the law of natural selection." That followed the style of his day, but today we call it "the theory of evolution by natural selection."

This theory is incredibly profound, yet quite simple. To understand its few sentences, we must first explore two words: heritability and fitness.

HERITABILITY

Heritability is easy to define. It means offspring resemble their parents more than if they were picked at random from the set of all offspring. For instance, most American children belong to the same political party as their parents, and blue-eyed children tend to be born more often to blue-eyed parents than to brown-eyed ones. It doesn't matter how a trait is inherited—on genes, by tradition, or any other way. As long as the phenotype is partly inherited, so will the fitness be. Heritability can be quantified, but we need not do it for this book.

FITNESS

Fitness is as hard to define as heritability is easy, for even when we understand it, we shall find it difficult to pin down except in the abstract. A full discussion of fitness requires the calculus, but we can understand it without that. To begin simply, let us say that fitness is the rate at which an individual reproduces.

The first complication arises because reproduction involves both living and producing living and fertile offspring. Both living *(viability)* and producing offspring *(fertility)* are involved. It does no good to survive and be sterile; it is of no benefit to inherit the potential for bearing a thousand young without the potential for surviving for the time necessary to do it. Similarly, bearing inviable or sterile young is worthless.

Now, if you think you have fitness mastered, tell me, what is the fitness of your neighbor's tomcat? You might say "bad" because he lives alone constantly locked in the house, or "good" because you happen to know he's already the grandfather of 276 kittens all over the neighborhood. But bad and good are only two classes. It would be much better to have a number which we could assign to any phenotype. This number would be its fitness.

There is one complication. Two different kinds of numbers have been suggested. One measures the number of descendants left after a period of time; the other compares this number to some arbitrary standard. The first is the absolute fitness; the second, the relative fitness. Both are important.

ABSOLUTE FITNESS

Suppose one algal variety grows and divides once every day. It is leaving two descendants every day. Another variety takes only twelve hours, so it leaves descendants at the rate of four per day. A measure of their absolute fitnesses is therefore two per day and four per day.

RELATIVE FITNESS

To get the relative fitnesses, we pick one absolute fitness (arbitrarily) as a standard, and divide all the fitnesses by it.

Suppose 2 is our standard; then, the first alga has a relative fitness of $2/2 = 1.00$; the second of $4/2 = 2.00$. Had we chosen the second as standard, then the first would have been $2/4 = 0.5$; the second, $4/4 = 1.00$. It doesn't matter which fitness is picked as the standard; in each case the second alga has twice the relative fitness of the first, and the standard has a relative fitness of 1.00. Relative fitnesses compare all the various fitnesses in a population to one another.

Why do we need relative fitnesses? Darwin's theory is frequently and popularly phrased "survival of the fittest." We need relative fitnesses because "fittest" is a comparative word. Our first algal variety, with fitness 2, reproduces well and can survive in its environment. But the second variety reproduces even better, and so as you will see in a minute, the second will replace the first. Being fit is not enough; one must be fitter than one's competitors to survive for long.

SURVIVAL OF THE FITTEST

Assume that different phenotypes have different fitnesses and that fitness is at least partly inherited; then, in a stable environment, the average fitness of the members of a population is always increasing. That's it. The theory that revolutionized biology in 1859 still stands, improved only a little, explaining a lot. We shall devote the remainder of this chapter to explaining it, understanding what makes it a theory, and showing how it can be tested.

Notice first what the theory doesn't say. There is nothing in it about man evolving from gorillas. That hypothesis does not derive from the theory at all. It is an educated guess based on the anatomical similarity of men to apes and the fossil record of man. (In fact, you recall, modern paleontologists feel man probably evolved from a species of ape but not a modern one and certainly not a gorilla.)

Now notice how subtly the theory predicts that evolution will occur. If each phenotype has a different fitness, then an increase in the average fitness can only occur by a change in the mixture of phenotypes. In other words, the phenotypes we see now in the population aren't the same (on the average) as those we would have seen had we looked last year or ten years ago. This is the change of phenotype we've called evolution.

Last, notice that it not only predicts evolution, but provides a mechanism to explain it—the heritability of different fitnesses causing the accumulation of higher fitnesses in the population. This mechanism is called natural selection.

EVOLUTION: A THEORY?

When many people think about evolution, they pass over it superficially with the statement, "Oh, that's just a theory." Indeed, it is a theory, but the word "just" is out of place. People who use it are confusing the theory of evolution by natural selection with something else: the hypothesis, or educated guess, that evolution has occurred.

You have read Chapter 10 and seen that there is impressive evidence that supports the occurrence of evolution. But you have also read the theory and seen that it is something else; it proposes the mechanism of evolution; it tries to explain how evolution is produced by life.

It is also very difficult to understand. No wonder Darwin took many years to develop it. "Just a theory" is hardly an appropriate phrase.

If you are willing to discipline yourself throughout this chapter and the next three, you will be able to do much better than Charles Darwin. You will come to understand this theory in only a week or two. And you will know why evolutionists are so sure of themselves.

WHAT IS
A SCIENTIFIC THEORY?

What makes the theory of natural selection a theory? The answer lies in an examination of theories in general. That will lay bare the structure of the theory of natural selection and point out all the ways it could be wrong. It will, in other words, instruct us how to go about testing the theory. I begin with an artificial example.

The scientist from the planet Kimdumani had learned perfect English from everyday Americans. "I have a theory," he pronounced carefully, "that earthly life runs on energy supplied by their star, which they call 'sun.' I say this because I have measured their need for energy and the rates at which various sources supply it to them. And the sun's energy is the only source large enough to do the job."

Whether or not our fictional character is right (and, of course, he is), he does *not* "have a theory." He has a hypothesis, a word which really means "educated guess."

To scientists who work with them, theories are rather special. *A theory is a set of deductions derived from a set of assumptions.* For instance, if we assume $x + 2 = 10$, then we may deduce that $x = 8$; also that $x - 4 = 4$; and that $x^2 = 64$. There is, in fact, an infinity of deductions which we can make from this assumption. There are also word theories. For example, assume that all members of the mammalian order Sirenia swim, and that manatees are Sirenia. Then "manatees swim" is our deduction. In this case it is hard to see any other possible deduction. Return to the discussion of natural selection and identify the assumptions and deductions in the theory of evolution.

DISPROVING THEORIES

Comparing deduction with reality. Every scientific statement is subject to disproof, and theories are no exception. In fact, theories have some subtle possible weak points which should be mentioned. One obvious way to disprove our Kimdumanian friend's hypothesis is to put some small sealed bit of life (say a terrarium) in a dark place. In most cases, its inhabitants would soon die and our friend's guess would not be disproved. We can (and should) do a similar thing with a theory, that is, compare its deductions with the real world. Go and look at a manatee. Does it swim? Measure something that you know to be x; is it 8? If not, there is something wrong.

Mistakes of logic. But even if the manatee swims, even if $x = 8$, the theory may be wrong. Suppose we had assumed $x + 3 = 10$ and deduced from this, $x = 8$. We measured x and it was 8, so we triumphantly announce the verification of our theory. But of course we have been victims of our inability to do algebra, followed by the unlucky accident that x is really 8. Every means of expression—language, math, geometry, even hand signals—has rules of deduction. By those rules, we made a mistake. If $x + 3 = 10$, then $x = 7$. Have you ever come up with the right answer for the wrong reason? That's what happened to us. Theories can be wrong, therefore, because their deductions are inaccurately drawn.

Since the rules of deduction are best worked out for number systems, theoreticians often use mathematics. Thus, they make their assumptions precise and their errors of deduction least likely. But being human, they still err, and the thinking man always insists that he be shown the logic.

Inaccurate assumptions. If the deductions of the theory are logically correct, why bother testing them? Because deductions correctly drawn from poor assumptions do not correspond to the real world, and it is measurable reality which concerns science. For instance, if x is really 8, and we assume $x + 3 = 10$, our assumption is wrong and our deduction useless. All assumptions must be tested.

Oversimplified assumptions. A more important cause (historically) of poor theories has been incomplete assumptions. The scientist dreads such systems, which he calls oversimplifications. The only way to defend against them is to test one's deductions again and again, until one gradually gains confidence that they do correspond to real life.

A famous biological example of an oversimplified system was arrived at by several men independently (Spencer, Volterra, and Lotka). The system involves exploitation in which one species (the predator) exploits another (the victim).

The deduction from this situation was that the numbers of victim and predator would constantly fluctuate—first rare, then common, then rare, then common again, and so on. Many have noticed that such fluctuations aren't usual in nature. Gause (and others) brought predation into the lab and showed that oscillations are hard to find there also.

The trouble with the theory was not its deduction process—this was perfect. The trouble was that theoreticians had ignored the fact that the prey are also alive and require nutriment, space, and energy themselves. This they omitted from their assumptions; they oversimplified their system

MacArthur and I have recently included this assumption and deduced that indeed fluctuations should be uncommon. We have also made many simplifying assumptions; only testing will tell whether they were over-simplifications or not. Properly deduced theories based on inaccurate or insufficient assumptions are often useless.

WHY THEORIZE?

Using theory to test assumptions. So far we have talked about theories whose main job is to make predictions about reality from known assumptions. Another important scientific use of theory is to work back-wards—eliminate poor assumptions by testing their logical predictions.

Notice I was very careful to say "eliminate poor assumptions," not "establish good ones." As we have seen, a theory that doesn't work is wrong; if its deductions are logically produced, then its assumptions must be defective. But a theory that does make accurate predictions may also be wrong. Even if it has escaped all the perils mentioned, it may rest on a set of assumptions which is only one of many sets producing the same predictions.

Here we may cite Bergmann's rule as an example: homoiothermic (warm-blooded) species have members with larger bodies in colder regions (farther from the equator) and smaller bodies in warmer ones. For a hundred years evolutionists accepted the argument that this rule followed from the assumption that it is fitter for an animal in a cold climate to have a lower rate of temperature loss per gram of body weight. This is an interesting assumption, and it does yield a deduction which is correct.

About 20 years ago, the physiologist Scholander began to look at other deductions from the same assumption. He found them inaccurate. He feels that animals are protected from cold by other means, such as insulation (fur, fat, feathers). Today evolutionists have discovered that many other reasonable assumptions yield Bergmann's rule as a deduction. They don't yet know which of the assumptions is (are?) valid.

Since even a theory which has been successfully tested may prove to be wrong because a new set of assumptions arises which makes a more accurate set of predictions and a more complete explanation of known phenomena, each theory remains forever unproved. Science reserves the right to modify it or replace it tomorrow. Meanwhile, scientists patiently chip away at alternative assumptions, eliminating them and becoming more and more confident that such changes will not have to be made or, when made, will be minor. If you can't stand that kind of uncertainty, then science and the measurable world are probably not for you.

Importance of theory. If all those things can go wrong, why bother with theories?

First, because theories share many pitfalls with hypotheses. Hypotheses can also never be proved, only disproved; hypotheses also can be tested "successfully" because of carelessness or ignorance; hypotheses also can be replaced by others which are just as good at explaining the facts. The only special risks of theories are careless deduction and oversimplification.

These extra risks are braved because, second, it has been the experience of scientists that theories illuminate problems and answers in unique, rewarding ways. By indulging in simplification they point to generalizations; that is, they tell us what parts of the world are really most important to understanding it. By requiring precise statement of assumptions and deductions, they help to focus experiments on those things likely to be most important.

Third, theories often produce surprising results. When assumptions are combined in logical ways and then operated on by logical methods, their deductions are often totally unexpected. The scientist in effect was simply unaware *before* he worked on the theory, that the few assumptions he was aware of had anything to do with the deduction which theorizing produced. For example, Einstein's theory of relativity led him to predict that time runs more slowly for objects which are moving rapidly (see Bronowski). This theory, in turn, led to some entertaining science-fiction stories about star-ship crew members who, because of the high velocities of their craft, lived to see generations of the earthbound pass by, but experienced no sense of living longer lives. Recently this theory of Einstein has received its first experimental test; the test involved two highly accurate clocks, one kept on the Earth, the other sent on a space voyage; the test tended to conform to Einstein's serendipitous prediction.

Finally, many scientists simply enjoy working on theories. Nothing else affords them as much intellectual satisfaction.

PROBLEMS

Generating hypotheses

11-1. In New Mexico, a black-rock lava desert runs right next to a white-sand gypsum desert. A black population of the rock pocket mouse inhabits the black desert. A very pale, almost white population of the similar apache pocket mouse lives on the sand. (See Fig. 11-1.) Construct an hypothesis to account for the mouse distributions. (In simple English: "Guess why the mice live where they do.")

11-2. Can you imagine why skunks are conspicuously patterned?

11-3. A few acres of grassland in southeastern Arizona were once fenced, and cattle were excluded. This land hasn't changed. The surrounding grassland, under intense grazing, changed to a mesquite (a thorny bush) and weed desert. Can you guess why? Can you devise a test of your hypothesis?

Constructing theories

11-4. Assume that populations isolated from each other tend to become genetically dissimilar and that genetically dissimilar populations have difficulty in interbreeding. Now define a species as an interbreeding population. What should happen

Fig. 11-1 The two deserts of south-central New Mexico and their pocket mice. (Courtesy of Museum of Vertebrate Zoology, University of California.)

133

to one species that is accidentally split into two or more isolated populations for a very long time?

11-5. Assume that there are two phenotypes, I and V, in a population; that the population lives in two environments, A and B; and that in A, the relative fitness of I is 0.8 and of V is 1.0. In B, however, the relative fitness of I is 1.0 and of V is 0.5. Assume also that the average fitness of a phenotype is the sum of [the proportion of time it spends in an environment times its fitness in it] plus [the proportion in the other times its fitness in it]. That is, if A is lived in 40% of the time, then the average fitness of I is (.40) (.8) + (.60) (1.0) or 0.92. Last, assume that the phenotype with best average fitness eliminates the other from all environments. What will happen if A is lived in 10% of the time? What if A is lived in 70% of the time?

11-6. Female frogs find mates by responding to the croaking males. Green frogs and pickerel frogs live in the same regions over most of North America, but John Moore has found that progeny of matings between these two forms or species are quite inviable—they all die in the early gastrula stage. Suppose a group of male green frogs were to croak a lot like male pickerel frogs, and attract half female pickerel frogs and half their own females. Now suppose they don't produce any more sperm nor differ in any other way from the group of "normal-sounding" males. Last, assume that their voices differ because of a difference in the anatomy of their voice-producing parts, which all their sons inherit. If there are 200 such frogs now and 800 of the normal ones, and the total male population doesn't change in numbers, how many will there be next generation when the males have all died and been replaced by their young?

12 genetics for readers of this book

Much of the modern development and testing of the science of evolution depends on a sister science, genetics, the science of inheritance. For you to understand and appreciate evolution, these modern developments must be understood. Hence, I must now offer you a brief exposition of some of the principles of genetics. Those already familiar with genetics may feel free to skip this.

This chapter is not a text in genetics and you should not treat it as such. It does not even explain all the genetic topics required for an understanding of all evolutionary thought and work. It deals only with those few ideas about genetics which are necessary background for understanding this book's discussion of evolution and population biology. Among its other omissions is the entire body of knowledge often called molecular genetics. It is simply not yet clear that knowledge of the molecules involved in inheritance helps us better understand evolution.

Permit me to apologize in advance for the rather didactic tone of this discussion. I am not a geneticist and am not going to pretend to be one. So I will simply recite the genetic facts of life second-hand, as it were, just as my teachers, living and literary, told them to me.

WHAT IS PARTICULATE INHERITANCE?

When Darwin wrote, biologists knew little of the true mechanisms of inheritance. Darwin shared their ignorance and escaped its consequences only through a combination of fortunate blind spots and more or less miraculous insights.

It was generally accepted that the organ of inheritance was the blood. To this day we preserve a vestige of this belief when we say "He has good blood," meaning: "His forebearers are a set of worthy people." The expression "blue blood" is similar.

Probably, people sought the material of inheritance in the blood for two reasons. First, unlike other tissues, blood is a liquid. Since people believed that the inheritance material of two parents mixed and blended to produce progeny, it was natural to seek a liquid to be that material: it is simply easier to think about the mixing of two bloods than, say, two hearts or two eyes.

Second, people believed that the material of inheritance carried with it all the information about the parent's body. If the parent had the unusual musculature of a blacksmith from working behind a forge with a heavy hammer, then his progeny would be born with superdeveloped muscles and the stuff of inheritance had to carry the directions for building a blacksmith's body. If the parent had turned to a life of crime, the child couldn't be trusted; it had inherited a tendency to do the same. In other words, people thought that the inheritance material was a blueprint drawn from all over the parent himself. What better tissue for this job than the blood, which might get information from literally everywhere within the body because it *is* everywhere? In a later chapter, we shall examine this notion, called "inheritance of acquired characteristics," in more detail.

Perhaps there are other reasons why blood was so widely believed to be the stuff of inheritance. For example, blood can be lost in small quantities without harm. And the females of many mammalian species produce a flow of blood when they are ovulating and capable of conception. With all these arguments pointing to it, it is no wonder that people were so ready to believe in the power of blood to bear the inheritance.

What really upset this conclusion was the discovery of nonblending, particulate inheritance. It turns out that there exist miniscule entities called genes or cistrons which parents donate to their children. Each parent donates one complete set of genes to each offspring. Obviously each child gets only two sets, and thus when children grow to be parents, they couldn't have more than two children of their own if their bodies couldn't copy their genes freely. In fact, genes are copied prolifically. Moreover, most single cells can copy their own genes with only the equipment that exists in virtually all of them.

Genes were first discovered in sweet peas by the Austrian monk Gregor Mendel. Later they were found in various insects and soon it became apparent that all living things have them. The discovery and exploration of the genes of bacteria and viruses capped the long attempt to show the universality of genes.

Genes carry much of the information that the progeny requires to build itself into a reproductive adult. Each gene carries a specific kind of message. Most of the genes we shall examine in this book code for the structure of the large, complex molecules called proteins. When the body builds a protein it first consults the blueprint by a particular gene.

Although each gene does only one job—carries only one blueprint—the product built with that blueprint may have many jobs in the body. Thus one gene can influence many different character traits. Such a gene is termed pleiotropic and the phenomenon, pleiotropy.

For instance the gene which gives the flowers of the sweet pea their red color also colors their leaf axils red and alters the coat of each pea from brown to gray. And in *Drosophila*, the vinegar fly, the vestigial gene renders the wings small and shriveled, changes two bristles on the fly's back, reduces its fecundity and its life span, and causes many other changes, as well.

Just as there are many ways to draw a blueprint ("Do you want a cedar shake roof, a slate one, or a tar-paper one?"), so there are many variant messages that can be coded into a gene. All the alternative genes, that is, the whole collection of all the blueprints for one job, are known as alleles. For example, the blonde-hair gene is allelic to the brown-hair gene; they are alleles. But blonde *hair* is not an allele of brown *eyes*. As in the above, genes are often named by the character trait they are known to produce.

DOMINANCE
AND GENE EXPRESSION

In many species, including *Homo sapiens*, each individual gets two complete sets of genes. Suppose one contains the blueprint for blue eyes and the other, its allele, the one for brown. Which blueprint is to be followed? How is the contradiction resolved?

There is not one answer, even for the same two alleles. For example, Ford has shown for a species of British butterfly, *Panaxia dominula*, that there are two alleles for spottedness: one for two spots, and one for eight. Those with two genes for two spots always have two spots; those with two genes for eight spots always have eight. But those with both have anywhere from two to eight spots.

If both genes are the same allele, their possessor is called a homozygote (from *homo*, meaning "same" and *zygote*, meaning "the fertilized egg"). If not, and the individual has two different alleles, it is termed a heterozygote (from *hetero*, meaning "different").

In general, for any two alleles, it is possible to predict the appearance of the heterozygote based on past experience. For example, a human with blue-eyed and brown-eyed alleles is almost always brown-eyed. The difficulty with the butterfly spots is that the butterflies were the product of a special experiment to prove that evolution could resolve the contradiction of heterozygosity in whatever way is best. In nature the butterfly heterozygotes are not so variable; they tend toward an intermediate number of spots.

When the heterozygote takes on the appearance, or phenotype, of one of the homozygotes, we say that the allele yielding the appearance is dominant and the masked allele is recessive. Often, dominance occurs because the gene has the job of specifying the structure of an enzyme (enzymes are proteins) needed for a color (say) to be synthesized. The recessive allele specifies an unworkable enzyme. But only one dominant is required to specify a satisfactory enzyme. So the dominant allele can work alone. It is like adding +1 (the dominant) to zero (the recessive); the zero has no effect at all.

In most cases heterozygotes are not identical to either homozygote. Sometimes they appear intermediate; occasionally they actually possess a phenotype different from either parent and are in no sense intermediate. As we shall soon see, heterozygotes are often superior to homozygotes in their ability to survive and reproduce.

WHERE ARE THE GENES?

Although genes were not actually seen until well after the invention of the electron microscope, they were located earlier in the twentieth century by a brilliant series of investigations. By the 1930s when a really breathtaking experiment by Curt Stern squelched the last bit of reasonable doubt, everyone concerned with genetics believed that genes are on the chromosomes. Their confidence was unshakable, despite the fact that they had never even seen a gene. (Later, investigators figured out the molecular composition of genes—and they, too, hadn't seen one.)

The chromosomes (on which the genes lie) are strands of organic material in the nuclei of cells. They readily take up certain colorful stains, hence their name (chromo, meaning "color," and some, meaning "body"). Because they stained so easily, they were quickly discovered. In fact, they were discovered before genes. It took quite a while before scientists linked the two.

Biologists had suspected they should have been looking in the cell's nucleus for genes. They could show that mother and father shared equally in donating genes to their offspring, but they knew the father's actual contribution, one sperm, was dwarfed by the mother's, one egg. If you think the situation disproportionate in humans, just think about chickens where the sperm is also microscopic, but the egg is somewhat larger even than a human egg (a human egg is about one-tenth the size of a pinhead).

What is equal about a sperm and an egg? Their nuclei. It has been said that a sperm is only a nucleus with a tail! But a whole nucleus it does have.

Knowing to look in the nucleus doesn't help much because the nucleus contains much more than chromosomes. Which nuclear element is to be associated with genes? Most scientists settled on the chromosomal element when they realized that the patterns of chromosomal copying and transmittal which they observed under the microscope were similar to the patterns of gene copying and transmittal which they inferred from their genetic experiments.

PATTERNS OF GENE
AND CHROMOSOME REPLICATION

If two sexual heterozygotes mate, their progeny will usually occur in one of two ratios. There might be three of the heterozygous phenotype for every one of the recessive homozygous phenotype; in this case a heterozygote's phenotype is determined by a dominant allele. Or there might be one of each homozygous phenotype for every two heterozygotes.

Such ratios were first obtained with various characteristics of sweet peas by Mendel. Plant height, flower color, pea shape, and surface texture all seemed to follow such rules. (See Fig. 12-1.) For example, in flower color,

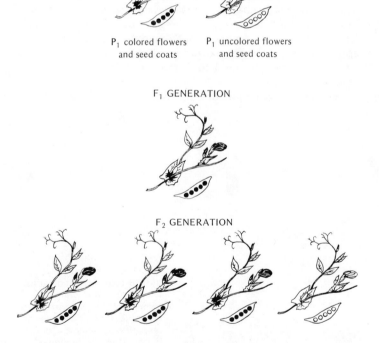

Fig. 12-1 The simple cross for color in sweet peas. The F_1 generation is both the progeny of the P_1 and the parent of the F_2. (From *Principles of genetics,* 5th edition, by Sinnott, Dunn, and Dobzhansky, Copyright 1958 by, and used with the permission of McGraw-Hill Book Co.)

a pure, red-flowered pea crossed with a white one produced a red hybrid, showing that red is dominant. When two of the red heterozygotes were crossed, 3/4 of the progeny were red, 1/4 white.

In snapdragons, however, a red-flowered plant crossed with a white produced pink hybrids, because there is no dominance. When the pinks are self-pollinated, their progeny are 1/4 red, 1/4 white, and 1/2 pink. (See Fig. 12-2.)

Examples also exist in animals. A pure, normal *Drosophila* mated with a vestigial-winged *Drosophila* produces all normal-looking heterozygotes. Heterozygotes mated to each other produce progeny 3/4 of which are normal and 1/4 vestigial. (See Fig. 12-3.)

A black Andalusian fowl mated with a white-spotted one produces all blue fowl (Fig. 12-4). A blue hen and a blue rooster have chicks 1/4 of which are black, 1/4 white-spotted, and 1/2 blue.

And finally, a blue-eyed wife and a brown-eyed husband (all of whose ancestors were brown-eyed, too) can expect only brown-eyed children. But a brown-eyed couple, each with a blue-eyed parent, can expect one of four of their children to be blue-eyed.

Mendel explained these results by postulating that each individual has two particles (genes) for each character, makes large numbers of copies for its potential offspring, and actually gives one gene per character to each offspring. Today, we know much more about the details of genetics, and there are exceptions to Mendel's generalizations. But for the most part he was right. How does that explain the 3 to 1 and the 2 to 1 to 1 ratios of previous paragraphs?

Suppose we examine the donation of each heterozygote. One-half the

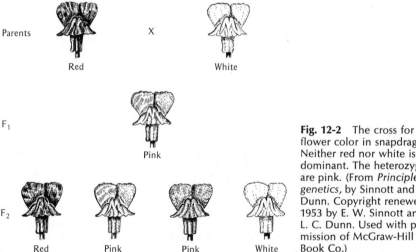

Parents   Red   X   White

F_1 Pink

F_2 Red   Pink   Pink   White

Fig. 12-2 The cross for flower color in snapdragons. Neither red nor white is dominant. The heterozygotes are pink. (From *Principles of genetics*, by Sinnott and Dunn. Copyright renewed 1953 by E. W. Sinnott and L. C. Dunn. Used with permission of McGraw-Hill Book Co.)

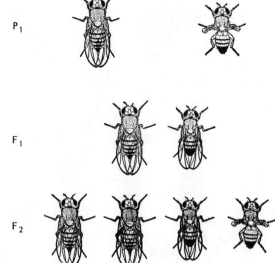

P_1

F_1

F_2

Fig. 12-3 The cross for wing form in the vinegar fly, *Drosophila melanogaster*. Males are smaller and have a solid abdomen tip. But the one of four F_2 that is vestigial could just as easily be female as male. (From *Principles of genetics* by Sinnott and Dunn. Copyright renewed 1953 by E. W. Sinnott and L. C. Dunn. Used with permission of McGraw-Hill Book Co.)

time it will be the dominant allele; 1/2, the recessive. Suppose the father contributes a dominant; this will happen half the time. In 1/2 of such cases, or 1/4 of the time, so will the mother; the other 1/2 will find the dominant sperm meeting a recessive egg to produce a heterozygote. Now suppose the sperm is recessive (as it will be 1/2 the time). It will fertilize a dominant egg in 1/2 the cases and a recessive one the other 1/2. Thus the following zygotes will each be produced 1/4 of the time:

1. Dominant sperm + dominant egg = homozygote
2. Dominant sperm + recessive egg = heterozygote
3. Recessive sperm + dominant egg = heterozygote
4. Recessive sperm + recessive egg = homozygote

The genotype is the term given to the genetic quality of an individual. So the heterozygotes have different genotypes from the homozygotes. Although this always affects their ability to be parents of various types of children, it may not mean anything to their own appearance. If there is a dominant allele, then the heterozygous phenotype is just like the dominant homozygote. Hence, 3 of the cases listed yield the same phenotype, the dominant; and 1 produces the recessive.

On the other hand, if there is no dominance (as in Andalusian-fowl color), then the phenotypes appear in the 2:1:1 ratio. There are two heterozygotes for each one of either homozygote.

The pattern of sexual reproduction in chromosomes exactly mimics this. Each parental cell has two chromosomes of each kind (there may be hun-

Fig. 12-4 The cross for plumage color in Andalusian fowl. Neither black nor white-spotted is dominant. Heterozygotes are blue. Compare this to the snapdragon cross (Fig. 12-2). (From *Principles of genetics,* 5th edition, by Sinnott, Dunn, and Dobzhansky. Copyright 1958 by and used with the permission of McGraw-Hill Book Co.)

dreds altogether). By a process called meiosis, parents produce myriads of sperm and eggs each with only one chromosome of each type. After union, the zygote has two full sets.

As the conceptus grows, it produces many millions of cells. Each is equipped with its own full set of chromosomes (and genes) in most instances. The process of complete cellular replication is called cell division, or mitosis. In between the production of each daughter cell, the cell doubles its chromosomal material. Thus, when it donates two full sets to its daughter by asexual reproduction (mitosis), it still has two full sets for itself. Single-celled organisms, such as algae and protozoans, often reproduce this way, avoiding meiosis and sexual reproduction most of the time.

The number of sets of chromosomes (and genes) possessed by a cell is called its ploidy. Cells with one set (like a sperm) are haploid. Cells with two are diploid. Bananas have triploid cells (as do some other things), and certain ferns are likely to be tetraploid (four) or even hexaploid (six). When a cell has more than two sets, but has *some* integer number of complete sets, it is called polyploid. When it has a number of complete sets and an incomplete set, it is aneuploid. Consideration of how polyploidy is initiated will occur much later in the book, when it is time to wonder how new species are formed.

THE LOCUS
OF A GENE
The Latin word *locus* means "place." It has given us our English word location. However, in genetics, it is used unchanged to mean the address of a gene on a chromosome.

Although genes are on chromosomes, the two things aren't exactly the same. There are many genes on each chromosome, and besides, chromosomes also contain nongenetic material. Also, some particles of inheritance aren't on chromosomes at all (although all the genes we shall study in this book are on chromosomes).

Genes are not thrown haphazardly onto chromosomes. Each occurs, as the term locus implies, in a very special position on the chromosome, a position reserved for it alone. Only another allele can occupy that same locus. Thus, when a geneticist speaks of studying two loci (loci is the plural), he means he is studying two sets of alleles, each with its own specific proper position on the chromosomal strands and its own job to perform. Look at the figure of the giant chromosomes in Chapter 13; that is a visible, graphic example of the precise way in which genes are ordered on chromosomes.

GENETICS PROBLEMS

12-1. In dogs, black is dominant to red. A red cocker spaniel is mated to a homozygous black mutt. What colors of offsprings are to be expected?

12-2a. In summer squash, flat fruit is dominant to round fruit. What are the expected progeny of a flat squash crossed with a round one?

12-2b. What are the expected progeny of one of these offspring when crossed with its round parent?

12-3. In cattle, red and white coat color when crossed yield all-roan calves. What would be the expected proportions of progeny of a roan bull and a white cow?

12-4a. All the offspring produced by crossing red four-o'clocks with white ones have pink flowers. What proportions of what flower colors will be yielded among the direct offspring of pink × pink?

12-4b. Of pink × red?

12-4c. Of pink × white?

12-4d. Of red × white?

12-5. In *Drosophila*, long wing is dominant to short wing. Two long-winged flies when bred together produced 48 short-winged and 146 long-winged offspring. What proportion of the long-winged offspring can be expected to be heterozygous?

13 testing Darwin's theory: are deductions and assumptions real?

Mathematics . . . was repugnant to me. . . . [But] I have deeply regretted that I did not proceed far enough at least to understand something of the great leading principles of mathematics; for men thus endowed seem to have an extra sense.

Charles Darwin, *Autobiography*

DEDUCTION: EVOLUTION OCCURS

Most of Darwin's famous book, *Origin of Species,* was devoted to stating the evidence in favor of evolution by natural selection. To the general reading public, the astonishment was evolution itself. Nowhere before had anyone amassed such impressive evidence that evolution had actually occurred. Darwin did that, of course, because he wanted to compare his deduction with reality.

Previously, a few men, including Darwin's grandfather, Erasmus, had believed in the reality of evolution. Others had even advanced possible theories of how evolution is fostered.

In fact, Alfred Wallace must share credit with Darwin for thinking of the mechanism of natural selection. Darwin would undoubtedly still be writing his book were it not for the fact that he was needled into presenting his theory with Wallace by the tacit threat of Wallace presenting it without him and stealing all the thunder. In his *Autobiography,* Darwin admits that the *Origin* would have been four times as long without the pressure of Wallace. And he adds, "Very few would have had the patience to read it."

Darwin's unique contribution, then, was to fill a book so full of data supporting this deduction that people could no longer ignore evolution. In the first chapter, I gave you a small but impressive sample of the evidence that evolution occurs. The rest of this book is full of more such examples.

ASSUMPTION: DIFFERENT PHENOTYPES
HAVE DIFFERENT FITNESSES

Critics admitted that a few things like wing color in a moth were good for camouflage and obviously would affect the chance that a moth would survive. But they maintained that most alternate phenotypes are selectively neutral, that is, each has the same fitness. What is the advantage of red hair over brown (or vice versa); of blue eyes over brown; of blood-type A over blood-type AB? These different aspects of the phenotype make no difference to the fitness! Or so they assumed.

Further, they said, look at all the energy going to waste on vestigial organs. What good is a thymus? Yet it develops. What good is the pineal body? But we all have one. How about the appendix? The coccyx? Body hair? Who needs them? If we don't need them, why doesn't selection get rid of them? Surely the energy would be useful for reproductive purposes. And people would no longer die of peritonitis following a ruptured appendix. No woman would any longer have trouble giving birth because she happened to have a broken or malformed coccyx that partially blocked a normal vaginal birth. Certainly this is fundamental to reproduction; why hasn't selection performed its work?

All the foregoing complaints are based on ignorance. Just because we don't know why something has lasted doesn't mean there's no reason for it, doesn't prove its uselessness. The only way to test these problems honestly is to measure the fitness of those with larger and those with smaller appendices. Are they different? No one has ever done it for blood type, hair color, or eye color, so we don't know.

But for some items on the list, the work has been done. And for some vestigial organs, we have now discovered a use. The thymus has been shown to be important to the development of the antibody system— important in battling disease. The pineal body—which was once an eye at the top of the head and still is in some reptiles—has become an organ associated with the measurement of time in mammals.

Anyone who has ever had gooseflesh on a cold morning is aware of the contraction of the tiny muscles around the base of each hair. My teachers once told me this was useless—it had once served to erect the hairs of the fur of our ancestors creating a larger air space in the fur and thus better insulation. It still does in any mammal with thick fur.

But is it really useless to us nearly naked apes? Remember what happens when muscles contract? ATP, the body's chief fuel, is used, and some of its energy is "lost" as heat. **That's** why we shiver; so our contracting muscles can warm us with the heat of ATP. However tiny those hair muscles, they do the same. And they do it gently, without causing us to lose our coordination. Gooseflesh is a mild way of obtaining heat from our ATP stores.

And the body hair itself? Well, no one knows all the answers and body hair remains a mystery, but I for one am no longer convinced of the existence of stagnant vestigial organs. Existing structures are probably either useful or on their way out because they depress fitness.

At one time, blood types were the favorite example of alternate phenotypes with identical fitnesses. What is the difference in fitness between a man of type A and one of type AB or O? None, used to be the answer.

But that was wrong. Researchers have now found that people with blood-type O get duodenal ulcers 1.38 times more often and stomach ulcers 1.19 times more often than other types. People with blood-type A are 1.19 times more likely than those with B or O to get stomach cancer; 1.26 times more likely than O's to have pernicious anemia; and 1.16 times more likely than O's to get diabetes mellitus. Lerner has summarized the data for these diseases and noted others which may influence people, depending on their blood type (see also Bajema). Blood types are anything but selectively neutral.

To be honest, it should be noted that a large body of workers are investigating the question of selective neutrality. However, they are working with miniscule differences in phenotype, mostly slight differences in the properties of proteins, differences that are detectable with only the most refined of methods. Perhaps such differences are selectively neutral or at least so minor as to prevent the action of natural selection from overcoming the accidents of life. Refer to the discussions of mutation, of genetic drift, and of group selection for examples of other evolutionary forces which, while usually very weak, can thwart natural selection if it, too, is very weak. (These forces are explained later in the text at various appropriate points.)

Theoretical workers have already produced a body of investigations to help us predict when and how often we should find neutral phenotypic differences. They have also produced much controversy among themselves. The main point is that the differences which may be neutral are so tiny as not to be ordinarily noticeable. And even these may have selective significances that are undreamed of. In any case, when we can readily sense differences in phenotype, such as when an organ is noticeably different in size or shape or a protein is absent or present or a behavior is variable, then the differences are probably important and cause important differences in fitness. Even scientists actively engaged in studying "neutral alleles" are quick to point that out.

ASSUMPTION:
FITNESS IS AT LEAST PARTLY INHERITED

To examine this assumption we could note that some of the phenotypic components we have already discussed, like wing color in moths and blood type in humans, are known to be inherited. But we shall attack this question directly by actually looking at the number of children born to a group of people: British peeresses (Table 13-1). These data were presented by R. A. Fisher, one of the first evolutionists to employ mathematical methods in his work.

From these data you can see that daughters who had been only children had the smallest families, an average of 2.97 children each. Daughters with four siblings had 3.99 children. Daughters with nine siblings averaged 4.38 children each. In general, the larger the fitness of the mother, the larger the fitness of her daughters.

If we now examine the number of children born to granddaughters, we should still find a heritable component. But a granddaughter receives only one-fourth of her inheritance from one of her grandmothers, whereas a daughter gets half her hereditary traits from her mother. So the heredity influence of grandmothers on the number of their great-grandchildren should be half as large as is the influence of mothers on the number of their grandchildren.

As Fisher pointed out, that is exactly what happens. For each additional child she has above the average number in her generation, a woman causes about 0.21 children above the average for her daughter's generation in her daughters' families and 0.106 children in her granddaughters' families above the average for their generation. The same numbers apply for fewer children than average. Fitness is certainly being inherited.

ASSUMPTION:
THE ENVIRONMENT IS STABLE

This assumption is not always true. The changing seasons, hot years and cold ones, and dry years and wet ones all violate it. Also, the very fact that there are different species of life alive at the same place and time produces a variable environment. One of the most important sources of environmental difference, in fact, is change in the abundance of any species, including one's own.

The reason that variation in environment is important is that it changes relative fitnesses. When the woods became black with soot, the black moths became more fit than the white. When the elk of eastern North America were driven from their land into oblivion, any animal that had specialized in eating elk was unfit. When the white man reduced the forest fires in the jack pine forests of Michigan, Kirtland's warbler nearly became extinct—it needs the young trees, which can grow only after the jack pine seeds are popped from their cones by fire. When the white man introduced fire control into the mountains of Arizona, the resinous, fire-resistant species became scarce thanks to the artificial boost we gave the fitnesses of their fire-susceptible competitors (Cooper).

When the environment changes, all we can say is that fitnesses will, too. The theory of natural selection would say, then, that while one environ-

TABLE 13-1   FAMILIES OF PEERESSES

Number of children born to mother	Number of such mothers	Average number of children born to their daughters
1	35	2.97
2	67	3.54
3	111	3.14
4	136	3.41
5	138	3.99
6	132	3.89
7	114	3.93
8	87	4.07
9	74	4.23
10	50	4.38
11	24	5.08
12	19	5.21
13	9	8.56
14	1	10.00
15	3	6.67

Source: Fisher.

ment reigns, average fitnesses will be increasing. A change in environment may well cause average fitnesses to plummet, but selection will never stop. Fitnesses will immediately begin rising again, but the fittest phenotypes may be very different from what they were before. Thus, the direction of evolution may change radically.

Environmental change is our first example of a nonselective influence on fitness. There will be others. In general, we shall usually conclude that selection increases the average fitness of a population, though other things may diminish it.

The effect of assuming a stable environment is to simplify the theory in order to handle those chunks of time in which an environment is relatively stable. This is almost never an oversimplification, for environments can last a long time (relative to the generation times of life). So deductions from the theory do agree with what we observe in nature.

DEDUCTION:
THE AVERAGE FITNESS INCREASES

This is the most difficult of the theory's contents to check against reality. You have already seen why. Evolution is a deucedly slow process. Remember the horse's tooth? The human brain?

Radical environmental change gives us one chance to test this deduction. Where man changes environments by design or by thoughtless pollution, the course of selection is altered and selection temporarily speeds up. Here we do see an increase in average fitness.

The moth population which evolves from peppered white to sooty black in sooty woods has improved its fitness. So have the bacteria which evolve resistance to antibiotics.

In one case involving the disease sickle-cell anemia, man himself has been improving in fitness. Sickle-cell anemia is fully discussed later. Watch later also for the many instances in which a population has responded to a laboratory environment with an increase in its mean fitness.

Biologists are not too upset at having so few examples of increased fitness. The reason is all around you. Life is marvelously adapted. Organisms seem to be doing just the right things to survive and reproduce. How could this be so if fitness had not been improved by the many changes that we call evolution? You will see many cases of adaptation in this book. Each one is an eloquent affirmation of this deduction.

IS THE THEORY LOGICAL?

There is a good chance you do not yet understand why natural selection should produce evolution. Darwin himself wrote, "I once or twice tried to explain to able men what I meant by natural selection, but signally failed."

The trouble is that the theory of natural selection is highly mathematical. It deals with rates of reproduction and the accumulation of reproductive ability. These are numbers. But Darwin tried to explain his theory in English.

To Darwin it was all rather obvious from the English. But to an ordinary mortal it is anything but clear. The deduction seems not to follow or else to have been produced by black magic.

In the 1930s, men (Fisher; Haldane; Wright) who later came to be called population geneticists and who understood both genetics and natural selection, added the math. They took the magic out of the deductive process. Now, anyone who knows the tiniest bit of algebra and genetics can follow the logic with ease.

In the next several sections, we'll build a mathematical model that realistically represents as complicated a situation as a year of algebra allows. Make sure you read these sections slowly and sternly; understand everything and don't let me sneak anything past you. Much of the confidence of the professional biologist in natural selection and much of his ability to understand it derives from mathematical studies like those that follow. First, we shall try to translate our knowledge of how things are inherited on genes into a set of numbers. Then, we can add some other numbers to represent selection and see how it changes the numbers representing genes.

The gene pool. The gene pool is an abstraction. It means the imaginary barrel containing all the genes of all the individuals of a population.

Let's ignore all genes in the gene pool except one kind—say, those that control blood type or those that control eye color or those that control anything. As long as our genes are at the same locus, they'll do.

Recall that a gene locus is an address on a chromosome where a particular kind of gene resides. Remember, too, that two genes that are supposed to do the same job but do it in different ways are called alleles (for example, blue eyes and brown eyes). Last, remember that each individual gets two genes for each job, that is, each "picks" twice from the barrel or gene pool when he is conceived.

We shall assume that our barrel of genes is so large that everyone approaching it to receive his genes has the same chances as everyone else, regardless of who has already picked what. We shall also assume that generations do not overlap at all; that instead, one generation goes to the barrel all at once and is conceived. Then the barrel's contents magically evaporate. The young generation grows to reproductive maturity, dumps all its genes into the barrel, and disappears. Then another generation lines up for its gene handout.

Natural selection in gene-pool terms. The main question we ask concerns the contents of the barrel. Are they the same when the second generation picks genes? If not, the second generation will not exactly resemble its parents. If we observe such a change, we'll call it evolution.

Our questions are: If different phenotypes have different fitnesses, and the fitnesses are heritable, can we deduce mathematically that the gene pool changes from generation to generation? And can we also deduce mathematically that the average fitness of each succeeding generation is higher than the previous one?

Symbolizing the gene pool. For the sake of concreteness, we shall name our two alleles yellow and blue, and symbolize them Y and B. If the total number of genes in the gene pool is N and the number of Y is n, then the number of B must be $(N - n)$. (Remember we assumed there were only two alleles.)

We shall name the fraction of genes that are yellow, p. Certainly, $p = n/N$. The fraction of genes that are B will be called q; $q = (N - n)/N$.

Notice that $p + q = n/N + (N - n)/N = N/N = 1$. This is a good thing, too, since p and q are the only two slices of the genetic pie we've got, and they'd better add to exactly one whole pie when we put them together.

Let's do that again with real numbers. Suppose there are 100,000 genes and 32,000 are Y. Then $N = 100,000$; $n = 32,000$ and $p = 32,000/100,000 = 0.32$. Similarly, since there must be 68,000 B alleles, $q = 0.68$. Of course $0.32 + 0.68 = 1.00$.

Make up your own numbers for n and N, and try it again until deep within your being you feel real meaning for p and q. They must be understood, since changes in p and q will be all we deduce to demonstrate that evolution is occurring.

Notice that since $p + q = 1$, therefore $q = 1 - p$. This means that if you tell me p, I can tell you q. (If $p = 0.16$, then $q = 0.84$, and so forth.) So we are really in doubt about one thing, p. This won't change, and we'll spend the rest of the chapter figuring out what happens to p under various biological conditions.

The Hardy-Weinberg distribution. The first set of biological conditions is the background for the others. It assumes four things:

1. All phenotypes have the same fitness.
2. There is no genetic mutation (see Chapter 14).
3. No phenotype either prefers or dislikes mating with any other. (Geneticists call this random mating.)
4. There is no way for natives to leave or foreigners to enter the system. (There is no migration or, in proper jargon, gene flow is zero).

Now condition (1) we have already gone to great lengths to disprove; and you probably know that (2) is wrong. The third and fourth can be right but usually aren't. So what are we doing? We are showing what would happen if all four *were* true. Then we'll compare this to what would happen if (1) and then (1) and (2) are false.

This sets up a kind of mathematical experiment with controls.

We will not bother with (3) and (4) in this book. Geneticists have worked out what happens when these assumptions are changed; briefly, the *values* of what natural selection achieves are different, but the *kinds* of selective achievements remain the same.

Imagine the first generation of souls lined up at the gene pool. Each steps up and picks one gene, then a second. What is the chance that the first will be a Y? It is p. In our previous example, the chance that the individual receives a Y is 0.32. Another way of expressing it is: 32% of the genes picked are Y. Since we assumed a huge barrelful of genes, this chance stays the same for the second pick. Similarly, the chance of getting B is 0.68 each time.

Fitnesses, however, belong to individuals, **not** alleles. So, what we really need to know is the chance of an individual being a certain phenotype.

There will be two or three different phenotypes to which we will want, later on, to assign a fitness. BB and YY will certainly look different, but BY may look blue if B is dominant or yellow if Y is. In either case, we shall have two phenotypes, hence two fitnesses.

But if BY is intermediate, say green, then we have a third phenotype to which we must also assign a fitness. We shall assume this to be true. The equations we'll get can easily handle cases of dominance, too.

We return to our unborn youth picking his alleles. We know the chance he got a Y his first pick was p. It was also p the second pick. But what chance was there to get Y's on both picks? (What is the chance he became a YY?)

We can easily figure this out. Suppose 1/4 got Y at first; that is, suppose $p = 0.25$. Then, only 1/4 of those would get them the second time, too. Hence, 1/4 of 1/4 get YY. Of course, $1/4 \times 1/4 = 1/16$. So 1/16 are YY.

Similarly, if 3/4 get B on the first pick, then 3/4 of *them* will receive a B on the second pick, too. So the fraction that are BB is 3/4 × 3/4 or 9/16.

This accounts for $9/16 + 1/16 = 10/16$ of the young. What are the other 6/16 like? They are the ones who received a B and a Y.

We can represent the fraction that are YY as $p \times p$, which is p^2. Those that are BB occur $q \times q$ or q^2 of the time. But how many are BY? Well, there are two ways to get to be BY. Either get B on the first round and Y on the second, or Y on the first and B on the second. What fraction does it the first way? $3/4 \times 1/4 = 3/16$. The second? $1/4 \times 3/4 = 3/16$. Either way? $3/16 + 3/16 = 6/16$. Hence, we can represent the fraction of the population that are BY as $qp + pq$ or $2pq$.

The three fractions we have just obtained, when taken as a set, are known as the Hardy-Weinberg distribution:

Phenotype	Fraction of newborn with the phenotype
YY	p^2
YB	$2pq$
BB	q^2

Now notice that these three fractions always account for 100% of the population: $p^2 + 2pq + q^2 = (p + q)^2$. But $p + q = 1$, so $(p + q)^2 = (1)^2 = 1$.

This time we have sliced the genetic pie into three pieces based on phenotypes. But the pieces still add up to one whole pie.

It is possible to deduce that because of our four assumptions, no change in p will take place. In each generation a fraction p of all alleles will be Y and fractions p^2, $2pq$, and q^2 of all phenotypes will be YY, BY, and BB, respectively. The principle that p doesn't change (that there is no evolution) if the four assumptions are true is known as the Hardy-Weinberg rule. Of course, we know now that evolution does occur; p does change. So the deduction made from the four assumptions is wrong. Soon we shall add a bit of natural selection and see if we get a more accurate deduction.

In summary, we shall use two alleles, B and Y. The fraction that are Y will be p; the fraction that are B will be q. $p + q = 1$. The fraction of individuals that are YY before selection is p^2; $2pq$ are BY, and q^2 are BB. This is the Hardy-Weinberg distribution. The Hardy-Weinberg rule says neither p nor these other fractions will change if there is no selection, mutation, or migration and if mating is random.

Allowing fitnesses to differ. In this section we shall not allow all fitnesses to be the same. Instead, we shall let the fitness of YY be y, of BB be b, and of BY be g. Then, we shall pick as our standard fitness g, and compare all the fitnesses to it. So the relative fitness of $YY = y/g$, of $BB = b/g$, and of $BY = g/g = 1$. Does this biological condition cause p to change?

Let us again begin with our gene pool of p and q. Again we dole out genes, two apiece, to the young. Again YY is p^2, BY is $2pq$, and BB is q^2 of the population. Now, however, we watch this generation as they grow and reproduce.

We notice that they are not equal in their chances of survival, nor in the number of young they have. In fact, when they throw themselves back into the barrel, when they reconstitute the gene pool, for every BY that goes in, y/g YY's go in and b/g BB's go in.

Suppose, for example, that $y = 1.5$ per generation, $b = 2.0$ per generation, and $g = 1.75$ per generation. Then, when the gene pool is reconstituted, for every one BY that started out, one goes back in. But 1.5/1.75 or only 6/7 of each YY will be added. And 2.0/1.75 or 8/7 of each BB will be added.

Let us see if p has changed. Suppose p started at 0.10. Then $(0.10)^2$ or 0.01 were YY, $(0.9)^2$ or 0.81 were BB, and 0.18 were BY at first. To make the math easy we will assume the population is 700. At first, then, there were 7 yellows, 126 greens, and 567 blues. When they went back to reconstitute the gene pool, for every 126 greens, there were 8/7 × 567 or 648 blues, and 6/7 × 7 or 6 yellows.

Each yellow contributes two yellow alleles to the barrel; each blue, two blues; and each green, a yellow and a blue. So there will be [(6 × 2) + 126] or 138 yellow alleles and [(648 × 2) + 126] or 1422 blue ones, a total of 1560 alleles in the barrel. Of these 1560, 138 are Y, so the new value of p is 138/1560 or 0.0885. In other words, p began the first generation at 0.100 and the second at 0.0885. Natural selection has indeed caused evolution.

We symbolize this change in p with the Greek letter delta, Δ, which stands for change. In this example, $\Delta p = 0.0885 - 0.100 = -0.0115$. That is, there was a decline in the frequency of the Y allele of 0.0115, or 1.15%.

Notice that the individuals with a double dose of Y had the worst relative fitness, 6/7. This change in p means there will be fewer of them around in the next generation.

Eventually, we will deduce that in a case like this, the trend will continue until $p = 0$, that is until all individuals are BB. At that point only the fittest will have survived! We shall also show that as p declines, the average fitness of the members of the population is improved, just as Darwin maintained. Study Fig. 13-1.

The general equation for Δp. Meanwhile, let's develop a general way to express Δp for any values of p, q, g, y, and b. In the previous example, after selection there were $(y/g)p^2$ yellows, $2pq$ greens, and $q^2(b/g)$ blues. Each individual contributed 2 genes, so there were $[2p^2(y/g) + 4pq + 2q^2(b/g)]$ genes after selection. Each yellow individual contributes 2 yellow genes; each green, 1 yellow gene; and each blue, no yellow genes. So there are $[2p^2(y/g) + 2pq]$ yellow genes. The new value of p is the new number of yellow genes divided by the new total number of all genes:

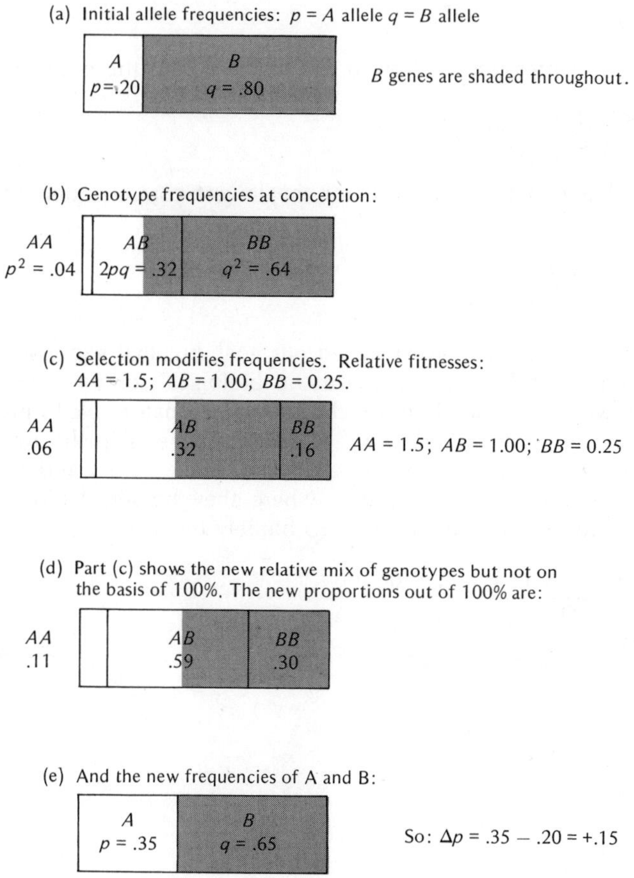

(a) Initial allele frequencies: $p = A$ allele $q = B$ allele

A $p =_{:} 20$	B $q = .80$

B genes are shaded throughout.

(b) Genotype frequencies at conception:

AA $p^2 = .04$	AB $2pq = .32$	BB $q^2 = .64$

(c) Selection modifies frequencies. Relative fitnesses:
$AA = 1.5;\ AB = 1.00;\ BB = 0.25.$

AA .06	AB .32	BB .16

$AA = 1.5;\ AB = 1.00;\ BB = 0.25$

(d) Part (c) shows the new relative mix of genotypes but not on the basis of 100%. The new proportions out of 100% are:

AA .11	AB .59	BB .30

(e) And the new frequencies of A and B:

A $p = .35$	B $q = .65$

So: $\Delta p = .35 - .20 = +.15$

Fig. 13-1 Selection working on a Hardy-Weinberg distribution.

$$\text{New } p = \frac{[2p^2(y/g) + 2pq]}{[2p^2(y/g) + 4pq + 2q^2(b/g)]}$$

But the 2 cancels out of the numerator and denominator and we have:

$$\text{New } p = \frac{p^2(y/g) + pq}{p^2(y/g) + 2pq + q^2(b/g)}$$

Go back very carefully over the numerical example and notice that all I did was substitute the algebraic symbols for the particular numbers. In that example, when we wanted Δp (the change in p), we subtracted p from *New p*. Algebraically:

$\Delta p = (New\ p) - p$

But now we have an expression for New p. Let's plug it into the equation.

$$\Delta p = \frac{p^2(y/g) + pq}{p^2(y/g) + 2pq + q^2(b/g)} - p$$

Now we use the denominator of New p for the lowest common denominator of Δp and we get:

$$\Delta p = \frac{p^2(y/g) + pq - p[p^2(y/g) + 2pq + q^2(b/g)]}{p^2(y/g) + 2pq + q^2(b/g)}$$

We could stop here since we have reached our goal, but that expression is awkward and sloppy, and besides, it makes no biological sense. So let's simplify it. Since we won't need to touch the denominator, we'll just replace it with the abbreviation "Denom." (If you trust me, skip the next steps. But if you're clever, watch me like a hawk to make sure I and my linotypist have got our minuses and pluses where they belong. Unfortunately, I've seen more than one math error go blithely on to press.)

$$\Delta p = \frac{p[p(y/g) + q - p^2(y/g) - 2pq - q^2(b/g)]}{Denom.}$$

$$\Delta p = \frac{p[(y/g)\ (p - p^2) + q - 2pq - q^2(b/g)]}{Denom.}$$

Now for a trick:

$(p - p^2) = p(1 - p)$.

But since

$p + q = 1$

$(1 - p) = q$

So

$(p - p^2) = pq,$

and

$$\Delta p = \frac{p[(y/g)\ pq + q - 2pq - q^2(b/g)]}{Denom.}$$

$$\Delta p = \frac{pq[(y/g)p + 1 - 2p - q(b/g)]}{Denom.}$$

One more trick:

$1 - 2p = 1 - p - p = (1 - p) - p = q - p$

So:

$$\Delta p = \frac{pq[p(y/g) - p + q - q(b/g)]}{\text{Denom.}}$$

And at long last:

$$\Delta p = \frac{pq[p(y/g - 1) + q(1 - b/g)]}{p^2(y/g) + 2pq + q^2(b/g)}$$

Maybe that doesn't look neat to you yet, but soon I hope to show you that every part of that expression translates into biological English. We have a lot to learn from it, and I think you'll agree, after I've interpreted it to you, that it is worth all the trouble you took to understand it.

Except for the symbols, it is an historic equation first derived in the early 1930s by one of the other founders of population genetics, Sewall Wright. I have tried to make only those changes in it which render it easier for you to understand.

The beauty of mathematics is that it often provides its own summary. In fact, the best summary of this section is that Δp, the change in p because of natural selection, is:

$$\frac{pq[p(y/g - 1) + q(1 - b/g)]}{p^2(y/g) + 2pq + q^2(b/g)}$$

where y is the fitness of yellows, g of greens, and b of blues.

The four possible fitness relationships. In this section you finally get to make use of the algebra you learned in the ninth grade and in the last section. One of my pet gripes right up to my last day in a math course was that I wasn't shown how to use what I had learned. (Perhaps I should have been clever enough to figure it out myself.)

In the last section, I promised to prove to you that if $y/g = 6/7$ and $b/g = 8/7$, then Δp would always be negative until the very last Y allele was gone. With the Wright equation, I can indeed prove it.

We need to realize two commonsense things:

1. p and q can never be less than zero or more than 1. What, after all, would be the meaning of $p = -.16$? When p reaches zero, Y is eliminated and that's as low as one gets in real life (and 100% is as high).
2. All the fitnesses, and therefore the relative fitnesses, can never be less than zero. When a phenotype leaves no one behind, it's gone. That's the worst it can possibly do.

Keep in mind that a negative Δp means p is declining. If Δp is positive, p is increasing. Now let's see what determines the sign of Δp.

A quick glance back at the Wright equation reveals that all the terms in the denominator are positive. $p^2(y/g)$ is the product of three positives, as is $q^2(b/g)$ and $2pq$. The sum of three positives is itself positive.

In the numerator, pq is always positive. But the terms in parentheses contain some minus signs, and so the whole parenthetical statement, $[p(y/g - 1) + q(1 - b/g)]$, may be positive or negative. Since everything else in the equation is positive, Δp will have the same sign as the parenthetical statement.

Remember that y/g is the relative fitness of a YY, b/g of a BB, and 1.00 of a BY. So our parenthetical statement is composed of relative fitnesses and gene frequencies! Let's now take the specific case of $y/g = 6/7$ and $b/g = 8/7$. Plugging these in, we see that Δp takes the sign of $-1/7$:

$$[p(6/7 - 1) + q(1 - 8/7)] = [-1/7p - 1/7q] = -1/7(p + q) = -1/7$$

Thus, Δp will always be negative (regardless of the size of p and q). So we prove what we said before: p decreases to the bitter end.

In fact, there are only four possible relationships of relative fitness. Our example was one in which the yellows were poorest, the blues best. Obviously, a second case would be: blues poorest and yellows best. Third, the greens could be poorest (heterozygote inferiority). Fourth and last, the greens could be best (heterozygote superiority). (In the third and fourth cases, it turns out not to matter much whether blue is better or worse than yellow).

Two of these general cases won't surprise you much: if blue or yellow are fittest, then only the fittest one survives. But the fourth case results in the survival of all three! And the third case results in either the survival of the fittest or the second fittest with no way to predict which!

I shall leave the general proof of case 1 (yellows worst, blues best) to you. It works just like the proof of case 2, which follows.

Case 2: heterozygote intermediate. One of the homozygotes (the blue) is poorest, the other is best; the heterozygote (the green) is intermediate. As always, Δp takes the sign of $[p(y/g - 1) + q(1 - b/g)]$. Here we've assumed y/g is bigger than 1 (remember 1 is the relative fitness of the heterozygotes, the greens) and b/g is smaller than 1. So $(y/g - 1)$ must be positive, and $(1 - b/g)$ must be positive.

Since a positive times a positive is also positive, our parenthetical statement is the sum of two positives. It is therefore always positive. So Δp is always positive. Biologically, this means that p increases until it reaches 1.00 at which point only the yellows, the fittest in this case, are left.

Case 3: heterozygote inferiority. Here the greens (the heterozygotes) are inferior. In mathematical symbols, y/g and b/g are both bigger than 1. This situation confuses us at first because one of the terms, $(y/g - 1)$, is positive and the other, $(1 - b/g)$, is negative. What sign does p have?

In this case and the next, the sign of Δp depends also on the size of p and q.

First, notice that Δp is on the positive-negative border when it is zero.

Then, notice that $\triangle p = 0$ if $[p(y/g - 1) + q(1 - b/g)] = 0$. If $\triangle p = 0$, p is at a value at which natural selection exerts no pressure at all. Such a value is called an equilibrium point or balance point.

The trouble with equilibria is that they don't always last. Suppose we try to balance a ball bearing on a pencil point. It can be done. But no one had better breathe, for one slip and the ball bearing goes crashing to the floor. This is called an unstable equilibrium. If it slips ever so slightly, there is no return. (See Fig. 3-6.)

Case 3 is just like this. If p is exactly the value at which $[p(y/g - 1) + q(1 - b/g)] = 0$, then $\triangle p = 0$. But if p gets even the tiniest bit larger by accident (say one blue allele fell off a cliff in a landslide), then there is no return. $\triangle p$ is positive and p grows until the blues are eliminated entirely.

If it was a yellow on that cliff, then $\triangle p$ becomes negative and it is the yellow that becomes extinct. There is no way to predict which will happen, and there is no assurance that it will not be the fittest phenotype that goes. To prove this, we need to recall that the negative term in the brackets was $q(1 - b/g)$. When p gets smaller than its equilibrium value, q must get larger ($p + q$ is a constant, namely 1.00). So when p gets larger, the positive term, $p(b/g - 1)$, gets larger and the negative gets smaller. This renders $\triangle p$ positive, and p takes off toward 100%.

But if p should get smaller, so does the positive term, and the negative one gets larger. Here $\triangle p$ is negative and q takes off for 100%. Unless we know the actual values of p, b/g, and y/g, we can't predict which way the alleles will go. (See Fig. 13-2.)

We can understand heterozygote inferiority logically. The rare allele has less chance of finding itself paired with another like itself and more chance of being paired with the common allele as a heterozygote. But the heterozygote is the least fit, so being rare hurts an allele. Conversely, being common helps, because the common allele is more likely to be paired with another like itself as a homozygote.

Biologically, this case is very difficult to understand. In fact, no case 3 has ever been documented. There is, however, one situation that at least mimics case 3 and is worth noting.

In humans, a complex blood protein called rhesus factor or *Rh* is often found. The genetics of *Rh* is extremely complex and unnecessary for this discussion, so we'll simplify it. Assume there is only one kind of *Rh* and it is inherited at one locus. Symbolize the dominant allele, *Rh*, and the recessive, *rh*. People who have the factor are either *RhRh* or *Rhrh*. People who don't are *rhrh*.

If an *Rh* man marries an *rhrh* woman, at least some of their children will be heterozygotes, *Rhrh*. These babies have the factor, but their mother doesn't. In some such cases, while the baby is in the uterus nearing its birth, some of its blood leaks into its mother's bloodstream. Its mother's disease-fighting system recognizes this as a foreign protein and builds antibodies against it. The mother thus destroys her own baby's blood. This condition is called *erythroblastosis foetalis* and until recently was a source

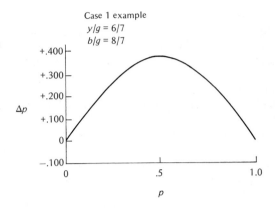

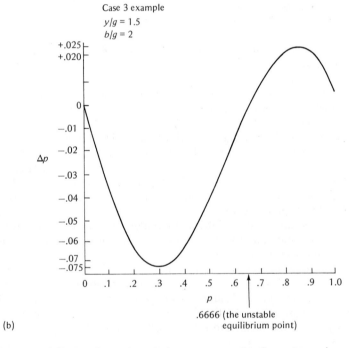

(a)

(b)

Fig. 13-2 Selective change in p during one generation for various values of p.

of much newborn and preborn death. Notice, however, that only hetero-zygotes can get erythroblastosis. All those that have it are heterozygotes in wombs of *rhrh* mothers. Thus the heterozygote is least fit with respect to erythroblastosis.

But neither the *Rh* nor the *rh* has disappeared. This makes us think that the *Rh* locus is not really a case 3, but probably a case where the heterozygotes possess some other advantage—an advantage which remains undiscovered. As I said before, no one has yet documented a case of heterozygote inferiority.

Case 4: heterozygote superiority. This case is also called heterosis. It results in balanced polymorphism. Polymorphism means many phenotypes. Balanced refers to the equilibrium; but in this case the equilibrium is robust. It's like one of those toy inflated clowns with a weighted bottom: no matter how hard you try punching it to the floor, it always rights itself. Using our ball-bearing analogy (Chapter 3), we should recall that a robust or stable equilibrium is like a ball bearing inside an empty ice-cream cone. Balanced polymorphism means that more than one phenotype remains in a population because the force of natural selection acts to increase any phenotype that gets rare.

We can understand heterosis biologically. As in heterozygote inferiority, the rare allele has more chance of being included in the heterozygous form. But this time heterozygotes have the advantage. So being more often heterozygotes leads to the increase of the rarer allele. The rarer the allele, the stronger the boost given it by natural selection. So whenever an allele accidentally gets rare, selection makes it more common again.

To demonstrate balanced polymorphism, we need only examine our parenthetical statement. This time $q(1 - b/g)$ is the positive term (why?), and $p(y/g - 1)$ is negative. So when p gets more common than its equilibrium value, the negative term gets bigger, the positive one smaller, and Δp becomes negative.

In short, if p accidentally gets too common, selection decreases it. Similarly, if p gets rare, selection increases it.

What is the exact equilibrium value in heterosis? Not necessarily 1/2. It is the value of p that satisfies:

$$[p(y/g - 1) + q(1 - b/g)] = 0$$

Since

$$q = 1 - p$$

we can substitute for q and get

$$[p(y/g - 1) + (1 - p)(1 - b/g)] = 0$$

This time I won't go through every step, but report the results of the simplification. The equilibrium value of p is:

$$p = \frac{1 - b/g}{2 - y/g - b/g}$$

which is 1/2 if and only if $y/g = b/g$. That is, $p = 1/2$ only in the unlikely event that homozygotes have identical fitnesses. Otherwise, p will be more than 1/2 if the yellow is more fit than the blue, but less than 1/2 if the blue is better than yellow. Since p is the frequency of the Y allele, this makes sense.

The logic of the deduction "evolution occurs." Those of you who are good at math probably noticed something. We have just shown that the deduction "evolution occurs" really does follow from the assumptions. The Wright equation had only four cases. In all but one (heterosis), Δp is not going to stay at zero; not, that is, until the work of selection is done and only one phenotype remains. When Δp is not zero, the gene pool is changing. That is what we hoped to show.

In the heterosis case, evolution quits, having left three phenotypes. There are different phenotypes; they have different fitnesses; their fitnesses are inherited. But there is no more evolution! Have we disproved the theory?

We have if the theory be that natural selection always produces change. Selection does not always produce evolution. In heterosis, it produced evolution, and then after an equilibrium was reached, it worked against further changes.

But Darwin did not insist on change. He insisted on improvement in fitness. Heterosis winds up leaving the members of a population at their highest possible average fitness. This fact is discussed at the end of this chapter.

An example of heterosis: sickle-cell anemia. In the first three cases, selection finished with only one phenotype. We have no reason (as yet) to expect any trace of selection in such cases. But in heterosis, selection is constantly at work maintaining variability. We therefore should be able to find some instance of heterosis in nature.

Like most people who have thought seriously about natural selection, you are probably thinking that it's o.k. for all life except people. So I'll relate the most famous example of heterosis. It just happens to be about people.

In parts of tropical East Africa, malaria has for too long been a real threat (Fig. 13-3). Particularly vicious complications known as cerebral malaria and blackwater fever frequently kill young children before they are five years old. I shall not go into the cruel and bizarre symptoms of the disease.

In these same regions, another even more often lethal condition plagues the youth. People die because of a defective kind of hemoglobin, hemoglobin S, in their red blood cells. Hemoglobin S molecules can stack up in the red cells, forming tactoids (liquid crystals). Such tactoids make the cells rigid and fragile. The rigidity produces blood which is too thick to flow freely through the tiny blood vessels where oxygen is actually delivered to the body's tissues, and those tissues consequently suffer. Also, the fragility of the cells causes them to die prematurely and their possessor becomes anemic. Because the red blood cells with tactoids have a peculiar, collapsed crescent-moon shape which resembles the blade of a sickle, hemoglobin S

THE
MOSQUITO DANGER.

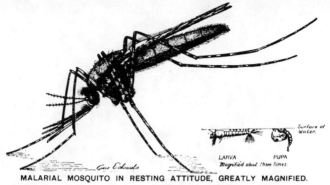

MALARIAL MOSQUITO IN RESTING ATTITUDE, GREATLY MAGNIFIED.

DANGER: Mosquitoes suck Malarial Fever from a sick man and give it to a sound man when they bite him.
DON'T LET THEM BITE YOU.

Fig. 13-3 The British Museum (Natural History) distributed posters like this to warn people of the possible consequences of mosquito bites.

disease is known as sickle-cell anemia (Fig. 13-4). It kills about 80% of its victims. Sickle-cell anemia turns out to be a congenital disease; people are born with it. Its inheritance is all too simple: everyone receives two alleles from the hemoglobin A gene pool. If he emerges with both A's or one A and one S, he is not troubled. But if he gets stuck with two S's, he is doomed to sickle-cell anemia.

People who are heterozygotes can easily be discovered by running a special blood test. Under certain laboratory conditions, their blood cells sickle up, too. But unless they are flying and the cabin pressure of their airplane falls too low, they never even know they're heterozygotes without the test. And any outward sign that they are is minor and soon overcome. One S is no risk at all.

To A. C. Allison, this looked like a case of heterozygote intermediacy. The heterozygote was much like one of the homozygotes, but the other homozygote was quite inferior. So the S allele ought to have disappeared. But it hadn't. In fact in some parts of Africa, 22% and more of the alleles in the hemoglobin A gene pool are S. That made Allison think of heterosis.

Since the areas where people got sickle-cell anemia were also the areas

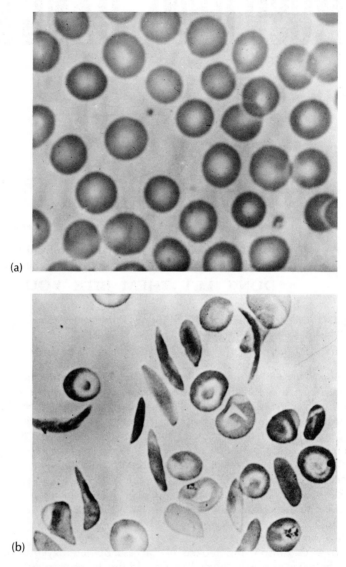

(a)

(b)

Fig. 13-4 Red blood cells from a normal person (a) and one who has sickle-cell anemia (b). Some of the cells of the diseased person show the sickled shape; others appear normal. (Courtesy of Dr. W. Hardy, Department of Medicine, University of New Mexico.)

where they died of blackwater fever, Allison hypothesized that the homozygote AA had the most trouble with malaria. This, if true, would make the
heterozygote most fit and generate heterosis.

To measure the harm done by malaria, Allison used the indirect technique
of counting the malarial parasites (a protist, *Plasmodium falciparum*) in the
blood of the people (Fig. 13-5). Of course, he also tested their blood to
see if they were homozygotes or heterozygotes. He had no trouble, unfortunately, in counting those with sickle-cell anemia.

Sure enough, people homozygous for hemoglobin A were almost always
the ones to die of malaria. Heterozygous people were not only less likely
to die, they were also less likely to get infected. Somehow, Allison convinced 30 people (half were AA, half were SA) to allow him to try to infect
them with malaria. He was able to infect all but one of the AA's but only
two of the SA's.

No really good measure exists of exactly how often malarial death occurs,
but Allison estimates the advantage of the heterozygote at up to 25%. It is
a bit difficult to translate this estimate into relative fitnesses—probably
because Allison never intended it to be so used. If Allison will excuse us,
we shall guess that this means $y/g = 0.80$. (Among other things, it might

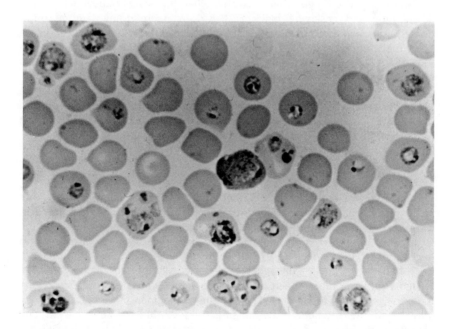

Fig. 13-5 A smear of human blood showing infection by *Plasmodium falciparum*.
The red blood cells are much as in Fig. 13-4, but contain small, dark streaks. These
streaks are the malarial parasite. (Courtesy of Dr. M. Rosales-Ronquillo and Prof. P.
Silverman.)

also mean $y/g = 0.75$, but you can work that case out yourself.) We already know that $b/g = 0.20$ (since 80% or more of SS individuals die). So, with p representing the fraction of alleles that are A, we are prepared to predict p using our heterosis equilibrium.

$$p = \frac{1 - (b/g)}{2 - b/g - y/g} = \frac{1 - 0.20}{2 - 0.20 - 0.80} = \frac{0.80}{1} = 0.80$$

Thus, the frequency of A should be about 80% and of S, 20%. We are certainly in the right ball park. The actual frequency of the S allele is around 22% in these areas of East Africa. So our equation did agree with our observation. Our prediction worked.

I. M. Lerner, in his book *Heredity, Evolution and Society* (which you might really enjoy reading), gives a whole list of other blood diseases which appear to be kept around because of heterozygote superiority. So the S allele is no fluke.

As an aside, what would you expect to happen if malaria were suddenly eradicated? This change in environment would change the relative fitness of the AA to 1.00 (same as SA). That would be a true case of heterozygote intermediacy, and the S allele should gradually disappear.

About 300 years ago, that's exactly what the slave traders who were kidnapping and enslaving black East Africans were doing (among other things). They were removing a whole people from a malaria-infested region to a malaria-free one. (I don't mean to suggest they knew this, nor that they were humanitarians. They certainly engendered far more hardship than malaria, and we are still witnessing the effects of their greed.)

Sure enough, the frequency of the S allele among American blacks has dropped to 4%. Partly, this is due to intermarriage, but most of this decline from 22% is apparently the effect of a case 1 selection. Unless medicine finds a remedy for sickle-cell anemia, the S allele should eventually disappear.

Laboratory tests of heterosis. As Bruce Wallace points out, though many scientists have obtained information on many genes which appear to be part of heterotic systems in nature, in only the human cases do we know much about why the heterozygote has the best fitness. In the rare cases when plants and animals have had their fitnesses measured, no experiments were performed to find out why they have the fitnesses they do.

Dobzhansky and his colleagues have tested, in the laboratory, heterotic systems in *Drosophila* species. They also aren't yet sure why *Drosophila* heterozygotes are superior. But often they are superior. And Dobzhansky has tested the prediction that a single equilibrium value exists in any environment. That is, if too many of one kind are accidentally introduced to an environment, selection will reduce them to a certain amount. If too few are present, selection will increase them to the same amount.

Before we examine Dobzhansky's results, we should know that in truth,

Dobzhansky did not work with different alleles, but with larger pieces of chromosome called inversions. An inversion is a segment of a chromosome that has been broken out and reattached in reverse order. Thus, if there are 1000 addresses on a chromosome, and they should be in strict numerical order, but instead a portion reads: 62, 63, **70, 69, 68, 67, 66, 65, 64,** 71, 72, we say that the gene loci in boldface type are an inversion (Fig. 13-6).

Inversions are not at all unusual. They tend to keep whole groups of genes together. In fact Lewontin has recently hypothesized that in most cases evolution works *not on the individual gene locus, but on large groups of loci like inversions* because these groups tend to hold together as if they were one locus. Hence, it is not bad science to transfer the formulas deduced for one locus, to inversions, which involve coherent groups of loci.

In most organisms inversions are rather hard to detect. But the salivary glands of flies (including *Drosophila*) produce very thick chromosomes each containing over 1000 strands. Because of this, the anatomy of the chromosome takes on the appearance of a banded strip. Each chromosome has its own peculiar banding pattern, and if a segment has been inverted, its bands can actually be seen to be inverted. Thus, under the microscope, Dobzhansky could actually see the genotypes of his flies.

In the following experiment Dobzhansky worked with the standard order, *ST*, and an inversion named arrowhead, *AR*. Thus, we can speak of three phenotypes: *ST,ST; ST,AR;* and *AR,AR.*

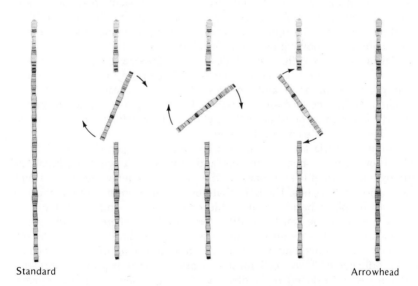

Standard   Arrowhead

Fig. 13-6 The inversion of part of a chromosome of *Drosophila psuedoobscura*. This depiction is only an idealization and is based on a drawing of this portion of a giant salivary-gland chromosome which appeared in Dobzhansky and Sturtevant.

Dobzhansky introduced populations of *Drosophila pseudoobscura,* a species very much like the more familiar fly, *Drosophila melanogaster,* into constant laboratory conditions. One of his populations began with the *ST* gene arrangement at a frequency of 0.698; the other with *ST* at 0.194. The rest of the chromosomes were *AR* in each population. After some months, each cage contained populations where the frequency of *ST* was about 0.55. This frequency remained almost constant for months until the experiment was stopped. (See Fig. 13-7.)

Superiority of the heterozygote had resulted in the achievement by the population of a gene pool in which *p* was at equilibrium. And this equilibrium was the same, whether the population had to increase *p* to reach it, or decrease *p* to reach it.

The importance of heterosis. Heterozygote superiority appears to be a major force for maintaining the variety of individuals that make up a population at one place and one time. Roger Milkman, a modern population geneticist, has recently shown how heterosis could account for most of the variety we observe in nature. His mathematical techniques are more advanced than this book requires. But much of common knowledge supports his conclusion.

Ever hear of hybrid vigor? Farmers have learned that if they plant varieties of corn, tomatoes, wheat, and other plants that have been produced from dissimilar parents, the crop is more resistant to disease, more bountiful, and faster growing. This is the basis for the Green Revolution discussed in Chapter 5. Population geneticists believe hybrid vigor is heterozygote superiority showing up in practical life.

Sarkissian and his colleagues McDaniel and Srivastava have investigated wheat and corn hybrids at the cellular level. They note that hybrid vigor in these grains is predominantly expressed by rapid plant growth. Their hypothesis is that the increased growth is due to an increase in the efficiency with which the mitochondria of the hybrid cells transform stored chemical energy into spendable chemical energy.

The mitochondria are the energy transformation organelles found in all cells. They contain special proteins and cofactors designed to break up carbohydrates and efficiently transfer their bonding energy into special high energy phosphate bonds. The phosphate bonds link phosphate to adenosine. The first phosphate bond contains little energy, the second more, the third quite a bit. Thus, the cell has AMP, ADP, and ATP (where A is adenosine, P is phosphate, M is mono or one, D is di or two, and T is tri or three); and most energy for spending is stored in the third bond of ATP molecules.

In producing ATP, the cell must use oxygen. That is why we breathe. The more ATP produced per molecule of oxygen used, the more efficient is the cell. The ratio of ATP produced to O_2 consumed is called the P/O ratio. If Sarkissian is right, hybrids should have higher P/O ratios than their parents. Here is some evidence that they do.

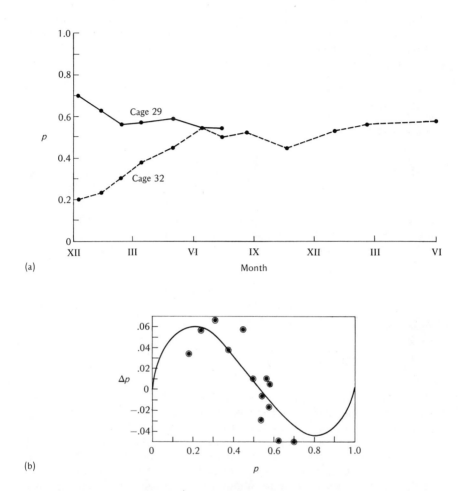

(a)

(b)

Fig. 13-7 One of Dobzhansky's experiments in attaining heterotic equilibria. (a) *ST* changes from either low or high values until it stabilizes at equilibrium. Equilibrium here was predicted to be 0.64/1.215, or 0.526. The frequency of *ST* is *p*. (b) Theoretical (curve) and actual values (dots) of Δp at various values of *p* in the experiment. The observed relative fitnesses were: *ST/ST* = 0.64, *AR/ST* = 1.00, and *AR/AR* = 0.575. This graph is like Fig. 13-2 but is typical of case 4 examples. (From Dobzhansky, 1948).

In their experiments, Sarkissian, McDaniel, and Srivastava carefully purify functional mitochondria from the cells of the various grain strains. They then supply the grain with a carbohydrate source and measure the P/O ratio while ADP is being converted to ATP. To discover if the difference is due simply to the two different kinds of mitochondria which are present in a hybrid, they also take mitochondria from the two pure parents, mix them in a test tube, and measure their P/O ratio. We shall examine an experiment done with corn mitochondria when the mitochondria were permitted to break down the carbohydrate α-ketoglutarate.

	P/O Ratio
Strain Oh 45	1.66
Strain Wf 9	1.44
Hybrid 9/45	2.19
Mixture 9 + 45	2.14

The hybrid is much more energetically efficient than its parents and this seems due to the simple combination of two types of mitochondria since the mixture is about as efficient as the hybrid. However, the hybrid is also more efficient at using other carbohydrates, whereas the mixture is only more efficient with α-ketoglutarate. This is not yet understood.

Now let's look at similar experimental results from wheat. As before, figures in the table are P/O ratios.

	Carbohydrate consumed		
	α-ketoglutarate	Malate	Succinate
Strain 31MS	3.8	2.6	1.9
Strain 28	3.2	1.8	1.4
Hybrid 31MS/28	5.8	3.8	3.4
Mixture 31MS + 28	5.4	3.5	1.8

In these data we see a clear superiority of strain 31MS over strain 28. One might think that hybridizing the two would be a mistake: diluting a good strain with a bad one. But instead the hybrid is clearly more efficient than either of its parents! As before, the mixture does about as well on α-ketoglutarate as the hybrid. But here it also does as well on malate. Succinate is not handled more efficiently by the mixture than by the pure strains, and we know no more about why than we did a paragraph ago when corn mitochondria produced similar results.

Sarkissian and Srivastava wondered if all these results were only to be found *in vitro* (that is, in glassware). Perhaps hybrids really don't transfer energy more efficiently. Perhaps they are only more resistant to the operation which separates the mitochondria? They checked this partially by measuring the rate at which oxygen is used by whole seedlings of the pure and hybrid strains. Sure enough there are significant differences. The hybrids use much more oxygen per hour. This is an indication both of their vigor and of a significant difference in their oxygen metabolism. Unfortunately, it is still impossible to obtain P/O ratios for whole organisms. But the speed and care of the methods of these investigators leave little doubt that what they have found is real. Hybrid grains are apparently much more efficient at energy transfer, and that allows them to grow faster.

Still, Sarkissian and Srivastava found other advantages in the hybrid besides increased efficiency. They poisoned the mitochondria with dinitrophenol, an agent that severely reduces a mitochondrion's ability to transfer energy to phosphate bonds. For reasons as yet unknown, the hybrid was more resistant to this poison than either of its parents. One would be misled to conclude that **all** heterotic advantages lie in increased energetic efficiency.

Ever hear the old saying about a pedigree dog being less vigorous, intelligent, and healthy than a mutt? Hybrid vigor again would be my guess, since of course pedigree animals are produced from very similar parents. The dog story has much less evidence behind it than the plant story. But many biologists have produced "pedigree" lab animals by a process called inbreeding. In this process, like are allowed to breed with like only. Such a procedure eliminates the heterozygotes. Whenever this has been done, the viability and fertility of the animals declines badly. This is more evidence that heterosis is a general and important constituent of the real world.

Final test of Darwin's theory. Should the average fitness in a population increase because of natural selection? Let us return to the language and rules of mathematics to check Darwin's verbal deduction. Again we shall incorporate what we know of genetics into our reasoning. What we need to do is find the average fitness of the members of a population in two successive generations. Then we'll subtract the average in the first generation from that in the second to get ΔF, the change in average fitness. Hopefully, ΔF will always be positive. If so, average fitness is always growing, and Darwin was right.

To keep things simple, we'll use exactly the same system and symbols we have been using all along. We'll add a new one though, F_i, which stands for the average relative fitness of the members of a population in the ith generation just after they are conceived. Thus $\Delta F = F_2 - F_1$. We shall also abbreviate (y/g) as y and (b/g) as b. And to avoid errors, we shall write Δ whenever we mean Δp. Yet, however we try, the algebra is a bit tedious. One can do the same thing with calculus in two or three lines! In fact one can do more, since with algebra, I won't even prove that ΔF is positive for all four cases.

The average fitness formula. We begin by evaluating F_1, the average fitness of the first generation of newly conceived young. In an average, we multiply each value by the number of times it occurs, and then divide by the total number of occurrences. So, if we want the average weight of five fish, and two weigh 3 pounds, one weighs 2 pounds, and two weigh 6 pounds, the average is

$$\frac{(2 \times 3) + (1 \times 2) + (2 \times 6)}{5}$$

Notice that this is the same as

$$\frac{2 \times 3}{5} + \frac{1 \times 2}{5} + \frac{2 \times 6}{5}$$

which is the same as

$(2/5 \times 3) + (1/5 \times 2) + (2/5 \times 6)$

In other words, to get an average, we multiply the fraction of times a value occurs by the value itself. We do this for all values, and the sum of these numbers is our average.

Thus, we can get F, an average fitness, easily. We simply multiply the fitness of each phenotype by its frequency, then add them together. The fitness of YY is y/g, which we're now going to write y; its frequency is p^2. The fitness of BY is g/g or 1; its frequency is $2pq$ or $2p(1-p)$. The fitness of BB is b/g, which we write b; its frequency is q^2 or $(1-p)^2$. So the average fitness must be:

$$F_1 = yp^2 + 2pq + bq^2$$

We now write F_1 using our alternate expression for q, that is, $(1-p)$:

$$F_1 = yp^2 + 2p(1-p) + b(1-p)^2$$

By multiplying everything out and gathering terms, you can easily (and should) show that this is:

$$F_1 = p^2(b + y - 2) + 2p(1 - b) + b$$

In order to get F_2, all we need to do is substitute the new value of p (after selection) wherever we had the old value. Since this new value is

$p + \Delta p$

which we now write

$p + \Delta$

then

$$F_2 = (p + \Delta)^2 (b + y - 2) + 2(p + \Delta)(1 - b) + b$$

THE FORMULA
FOR CHANGE IN FITNESS

Now ΔF is $F_2 - F_1$, which you can see is:

$$[(p + \Delta)^2 - p^2] (b + y - 2) + 2[(p + \Delta) - p] (1 - b) + b - b$$

Of course, we can cross out the $(+b - b)$ at the end, and notice also that

$$[(p + \Delta) - p] = [p - p + \Delta] = \Delta$$

So

$$\Delta F = [(p + \Delta)^2 - p^2] (b + y - 2) + 2\Delta(1 - b)$$

Do you remember that any algebraic expression like $(a^2 - b^2)$ factors to $(a + b)(a - b)$? If you imagine that $(p + \Delta)$ is like a and p is like b, you will see that

$$[(p + \Delta)^2 - p^2] = [(p + \Delta) - p][(p + \Delta) + p] = \Delta(2p + \Delta)$$

If you didn't remember that trick, you can check on it by multiplying the factors together. Now ΔF is getting simple.

$$\Delta F = \Delta[(2p + \Delta)(b + y - 2) + 2(1 - b)]$$

or

$$\Delta F = \Delta[(2p + \Delta)(b + y - 1 - 1) + 2(1 - b)]$$

or

$$\Delta F = \Delta[(2p + \Delta)(y - 1) + (2p + \Delta - 2)(b - 1)]$$

PROVING THE HETEROZYGOTE
INTERMEDIACY CASE

At this point, we can prove cases 1 and 2. Δ is a change in p, and whatever p changes to, it cannot exceed one nor be less than zero. Moreover, if $\Delta < 0$, then $-\Delta \leq p$. So $(2p + \Delta)$ must be positive.

Yet $(2p + \Delta)$ cannot ever be as large as 2: if p is almost one and reaches one in the next generation, then $p + \Delta = 1.00$, and p is less than 1.00 and $p + (p + \Delta)$ or $(2p + \Delta)$ is less than 2.00. This shows that $[(2p + \Delta) - 2]$ is always a negative number.

In case 1, the heterozygote was intermediate, and YY was the least fit. So b was greater than one, making $(b - 1)$ positive. But y was less than one, making $(y - 1)$ negative. We deduced that Δ (or Δp) was also negative. Thus, we can write the signs of the number of ΔF as

$$\Delta F = (-) [(+) (-) + (-) (+)] = (-) (-) = +$$

So in case 1, ΔF is always positive.

Case 2 is just as readily handled. In case 2 it was YY that was best, so b is less than one and y greater than one. In ΔF this makes $(1 - b)$ positive and $(1 - y)$ negative. In case 2, Δ was always positive. The signs of ΔF become:

$$\Delta F = (+) [(+) (+) + (-) (-)] = (+) (+) = +$$

Again we have deduced that ΔF is always positive. (See Fig. 13-8.)

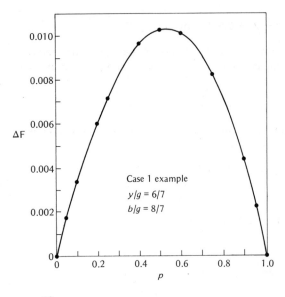

Case 1 example
$y/g = 6/7$
$b/g = 8/7$

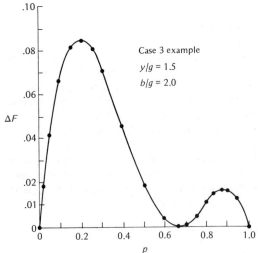

Case 3 example
$y/g = 1.5$
$b/g = 2.0$

Fig. 13-8 Changes in average fitness at various values of gene frequency. Notice that ΔF is always positive; that is, the average fitness in the population is always increasing. Examples are the same ones as in Fig. 13-2.

Proving the heterozygote inferiority case. To do case 3 requires using the facts that $(1 - b)$ and $(1 - y)$ are both negative (why?); and that Δ is negative if p is less than $(1 - b)/(2 - b - y)$; whereas Δ is positive if p is greater than $(1 - b)/(2 - b - y)$. Can you do it? It might be helpful to recast the ΔF equation as:

$$\Delta F = \Delta[(b + y - 2)\,\Delta - 2p(2 - b - y) + 2(1 - b)]$$

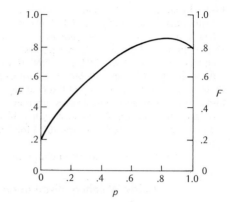

Fig. 13-9 The average fitness of populations with various frequencies of the allele for the normal hemoglobin. The only other allele is assumed to be the sickle-cell allele. It can be seen that the final value of p is at that value generating the highest F.

The case of heterosis. If you can do case 4 using simple algebra, write me. I haven't been able to do it yet. I'll be happy to include your proof in the next edition of this book. Don't worry about Darwin, though. Calculus easily proves case 4, too.

Meanwhile, let's check the example of a case 4 that we already discussed: sickle-cell hemoglobin. We know that the equilibrium frequency of S should be 0.20. Is that the gene pool with the maximum average fitness?

To find out, all we have to do is calculate F for all possible values of p using our equation.

$$F = p^2(b + y - 2) + 2p(1 - b) + b$$

Remember

$$b = 0.20 \quad \text{and} \quad y = 0.80$$

for this case, so

$$F = p^2(0.20 + 0.80 - 2) + 2p(1 - b) + b$$

or

$$F = -p^2 + 1.6p + 0.20$$

I have solved this equation for all possible values of p and plotted the results in Fig. 13-9. (You should check one or two. What is F for $p = 0.5$? For $p = 0.1$?) Sure enough the highest value of F is attained by the population in which $p = 0.80$ and $q = 0.20$. Here, $F = 0.8400$. Since "$[p = 0.80]$" is the population which selection always produces, we conclude that selection always increases the average fitness of humans in this case.

PROBLEMS

Gene frequency

13-1. In a population of 1000 *Drosophila*, there are 622 alleles for normal wing (+) and 1378 for vestigial (*vg*). What are the gene frequencies?

13-2. In chickens, *F*, the allele for feathered shanks, is dominant to *f*, the allele for featherless. In a coopful of 100 chickens, 23 are heterozygous and 65 are featherless. What are the gene frequencies?

13-3a. In man, there is a blood-type system called *MN*. There are three genotypes and phenotypes: *MM*, *MN*, and *NN*. If frequency of the *M* allele is 0.70, and there are 100 *MM* and 10 *MN* in a group, how many are *NN*?

13-3b. What is the frequency of the *N* allele?

13-4a. In snapdragons, red flowers are homozygous *RR*; white flowers, homozygous *rr*; and pink flowers are heterozygotes. In a group of 500 plants where the frequency of *R* is 0.20, there are 100 pink-flowered plants. What is the frequency of *r*?

13-4b. How many white-flowered plants are there?

Hardy-Weinberg distribution

13-5a. A population of 2000 Ute Indians has only 4% with blood-type *A* and none with *B* or *AB*. Assuming that their blood types fit a Hardy-Weinberg distribution, and that *p* is the frequency of the *O* allele, and *q* of the *A*, what is *q*? (Hint: convert percentage to proportion before you take the square root.)

13-5b. What fraction of the Utes are heterozygous *AO*?

13-6. In deer mice, the allele for buff coat color, *G*, is dominant to the one for gray, *g* (and is *not* sex-linked). Of 108 mice collected by Blair in New Mexico, 20 were gray. Assume these phenotypes fit the Hardy-Weinberg distribution. What is the frequency of *G*?

13-7a. In humans, *T*, the gene for the ability to taste PTU is dominant to *t*, its nontaster allele. (It is not sex-linked.) Suppose the frequency of *t* is 0.70. Which is the more common phenotype, tasters or nontasters?

13-7b. What is the nontaster frequency?

13-8. In humans, the frequency of the recessive allele *rh* varies from population to population. Black Americans are 7.4% *rh* negative, and whites are 14.7%. What is the difference in the *rh* allele frequency between these two groups?

Fitness

13-9. In an unpolluted woodland, Kettlewell released 473 black moths and 496 peppered. He recaptured 30 and 62, respectively. Assume that the birth rates of the moths and all the rest of their biology is the same for both forms. Then, estimate the relative fitness of the peppered variety in this woodland. (Hint: black forms are both homozygotes and heterozygotes.)

13-10. Hemophiliacs have blood that does not clot properly. The slightest accident can be fatal. Records of humans with hemophilia (a recessive genetic disease) show that every ten hemophiliacs can be expected to live to have only about three children. Nonhemophiliacs average 11 children per 10 potential parents. What is the relative fitness of a hemophiliac?

13-11. David Lack found that chimney swifts did not all rear the same number of young per year. Swifts which laid 1 egg reared about 1.0; swifts which laid 2 eggs about 1.8 young; 3 eggs, 2.4 young; and 4 eggs, 2.4 young. What are the relative fitnesses of the four phenotypes compared to the 3-egg phenotype?

13-12a. Dobzhansky placed three types of fruit flies in one population cage: 110 mixed, 200 standard, and 200 chiricahua. After one generation, there were 250 mixed, 450 standard, and 200 chiricahua. What were the absolute fitnesses of the three varieties?

13-12b. What were their fitnesses relative to the mixed?

13-13. Red-scale insects destroy citrus. Orchardists attempted to control the scale by spraying with the poison HCN. In 1914, one spraying in one place in California did almost no good. It was found that this population had a new allele (heterozygote is intermediate) which confers resistance to HCN. At one concentration of the poison, 96% of nonresistant scale are destroyed, but only 55% of resistant. Assume that 70% of heterozygotes are destroyed. Assuming resistance to HCN is the only heritable biological difference between these genotypes, what are their relative fitnesses at this HCN concentration, and what will happen if HCN is administered continually?

Using Δp and ΔF

13-14a. In the fruit-fly problem (13-12), the mixed were really heterozygotes, ST/CH. Let the frequency of ST be p. Using the data and your answers to the problem, what was Δp in the problem? What should it have been, given the gene frequencies of the problem? Why the discrepancy?

13-14b. Using the same selective values, predict Δp if $CH = 0.8$. If $CH = 0.01$. *Watch your signs.*

13-14c. What do you predict will be the outcome of this selection? What will be the final equilibrium value of CH?

13-15a. Selection for wing pattern is proceeding in an imaginary butterfly species. There are three phenotypes (and genotypes): striped, SS; spotted, Ss; and clear, ss. The relative fitnesses are $SS = 1\ 1/3$ and $ss = 1/2$. What will be the outcome of natural selection?

13-15b. What is the value of Δp if p, the S allele frequency, is 0.40?

13-15c. What is the mean fitness of the population before and after this change? What is ΔF for the generation?

13-16. A large population of *Drosophila "imaginarius"* has two body colors, ebony and gray. These phenotypes are controlled by one locus with two alleles: EE or Ee is gray; ee is ebony. In one generation, the ebony allele frequency drops from 0.200 to 0.175. What is the relative fitness of the ebony phenotype? (Hint: EE and Ee have the same phenotype.) What is the eventual outcome of natural selection? What will be the mean relative fitness then? What is it now (at $0.20 = e$)?

14 the role of mutation in evolution

MUTATION FROM THE EVOLUTIONIST'S POINT OF VIEW

The late Sir Ronald Fisher gave the best definition of mutation. *"Mutation is the initiation of any heritable novelty,"* he wrote in 1930. Now, of course, that was 15 years before people began to suspect that DNA was the stuff of genes and over 20 years before they "proved" it. In 1958, a revised edition of his 1930 book emerged. Much was altered and added, but the definition of mutation stood unchanged. Fisher felt no need to change his definition even with knowledge of DNA. "Mutation is the initiation of any heritable novelty," he repeated.

The remarkable thing about this definition, of course, is its total freedom from any mechanism of inheritance. Fisher didn't care whether genes were DNA or Kool-Aid. As a matter of fact, he realized that the mutation didn't even have to occur to the genes to be important. As long as it was heritable, it provided a new phenotype that could increase in frequency by the agency of natural selection.

Fisher is showing us by his definition that there is a particular class of events which provides the raw material for natural selection. It is this class of events he calls mutations.

We, of course, can modify the word. A genic mutation is the initiation of any heritable novelty by a change in the DNA. There can be cytoplasmic mutations, traditional mutations, and others. As long as the new phenotype can be transmitted to future generations, selection will militate either against or in favor of it.

178

MUTATION AND SELECTION
IN HARNESS TOGETHER

Natural selection is powerless without variety. If there is no variation in the phenotype of a population, what is selection going to select? Why bother with a menu when there is but one thing for supper?

Fisher clearly recognized that selection was not worth studying unless there was a force for the addition of heritable variety to a population. In fact, one of Fisher's major contributions, his fundamental theorem of natural selection, is the deduction that *the greater the heritable variety in a population, the faster selection improves the average fitness.* (Because his proof requires calculus and statistics, we shall omit it.) Mutations are the original source of the variety.

One of the early criticisms leveled against natural selection was that it lacked creativity. How could it have created the marvelous and varied world of life, when it was only a force for picking and choosing? This is certainly true. Selection only modifies phenotypic frequencies. It never starts from zero. The new phenotype must already exist before selection can act. (Try plugging $p = 0$ into our equation for Δp. What happens?)

With Fisher's definition of mutation, we can see the creative side of the process. Evolution may be understood as a team effort. *Mutation provides the menu; natural selection picks the dinner.*

Many early evolutionists weren't satisfied with this view of an evolutionary team. Most weren't even aware of it. They believed that evolution proceeded by mutation only. There are two kinds of evolutions by mutation: adaptive and random. Adaptive evolution is evolution which increases fitness. Random evolution is just change by accident; it may or may not increase fitness. They believed in adaptive evolution by mutation.

ADAPTIVE EVOLUTION
BY MUTATION ALONE?

If only organisms could have mutations according to their needs; if only mutations were helpfully directed toward increasing fitness, then the theory of evolution would be: mutations do not just happen, they happen because they are needed to improve fitness. And most of them do improve it, because they are the only ones allowed to happen, or they are the only ones encouraged to happen.

But is that the way mutation really works? Are mutations helpfully directed? There is abundant evidence that this is not true for genic mutation at all. Before we examine this evidence, we shall have to define one more division of opinion.

TWO HYPOTHESES OF INHERITANCE

All those that have believed in evolution by mutation have not believed in the same sort of inheritance mechanism. Some have believed in the continuity of the germ plasm, others that it is reconstituted in each generation from the body of the organism.

Let's not go too deeply into the details of all this. What the continuity people say is what most biologists agree on today: there is a special tissue called germ plasm which contains the instructions for constructing an adult. This tissue is passed on through the generations, but is always present and is never made from scratch. Today we call this tissue the germ cells, and the set of instructions, the genes.

According to the continuity people, then, evolution by mutation would work like this: There is a special device which goes around measuring the environment and pressuring the genes to change in a direction which better adapts the organism to the environment. The change would appear in the phenotype of the next generation.

The reconstitutionalists believe that the germ plasm is dismantled after development and then rebuilt when the organism reproduces. The reconstituted instructions call for building an organism just like the one in which they were formed. If an organism has lost a leg, its progeny will also lack the leg. So the reconstitution theory leads to a prediction that acquired characters will be inherited. (See Fig. 14-1.)

LAMARCKIAN EVOLUTION

The "reconstitutionalist" theory of evolution is often termed Lamarckism, after Lamarck, the famous French paleontologist of about 1800 who is given credit for it. Since these people believed acquired characters to be inherited, the acquisition of a new phenotype was tantamount to mutation. Now, if only those mutations increase fitness. . . . Of course, Lamarckians believed they did, and so they believed in evolution by mutation.

The favorite story of Lamarckian evolution is the elongation of the giraffe's neck. Each generation of giraffes, it seems, stretched their necks a little in the effort of reaching for the leaves at treetop level. Each successive generation was therefore born with slightly longer necks. This continued until stretching was no longer necessary. Try retelling this story in Darwinian form.

Don't laugh at the Lamarkian story though. Maybe such things can actually happen. Until all the evidence is in, we won't know.

Don't become angered by Lamarck either. Weismann, a famous scientist of the nineteenth century did. He decided to put the three blind mice to work for him. He cut off their tails with a scalpel and allowed them to reproduce. All their young had tails. Then he cut off these and allowed this generation to beget a third. Still tails. And again. Still tails. And tails. And tails. Aha! Acquired characters are not inherited.

Poor Weismann. All that work and it turns out that some acquired characters are inherited after all, although not taillessness in mice. But Jennings and his student Sonneborn have grafted a second mouth onto Paramecium. All such Paramecium then gave rise to two-mouthed daughters. Forever. And certainly the traditions that people acquire are passed on to their children.

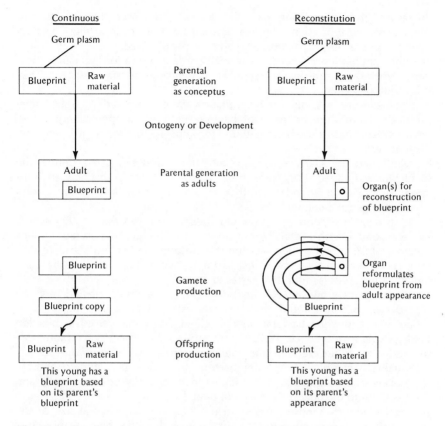

Fig. 14-1 Continuity vs. reconstitution: two views of the germ plasm.

So some acquired characteristics can be inherited. But are they acquired because they're more fit? I suspect the two-mouthed *Paramecium* isn't, but what about civilized people? If people have indeed become wise to the point where they can modify their culture in order to increase their fitness, then they must be evolving a la Lamarck! Are they that wise?

Of course Weismann's work is far from all wasted. He did show that taillessness in mice was not inheritable as an acquired character. In fact there is a huge class of characters just like this. All the ones inherited by genes are such. For them, Lamarck is certainly wrong. For them we must return to the basic idea: are mutations helpfully directed?

ANTIBIOTIC RESISTANCE IN BACTERIA

The wartime injuries of 1939 spurred the attempts to purify penicillin and make a useful drug from it. In 1940, Florey and his team of colleagues dramatically rescued several hospitalized people who were literally in the act of dying. Bacterial disease had caused their illness, and the new medication, penicillin, was quite a bit more toxic to most bacteria than to people. So the bacteria died and the people lived.

Other antibiotics followed. Soon a discordant indication appeared. Bacterial types that were once susceptible to penicillin became resistant. They thrived in penicillin.

The believers in evolution by mutation were heartened. "Surely," they insisted, "there were no resistant bacteria before. The 'penicillin-infested' environment had *caused* mutations to appear—mutations to penicillin resistance."

"No," said the Darwinists, "the mutations already existed before the penicillin was added. They were just rare. Putting them in this new environment simply changed relative fitnesses around. Penicillin-resistant alleles then became quite common."

In an elegant experiment, Luria and Delbruck proved that the Darwinists were absolutely right. Later, by developing a technique they called "replica plating," Joshua and Esther Lederberg were able to confirm these results. The Lederbergs' experiment is just as impressive as the one done by Luria and Delbruck. But it's infinitely easier to explain.

Two ways to grow bacteria in the lab are on a disc of jellied medium called agar and in a liquid medium in a test tube. Each medium contains nourishment, but the bacteria on the jellied disc remain fixed in position and grow on the surface. Penicillin or streptomycin or any antibiotic can be added to either medium. But then all nonresistant bacteria die.

Usually, bacteriologists transfer bacteria from one agar disc to another by means of a single platinum loop. The loop picks up some cells and carries them to the new surface for continued growth.

The Lederbergs' innovation was to use a piece of velvet the size of the disc, instead of a platinum loop. Velvet is a cloth with a high-cut pile. It is like thousands of tiny needles, each picking up a few cells and moving them to the new surface. Of course the velvet gets far more cells than the loop, but that is not why the Lederbergs used it.

Since the bacteria do not move around on an agar plate, the ones that are close together must be sisters or cousins. When the velvet touched the surface of the new agar plate, it was thus making a replica of the old one. Each bacterial family near the center of the old agar donated some members to the center of the new plate. Each family on the eastern edge donated some members to the new eastern edge, and so on. The Lederbergs could locate the relatives of bacteria anywhere on the new plate by looking at the same spot on the old one.

The Lederbergs proposed proving that the mutation for antibiotic resistance occurred before exposure to the antibiotic. Their idea was to subject some members of many bacterial families to a drug. Meanwhile, they'd hold back the rest of the families' members in a protected, benign environment. First, they'd see which exposed bacteria proved resistant to penicillin. Then, they'd test their relatives (previously unexposed). If these bacteria were resistant because of a family trait—that is, an inherited mutation which occurred before exposure, then their relatives should also have the mutation and should be resistant. Instead of most of their relatives dying upon exposure to penicillin, most should live. The mutation could not possibly have been helpfully directed by the pressure of penicillin.

On the other hand, if the mutation was helpfully directed, then the family wouldn't have it. Its members would stand no better chance than others of becoming resistant. It would be just luck that their cousin happened to be the one to mutate properly in the terrible new environment. When other members of these lucky bacteria's families would be cultured with antibiotics, most should die.

Here, briefly, is the actual experiment. They grew some *E. coli* on a plain agar plate. Then they made a replica on a plate full of streptomycin. Only a few bacteria lived. These bacteria were discarded, but the Lederbergs sought out their families on the original plates by looping off some bacteria from the spots where they had obtained the resistant ones. These loopsful were placed in a liquid medium for rapid growth. Then they were plated onto new, but harmless plates. Remember they had never been exposed to streptomycin. Nor had any of their direct ancestors. The exposed relatives had all been discarded. Replicas of these new plates were produced on plates full of streptomycin. Sure enough, far fewer bacteria died. The unexposed relatives of the resistant bacteria did contain the mutation. (See Fig. 14-2.)

The Lederbergs then discarded the second replica plate and looped out corresponding parts of the second harmless plate. These second loopsful contained a far higher proportion of resistant relatives than the first did. They grew the second loopsful in liquid, and replated. When they exposed this third round to a toxic replica plate, an even larger number of resistant bacteria were present. The third replica plate was dense with resistant bacteria. And none of their mothers or grandmothers of great- or great-great-grandmothers had ever stared a streptomycin molecule in the face! The mutation had occurred **before** the new environmental pressure. By the fourth round of replica plating, every single bacterium was resistant! This mutation had certainly not been helpfully directed.

Each such step of this experiment enriched the population of bacteria with resistant alleles. In effect, the Lederbergs tamed natural selection and brought it into the laboratory. Here it is called artificial selection because the fitnesses are determined by man (artificial means man-made).

The Lederbergs tested other antibiotics and found similar results.

MOST MUTATIONS ARE HARMFUL

Only rarely are mutations helpful. The most damaging evidence against the hypothesis of helpfully directed mutation is that virtually all mutations are harmful! G. L. Stebbins reports that less than 1% of the hundreds of observed mutations of barley have been any good. Lerner lists

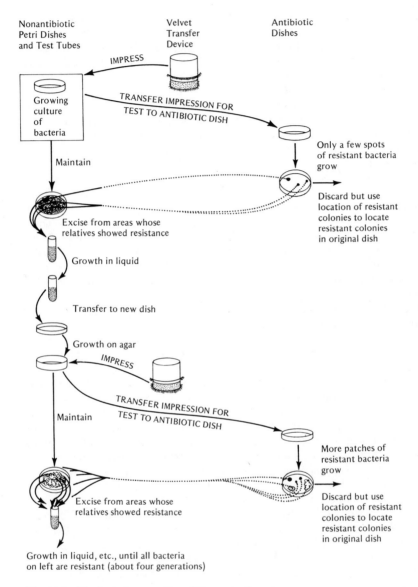

Fig. 14-2   The Lederberg replica-plating experiment.

10 different human mutations whose mutation rates are known. They have low relative fitnesses from 0 to 0.33 except for albinism (fitness unknown) and aniridia (no iris in the eye; fitness unknown). It is hard to believe under most circumstances that either renders its bearer as fit as its normal counterpart.

(One exception, albinism, is interesting. A very high frequency of this allele occurs in the Hopi, a culture of Pueblo Indians. The Hopi live in and have mastered the harsh northern Arizona desert. Their oldest towns, Oraibi and Walpi, are about a millenium old. Each day during the growing season the men descend from the mesas on which they have perched their towns, to farm the desert below. Albino men cannot stand the sun and are left behind with the women where they engage in respectable occupations that can be done indoors. They apparently also engage in a bit of less respectable extracurricular activity with the wives of the men in the field. Anyway, far more albinos are born into the Hopi nation than can be accounted for by mutation.)

Bruce Wallace has run an exhaustive test of the proposition that most mutations are harmful. He used laboratory populations of *Drosophila melanogaster*. The portion of the fitness he measured is called preadult viability. This is the relative chance that an egg will live to become an adult, so it is a very important part of the overall fitness.

To increase the rate at which mutations occur, Wallace subjected his flies to doses of x-rays. The x-rays caused many lethal mutations; in fact, Wallace compared his treatment of the flies to "an atomic disaster" (x-rays are the same as the gamma rays of nuclear explosions). He estimated that about 95% of all eggs did not survive because they had a dominant lethal mutation. Look how easy it is to change things for the worse!

Sublethal mutations. What about the 5% that did survive? Wallace felt that many of these had had small mutations. He wanted to discover whether they were preponderantly good, bad, or indifferent. These mutations were so small that it would have taken too much time and effort to find them. But he wasn't interested in finding each one. What he wanted to know was their usual effect on preadult viability. To find this, Wallace used a complex test.

CyL, or Curly Lobe (curly wings and lobelike eyes), are two known mutations of the fruit fly's second chromosome. There is a way to get these to be inherited as if they were one locus, always fastened together. Wallace used this way, called crossover suppression, and so was able to call his phenotype CyL, as if it were one mutant allele.

CyL is called a semidominant lethal. Some of its effects are dominant, but its lethal effects are recessive. Homozygous CyL/CyL flies always die. Flies heterozygous for it do not die, but appear curly and lobed. So a cross between two heterozygotes—CyL/+ × CyL/+—should result in two living heterozygotes (CyL/+) for every one wild type (+/+). (See Fig. 14-3.)

Wallace noticed that these progeny of a CyL/+ heterozygote cross would differ in one important respect: the heterozygotes would have only one of the + chromosomes, whereas the homozygotes would get two. If these + chromosomes had any deleterious effects on viability, the homozygotes would be in a worse situation than the heterozygotes; they would have double trouble. (Of course, if the mutation were helpful, they would have a double boost).

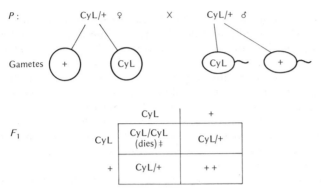

Ratio of living F_1: 2/3 Curly Lobe (CyL/+) to 1/3 wild type (+ +)

Fig. 14-3 A heterozygote CyL/+ cross and its theoretical output of progeny.

Naturally Wallace, being a fine experimentalist, had saved for comparison a control group of flies that had not been x-rayed. Bearers of x-rayed + chromosomes appeared to be identical to bearers of control + chromosomes. But were they really? They should have contained some of those small, hard-to-spot mutations. How were these mutations affecting preadult viability?

Because he had controls, Wallace easily answered this question. To see whether the x-rays had induced harmful but nonlethal mutations, all he needed to do was work up two separate sets of heterozygote crosses: in one set the mated flies were CyL/control +; in the other set they were CyL/x-rayed +. Then he simply compared the fraction of surviving x-rayed homozygotes. Wallace did this many times for two years (see Table 14-1). In his first comparison, the control homozygotes constituted 32.08% (on the average) of the living children of their parents, but x-rayed homozygotes averaged only 30.66% of the living children of theirs. In the eighteenth comparison, control homozygotes were 31.58%, whereas x-rayed were only 29.06% of the surviving progeny of their respective parents. In 21 of the 22 such comparisons Wallace made, the x-rayed homozygotes did worse than the controls. This definitely confirmed the preponderance of harmful small mutations over helpful ones (Fig. 14-4).

(As an aside, notice that in no case did the homozygotes attain the expected average frequency of 1/3. The very highest was 33.17%. While this is indeed close to 33.33% (1/3), it is the closest of 44 large groups of young flies. If the true frequency is 33.33%, you'd expect a few cases to be higher, a few lower, and most fairly close to 1/3. Doesn't this suggest that the CyL/+ heterozygote is exhibiting hybrid vigor and has superior preadult viability?)

Beneficial mutations. How can mutation be good at all if its results are more often harmful than helpful? The answer is that however

TABLE 14-1 THE EFFECT OF SMALL,
            DELETERIOUS MUTATIONS ON
            THE VIABILITY OF DROSOPHILA

Percentage of flies that are homozygous wild type	
X-rayed	Control
30.66	32.08
31.94[a]	31.65
31.11	31.46
30.39	31.49
30.79	32.14
29.63	31.64
29.85	31.40
30.81	31.79
29.99	30.84
29.90	30.87
29.26	32.25
30.33	32.77
30.63	32.04
30.83	32.77
29.72	30.19
29.60	31.00
31.07	31.59
29.06	31.58
31.35	33.17
29.87	31.37
30.78	31.27
31.38	31.39

Source: B. Wallace.
[a] This is the only case where the wild types composed more of the progeny of x-rayed parents
than of control parents sampled at the same time.

rarely a good mutation occurs, once it does, selection increases the proportion of the population that has this new beneficial allele. Similarly, selection
keeps down the frequency of the deleterious alleles that usually result from
mutation.

In fact, if you think carefully about it, you will realize that it is the very
efficiency of selection, its great power to increase fitness, that creates the
situation where most mutations are harmful. If a population is composed
of very well adapted individuals, why should changes help them? They
should hurt. If you're doing everything almost perfectly, doesn't it make
sense that trying a different way is almost certain to impair your perfor-
mance?

Wallace knew this and as few evolutionists have, he took full advantage
of it. He realized that putting members of Drosophila in the laboratory
subjected them to a new environment, an environment to which they'd not
had a chance to adjust fully. He thought a few of their smaller, nonlethal

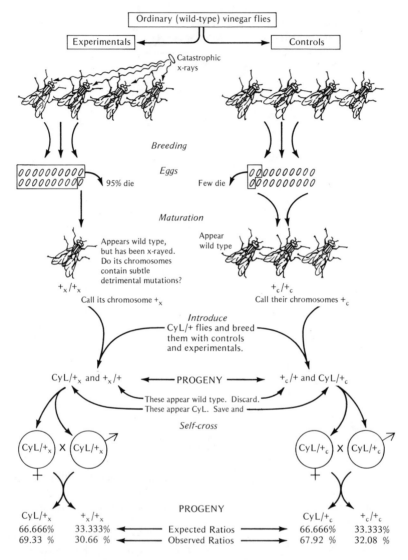

Ordinary (wild-type) vinegar flies

Experimentals ←————————————→ Controls

Catastrophic
x-rays

Breeding

Eggs

95% die   Few die

Maturation

Appears wild type,
but has been x-rayed.
Do its chromosomes
contain subtle
detrimental mutations?

Appear
wild type

$+_x/+_x$
Call its chromosome $+_x$

$+_c/+_c$
Call their chromosomes $+_c$

Introduce
CyL/+ flies and breed
them with controls
and experimentals.

$CyL/+_x$ and $+_x/+$ ←———— PROGENY ————→ $+_c/+$ and $CyL/+_c$

These appear wild type. Discard.
These appear CyL. Save and

Self-cross

$\left(CyL/+_x\right)$ X $\left(CyL/+_x\right)$

$\left(CyL/+_c\right)$ X $\left(CyL/+_c\right)$

PROGENY

$CyL/+_x$	$+_x/+_x$		$CyL/+_c$	$+_c/+_c$
66.666%	33.333%	←—— Expected Ratios ——→	66.666%	33.333%
69.33 %	30.66 %	←—— Observed Ratios ——→	67.92 %	32.08 %

Fig. 14-4 A diagram of Wallace's discovery of small, harmful mutations in x-rayed
Drosophila chromosomes.

mutations would help. So he ought to find that the survivors of x-rays
would evolve to fit their new environment faster than the controls. Why?
Because both groups needed to adapt, but the x-rayed flies had been given
a larger supply of variation—a bigger menu. Eventually the slow, natural

mutation rate of the controls could be expected to catch up—to provide similar new choices—but they would take much longer.

In addition to his controls and "atomic disaster" flies, Wallace had three other populations of flies which were constantly receiving x-rays under three different experimental regimes. We need not examine the exact nature of those regimes here. In each of the five populations, Wallace counted the average number of flies that survived to adulthood per test sample. The higher the number, the better the fitness of the parents of the flies.

Each of the four x-rayed populations should have done better than the control. Each did (Table 14-2). It took the nonirradiated flies over 40 weeks to catch up to the other four populations. For instance, the weeks 30 through 39 showed the control yielding only 147.1 live flies for every 164.8 or 165.4 or 154.2 or 157.2 live flies from each of the four irradiated groups. A few small useful mutations had indeed occurred.

As you might have guessed, the five groups of flies continued to evolve in the laboratory and their fitness continued to increase. After almost two years of work, the same five groups were yielding much larger numbers of survivors: 455.2, 404.6, 374.7, 383.2, and 364.8 live flies per sample (where the samples were taken the same way as at weeks 30 through 39).

After the first year to year and a half, the x-rays proved harmful in effect. The helpful mutations had been incorporated into the gene pools and more were unlikely to occur. The three populations that continued on x-ray doses never developed as good a fitness as the two that were not treated this way. These three were outstripped after about one and one-half years and were never again superior.

The population that suffered the "atomic disaster," however, was just as good as the control: it recuperated rapidly by natural selection, though at great cost to individual life. Is it any wonder that biologists fear nuclear devices and maintain a cautious respect for the energy of x-rays?

GENETIC ASSIMILATION
OF ACQUIRED CHARACTERISTICS

Indeterminate phenotypes. What we inherit from our parents is a potential, no more. With this potential as a guide, we grow into reality. We may have the potential to live in Indiana, Iowa, or Idaho, but if we actually live in Boise City, that is our reality, that is our phenotype. We may have the potential to weigh anywhere from 98 to 300 pounds, but if we weigh 153.6, that is our phenotype.

The guidelines set by our inheritance may be narrow or broad. There is quite a bit of leeway in our weight, but little or none in the composition of our hemoglobin. Often our environment determines our phenotype within these guidelines.

For instance, there is abundant evidence that life span is inherited. But within groups of individuals possessing similar inheritance, there is much

TABLE 14-2 WALLACE'S FIVE POPULATIONS AND THEIR YIELDS[a] OF FLIES DURING TWO YEARS

Time (in weeks since start of experiments)	Population treatment				
	No x rays (large pop.)	"Holocaust" at time 0 (large pop.)	Chronic high-dose x rays (large pop.)	Chronic high-dose x rays (small pop.)	Chronic low-dose x rays (large pop.)
30s	147.1	164.8	165.4	154.2	157.2
40s	221.1	237.1	276.3	273.5	287.2
50s	215.1	203.4	205.9	204.6	204.6
60s	314.7	323.7	301.6	306.9	295.4
70s	374.5	397.8	374.4	379.8	347.5
80s	397.9	340.8	296.6	362.8	336.8
90s	408.3	373.2	388.5	430.1	392.0
100s	399.5	420.6	353.7	376.4	357.9
110s	477.4	463.1	404.4	418.4	394.8
120s	455.2	404.6	374.7	383.2	364.8

Source: B. Wallace.
[a] The yield is the number of flies hatching from standard test situations.

evidence (from all sorts of animals) that the longest lives are lived by those that receive the minimum essential nutrition. Abundant food apparently contributes to earlier death.

Another case is callouses. We are all born (to a varying degree) with the ability to develop callouses providing we often rub our hands against rough surfaces. If our environment includes a need for manual labor, our hands are calloused. If not, they are not.

The ostrich hatches with callouses. They are underneath the bulk of his body where he normally rests on the ground and they are obviously useful. There callouses prevent the broken blisters and subsequent infections that might occur if the young ostrich had to acquire callouses by resting on his bottom on the abrasive earth. (See Fig. 14-5.)

At this the Lamarckians roar approval. Here is a case of evolution by the inheritance of acquired characteristics.

Or is it?

Let us hear their argument. The ostrich acquired callouses as an adult. These were passed on to his young. Now that is not much of an argument. Are the sons of cowhands born with callouses on their posteriors? Are the sons of lumberjacks possessed at birth with the callouses of their fathers? No.

Lamarckian evolution mimicked by natural selection. The young ostriches' callouses are easily explained by the action of natural

Fig. 14-5 The underside of an ostrich. The ischial callosities appear as egglike protuberances on the midline. (From Waddington.)

selection. The development of callouses is inherited, but there are genes which modify the amount of environmental friction required to produce them. Consider the ostrich with the genes which specify: *callouses, right away, even without friction*. Won't he be more fit than his neighbor who needs to raise three blisters to get his callouses?

Waddington and Bateman, using *Drosophila*, have actually brought two callouslike systems into the laboratory. They have confirmed that characteristics, at first acquired by interaction with certain environments, can become fully determined by genes. Waddington has dubbed this "genetic assimilation of acquired characteristics." All that is required to achieve it is to create selective pressure for the early development of the characteristic.

At first, Waddington and Bateman used a characteristic called posterior crossveinlessness. This is an anomalous pattern of blood vessels in the wings; a small vein is actually missing (Fig. 14-6). In all common populations of *Drosophila*, crossveinlessness is produced if the developing flies, as immature forms called pupae, are subjected to an extraordinarily hot environment. Without such heat shock, flies develop the standard vein pattern.

What Waddington and Bateman wanted to show, of course, was that by selecting for flies who needed less and less heat to produce crossveinlessness, they could eventually get a strain whose members were all crossveinless even without high heat. As we shall see, they were quickly successful (Fig. 14-7).

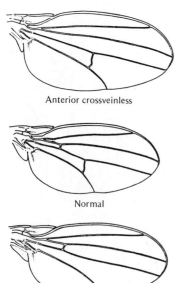

Anterior crossveinless

Normal

Posterior crossveinless

Fig. 14-6 Normal and crossveinless patterns of *Drosophila* wing blood vessels. (Adapted from Waddington.)

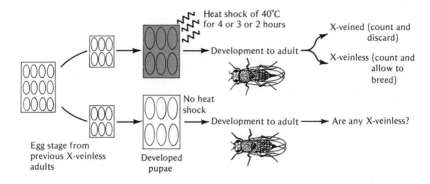

Fig. 14-7 One generation of the experiment of Bateman. After fourteen such generations, flies began to appear without crossveins even though not heat shocked (their ancestors had been heat shocked).

Waddington and Bateman's heat shock temperature was 40°C (104°F). At first they subjected pupae to four hours of shock. When the pupae emerged as adults, 56% had no posterior crossveins. They selected these for breeding and discarded the others. Offspring were divided into two groups. Group one was shocked; group two developed without shock.

In the first generation, not one unshocked pupa became a crossveinless adult. But a slightly higher fraction of the shocked ones became crossveinless. Waddington and Bateman repeated their selection of only these as breeders. Again they divided their offspring into a group to be shocked and a control group. Again the fraction of the shocked flies that became crossveinless was higher. But again all unshocked flies were normal.

After five generations, about 74% of shocked flies became crossveinless. At that point they lowered the shock time to three hours. With the smaller shock, only about 42% of the sixth-generation flies became crossveinless.

Soon the percentage had climbed back near 65%. So they lowered the heat shock still further to two hours. By the tenth, eleventh, and twelfth generation, the fraction responding to this heat shock had leveled off at about 90%.

Furthermore, in generation 14, there appeared in the unshocked flies the first few crossveinless ones. These flies were genetically crossveinless. Their genotype had assimilated as fixed, a phenotypic character that once was acquired! Breeding from them results in a genetically crossveinless race (Fig. 14-8).

With extreme care, Bateman repeated this experiment. She showed that the variation that selection was working with was not due to mutations while the experiments were in progress. The mutations had all occurred beforehand. She showed that another phenotypic anomaly, called bithorax, could also be assimilated—this one in 28 generations.

Genetic assimilation of environmentally induced characters was certainly

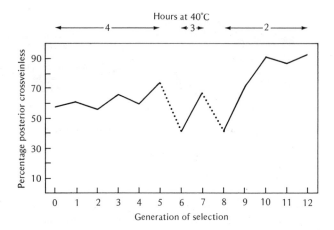

Fig. 14-8 Bateman's results with selection for crossveinlessness. (Adapted from Waddington.)

happening in the lab. And it was happening by Darwinian selection, *not* by Lamarckian evolution. As Waddington explains, what had occurred was a change in the indeterminacy of a phenotypic characteristic. Whereas once the environment had played an important role in determining it, now it was solely a product of the genes.

RANDOM MUTATIONS

Evolution by random mutation. Even though mutations often harm fitness, they do occur. And they are change. And change is evolution. So mutations do cause evolution.

What is the evolutionary pressure generated by mutation? Even though we talk herein of genic mutation, you should remember that these same principles can be applied to traditional mutation, chromosomal mutation, or any other.

Suppose there are two alleles at a locus, Y and B. There is a chance that a B will become a Y and another chance that a Y will mutate to a B. These chances may be small, even near zero, but they do exist. What is the net result of evolution by these mutations (assuming no selection)?

Imagine two barrels: one for B and one for Y alleles. Imagine also two mutator genies: one picks out B's, changes them to Y's, and throws them in the Y barrel. The other does the reverse. The only rules are that the $B{\rightarrow}Y$ genie must change exactly $x\%$ of the B genes per generation; whereas the $Y{\rightarrow}B$ genie changes $z\%$ of the Y genes in that time. Which genie wins? Neither.

When the $Y \rightarrow B$ genie is winning, he will have depleted his own stock of Y genes. That gives the $B \rightarrow Y$ genie the advantage in the next round. In fact, when the number of Y genes converted equals the number of B genes converted, we have a stable equilibrium. Notice I said actual number, not percentage. Later we shall see that adding selection to this system destroys the equilibrium. But for now, if p is the frequency of the Y allele, and q, that of the B, then when

$$xq = zp$$

there is an equilibrium of mutation. Let's try this equation with some sample values.

Geneticists have found that the actual rates of genic mutation are very, very small: five per million or 8 per hundred thousand or so. Since mutations tend to be harmful, these low rates are fine with me. In fact, many evolutionists believe they have evolved to be low, since organisms with high rates tend to be less fit. (Yes, there are genes known which influence mutation rate.) However, for a sample calculation, we'll use high rates. They're easier to multiply.

Suppose $x = 0.10$ (that is, 10% of the B alleles becomes Y) and $z = 0.25$ (25% of the Y alleles become B). If $p = 0.50$, then (0.25×0.50) or 12.5% of all alleles are changing in that generation from Y to B. Similarly (0.10×0.50) 5% of all alleles are changing from B to Y. So the net change is the difference between the two: 7.5% of alleles become B. We can see that in the next generation q will be 57.5%. There will be a change in p, a Δp due to mutation, of minus 0.075.

Now suppose p gets very small; say 0.01% or $p = 0.0001$. Then mutation will increase its frequency. $zp = 0.25 \times 0.0001 = 0.000025$. And $zq = 0.10 \times 0.9999 = 0.09999$. Thus, 9.999 of every hundred alleles are switching from B to Y, but only 0.0025 of every hundred are going the other way. $\Delta p = +0.09999 - 0.000025 = +0.099965$. From this you can see that when a gene becomes rare, most mutation is in its favor. And its increase due to mutation is very near the rate at which its allele mutates to it.

Just for fun, let's calculate the equilibrium value. It is $(1 - p)x = pz$ or $p = x/(z + x)$. In the case above, equilibrium of mutation is reached when $p = x/(x + z) = 0.10/0.35 = 0.286$. But as we said before, this matters little. Selection does not allow such equilibria to last. The important conclusions about mutational evolution are that (1) when an allele is rare, mutation will be adding to its frequency and (2) the change of p owing to mutation may be symbolized Δp_m and equals $[(1 - p)x - pz]$ or $x - p(x + z)$. This last formula vividly underlines the fact that Δp_m is positive and close to x when p is very, very small.

Rare, harmful alleles. In Chapter 13 we predicted that in all cases but heterosis, one of the alleles would become extinct owing to selection against it. From the previous section, however, we learn that extinction of an allele is not final. It is an abyss from which return is

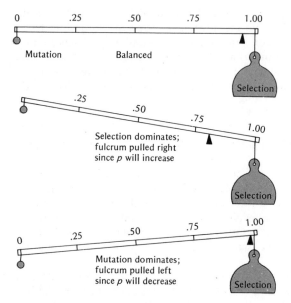

Fig. 14-9 The balance between strong selection and weak mutation may be compared to two weights suspended from a rod. One weight (selection) is heavy. The other (mutation) is miniscule. In the diagram, the frequency of the favored allele is represented as the distance from the light weight to the fulcrum. Thus, the rod represents all possible values of p; the fulcrum is on the actual value.

predictable. When an allele is absolutely gone, it is produced from another allele at the prevailing mutation rate. If $p = 0$, $\Delta p_m = x$.

In this section we shall examine the balance that exists between selection and mutation. From selection theory we predicted that an unfavorable allele would disappear utterly. From mutation theory we concluded the allele would occur at a mutational equilibrium, $p = x/(x + z)$. This sets up an evolutionary tug of war between selection and mutation.

We shall see that the forces of selection are usually so strong and those of mutation so weak, that selection completely dominates the picture. But that is precisely what you'd expect, isn't it? What would be the fitness of a phenotype with a high mutation rate? In effect, selection for low mutation rates has attenuated the strength of Δp_m to the point where all mutation can do is stave off that final oblivion. It just barely prevents deleterious alleles from becoming totally extinct.

Being interested in expressing ourselves precisely, we symbolize the equilibrium in the tug of war as

$$\Delta p_s + \Delta p_m = 0$$

where Δp_s is the old Δp of the Wright equation, the change in p caused by selection (Fig. 14-9). Remember, this equilibrium does not apply to a heterosis (case 4). There, selection alone maintains both alleles at a high frequency. At such high frequencies, weak mutation rates play almost no role. Of course, we could figure in mutation there, too, but that would mostly be a waste of time.

E. T. Morch, a Danish investigator, tested this theory using a detrimental human allele, an allele that is a semidominant lethal. People with a double dose do not live, so their fitness, y/g, is zero. People with one normal allele and one harmful one do not grow to acceptable heights; this allele is thus one cause of dwarfism. It is called chondrodystrophy or achondroplasia (Fig. 14-10).

Most such dwarfs have normal brothers and sisters. So Morch interviewed these families to discover the relative fitnesses of the dwarfs. One hundred eight dwarfs had produced 27 living children. Their 457 normal brothers and sisters had 582 children. Thus, the fitness of a dwarf, g, is 27/108 or 0.25, and of his brother, b, it's 582/457 or 1.27. This makes $b/g = 5.0$. Of course, the dwarf's relative fitness is $g/g = 1.00$ (the dwarf is the heterozygote). Now we are ready to write Δp_s (p is the frequency of the dwarf allele):

$$\Delta p_s = \frac{pq[p(0-1) + q(1-5)]}{p^2(0) + 2pq + q^2(5)} = \frac{pq(-p-4q)}{2pq + 5q^2}$$

Note that Δp_s is always negative.

Next, Morch needed to know the mutation rates. He collected the records of 94,075 live births in a Copenhagen hospital. Of all these babies, only 10

Fig. 14-10 Three types of abnormally small adults. The two dwarfs to the immediate left of the normal adult are chondrodystrophic. All these individuals were older than 20 when the photo was taken. (From Major.)

were chondrodystrophic dwarfs. But two of the 10 had been born to dwarf parents, so they were not produced by mutation. The other eight were. This gives 94,073 potentially normal births, with eight of these astray by mutation. Since each of the 94,073 have two genes for this locus, there were 188,146 loci. Eight mutated so the mutation rate, x, is 8/188,146 or 42.5 mutations per million genes. This low rate isn't at all unusual. No mutations to normality were observed, so we will have to assume $z = 0$. This won't introduce much error though (why?). Morch now has Δp_m:

$$\Delta p_m = q \frac{42.5}{1,000,000}$$

and is thus capable of finding the value of p at selective and mutational equilibrium. This will be the value of p that satisfies the equation:

$$\Delta p_s + \Delta p_m = 0$$

or

$$\frac{pq(-p - 4q)}{2pq + 5q^2} + q \frac{42.5}{1,000,000} = 0$$

Morch already knows what the answer should be, though. Of 94,075 babies, 10 were dwarfs. So the frequency of the dwarf allele is 10/188,150. That should be very close to the value of p that satisfies our equation.

To solve the equation, we must first substitute $(1 - q)$ for all the p values or else a $(1 - p)$ for all the q's. From that point we eventually reach the equation:

$$3.0001275 \, q^2 - 1.999915 \, q - 1 = 0$$

This is a rather messy quadratic equation. Usually geneticists make a few simplifying assumptions and get an approximate answer which avoids such complex work. However, just this once I've worked it through without introducing any more error than we've already been saddled with. The positive value of q that solves this equation is $q = 188,140/188,150$. Thus the equilibrium value of p is precisely what Morch measured: 10/188,150! It appears that the equations explain perfectly the low frequency of this harmful allele. The balance between selection and mutation is real.

MUTATION PROBLEMS

14-1a. *Drosophila* genes mutate to white eye from red eye about 2.9 times per 100,000 gametes. Assuming there are 500,000 red-eye genes in one generation, how many will change to white? How many would change if there were 5,000,000 red-eye alleles?

14-1b. If there are 125,000 white-eye alleles and 500,000 red-eye, what must be the white's mutation rate to red in order to balance exactly the changes to white?

14-2. Retinoblastoma, a fatal eye tumor in humans, is caused by a dominant allele, R. This allele is produced from r at a mutation rate of about 20 per million gametes. Of the next 50 million babies born, how many might be expected to die of retinoblastoma?

14-3. Cut wings is a sex-linked allele in *Drosophila*. That means each male has only one chromosome with a cut-wing locus. In 60,000 male offspring of normal parents, only nine were cut-winged. What is the mutation rate of normal wing, Ct, to cut wing, ct?

14-4a. Tay-Sachs disease or infantile amourotic idiocy is a recessive lethal disease found mostly in Jews. The heterozygote is as fit as the dominant homozygote. The change at equilibrium caused by natural selection has been found to be 11 per million alleles. That is, if p represents the frequency of the normal allele, +, then $\Delta p_s = 0.000011$. What is Δp_m at equilibrium?

14-4b. What is the frequency of the Tay-Sachs allele at equilibrium?

14-4c. What fraction of the population is heterozygous for it?

15 adaptation: main product of evolution

*If a beaver two feet long with a tail a foot and a half long
can build a dam twelve feet high and six feet wide in two
days, all you would need to build Boulder Dam is a beaver
sixty-eight feet long with a fifty-one foot tail.*

Norton Juster

Distinguish evolution from the forces producing it. Evolution
is the actual change in the population's phenotypes, whereas the forces
are the mechanisms which cause the change, like natural selection and
mutation.

Now distinguish evolution that increases predictably the average fitness—
adaptive evolution—from evolution that doesn't—nonadaptive evolution.
As we have seen, natural selection produces adaptive evolution. Evolution
from mutation is almost always nonadaptive.

There are other mechanisms that might produce nonadaptive evolution.
In the first part of this chapter, we shall examine one of them. Then in the
second part, you will learn of some very strong evidence that evolution is
primarily adaptive. We shall conclude that evolution has only rarely been
influenced by nonadaptive mechanisms.

Why go to the trouble of explaining nonadaptive evolution at all if it is
and has been unimportant? Because there are some who disagree with
me that it is weak. Perhaps one day you will be one of them.

200

GENETIC DRIFT

In Chapter 13 we made an implicit simplifying assumption about the size of the population. We assumed it was so large that the frequency of each allele in every new generation would be the same as the allele's frequency in the gene pool. Often that is inaccurate. Often a population is small. Does smallness influence its evolutionary fate?

To answer this question, Sewall Wright developed the theory of genetic drift. Drift is the evolutionary effect produced by the *smallness* of a population. It is a mechanism for nonadaptive evolution. It is called drift because when a population is very small its allele frequencies undergo unpredictable changes; they appear to drift aimlessly.

The theory of drift is complex and one must use statistics to attain predictions from it. But it is easy to understand that drift is both reasonable and nonadaptive.

Suppose—for the extreme case—that an island is free of birds. Perhaps once in a hundred years a storm of just the right size and direction, at just the right season, blows a few birds to the island. If the birds survive their unwanted voyage, they are Fletcher Christians. They have no better chance of returning to the mainland than they had of arriving in the first place. And they certainly waste no time waiting for the return storm. If the habitat is at all suitable, they, like the shipwrecked souls of Pitcairn Island, found a new colony.

Soon the island is teeming with this bird species. But all the members of the population can trace their ancestry back to those first founders, whose tiny gene pool began the whole population. These founders couldn't carry all the variety of their parental mainland population with them. They had only their own few genes. These genes were necessarily a small sample of those available. So the new colony may look very different from the mainland population. If there were, for example, 100 alleles at a particular mainland locus and only 5 Fletcher Christians, then immediately at least 90% of the mainland alleles would be extinct on the island. The genetic drift that results when a few members of a large population establish a new population in some isolated spot is known as the founder principle.

Several examples of the founder principle at work in isolated human populations are known. Some have been noted in the strict Amish communities because these people tend to intermarry. One, a genetic disease, was first described in 1860. Since then, only 100 cases are known to have occurred, and 55 of them were Amish from a small (8000 people) group of Pennsylvanians. The ancestors of all 55 were a couple who came to America in 1774. Lerner estimates the frequency of the allele in this group at about 0.065. This is far higher than in any other known human population. Naturally, the average fitness of these people must be lower than it would be if the drift hadn't occurred.

From the extreme of the founder principle, you can imagine the less extreme case of the generation-to-generation replacement of a small population. Each generation is small so there is a great chance that each succeeding generation will be different from its parent just by accident. In essence, there aren't enough members in the population for the law of averages to work out.

There are simple ways of showing this in the laboratory. One of the simplest is to get a good coin. Imagine a population of 10 diploid individuals; now imagine that each receives one of two alleles, H or T, at $p = 0.50$, $q = 0.50$. Then actually construct the population by flipping the coin to determine each allele. Only rarely will your result consist of 10 heads and 10 tails. When it doesn't, the population has drifted from its gene-pool values just by accident.

You can probably accept the fact that the smaller the population, the greater is the average absolute value of Δp due to genetic drift. Genetic drift may now be formally defined as any change in p which results from random sampling accidents when a new generation is receiving its genes.

Has genetic drift occurred often? Does it form an important part of the forces which determine p? Some cases do exist but on the whole, drift results in nonadaptive evolution. Since evolution is primarily adaptive, we will not be able to account for much of it by drift. We can thus relegate drift to the relatively unimportant status of an interesting subtlety—a grace note that permits us to predict p to the second or third decimal place. But, ordinarily, drift is unnecessary to our grasp of the major forces of evolution.

THE PREDICTABILITY OF EVOLUTION

Already we have seen cases in which natural selection dominates other, nonadaptive forces. Also, we've noted the great difficulty in finding potential and real cases of nonadaptive evolution. We could keep on doing this forever, collecting examples in which only adaptive evolution appears to be capable of explaining the patterns we find. But science prefers the experiment if it is possible.

Parallelism and convergence. The ideal experiment would be to place several populations in the same new environment (separately). If evolution is truly adaptive, then each population should evolve to be the same as all the others. One can imagine some best way to occupy this environment; adaptive evolution should achieve it. Nonadaptive evolution, especially random evolution, should not yield the same result in all the separate replicas of the environment.

It turns out that nature has performed such experiments for us innumerable times. When she has, sometimes the results are observable as parallelism or, even more spectacularly, as convergence. In *parallelism*, separate populations begin with similar phenotypes and change markedly, but always resemble each other (Fig. 15-1b). In *convergence*, they start out quite dissimilar and evolve to look (often extraordinarily) alike (Fig. 15-1a).

These "experiments" can be noticed because similar environments tend to develop in many different parts of the world; but the populations that are forced to adapt to them from place to place are often from different species. For example, we might have a population of roses forced to adapt

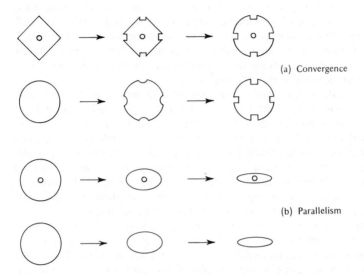

(a) Convergence

(b) Parallelism

Fig. 15-1 An idealization of convergence and parallelism.

to a new desert in Mexico and a population of euphorbias forced to adapt to a similar new desert in Tanzania. If the two populations converge, it must be due to the predictability of evolution. The fact of their convergence is preserved, however, because the two species were so dissimilar to begin with that they each are likely to have kept some fundamental traits which expose their true relationship.

Marsupials and placentals. Do you know not to rub a cat's fur the wrong way? This has given rise to our popular idiom "to rub the wrong way." You never have to worry about a mole, though. Try the next mole you meet. You'll find his fur doesn't have a wrong way. Imagine the mole in his tunnel home. He can't turn around, so he must be able to go in reverse as easily as forward. Backing up could be slightly tougher if his fur stuck out stiffly to the rear. So instead, his fur lies any way it is pushed.

Burrowing underground is an opportunity that exists in many parts of the world. But moles are not so widespread. In Australia and Africa, their place is taken by other groups of animals.

In Australia, most of the native mammals are marsupials. (In contrast, the only marsupial in the United States is the opossum.) Marsupials suckle their young with milk, but they bear them at a very early stage of development, and the young grope into a pouch (the marsupium) covering their mother's nipples. There, warm and well-fed, they grow to the stage at which they can emerge and successfully withstand the elements. To help support this pouch, marsupials have a special bone, called the *epipubic bone*. It is part of their pelvic girdle, but it is not found in other mammals. Marsupials also all have several unusual features of the bones of their skull. All things considered, marsupials are a diverse group of mammals which share many features found in no others. It is reasonable to interpret this as being caused by their having descended from one common ancestor in the remote past (actually, about 100 million years ago).

One of Australia's marsupials looks remarkably like a mole. Not only does it have weak eyes, short tail, rotund body, and broad digging front feet; but, it also resembles the mole in the reversibility of its fur. Apparently, to live successfully like a mole, you've got to look like one. Even though we can't yet say we could have predicted the evolution of the mole, we know from this spectacular convergence that someday we should be able to. One way to explain this is to hypothesize that evolution is primarily adaptive. If evolution were mostly random and nonadaptive, such convergence would be extremely rare or perhaps totally nonexistent.

In addition to the marsupial mole, marsupials have evolved to exploit many other environments similar to those of New World and Old World placentals (placentals are mammals whose young are nurtured for a long time within their mother's womb in placentae—sacs which provide the developing young with a constant, perfect environment). The Tasmanian wolf is the marsupial version of the dog-family carnivore. He runs on his toes to pursue his prey as do wolves. There is a marsupial "flying squirrel" and marsupial "rats" and "mice." (See Fig. 15-2.)

Perhaps the most startling convergence of marsupials and placentals occurred in some animals recently extinct: the saber-toothed carnivores (Fig. 15-3). Sabertooths could open their mouths to a wide enough angle so that their long, sharp saber teeth stuck out. Then, mouths agape, they could plunge their teeth deep into the prey with the strength of unusually powerful neck muscles. That obviously took some doing. There is a long list of special adaptations of the skull that made it possible: the long canine teeth, the sheathlike extensions of the lower jaw that helped prevent the teeth from breaking, the modifications of the skull which permitted the jaws to be held wide open so the teeth protruded, and very robust bones for attachment of the neck muscles.

The placental sabertooths and the marsupial ones (they lived in South America) shared all these adaptations. Imagine how many muscular convergences must have accompanied the skeletal ones! But an identifying feature of the marsupial—the peculiar spilling out of the lacrimal (or eye) bone onto the outer surface of the skull—didn't need to change. And so by looking at the skulls we can easily determine that these sabertooths were descended from ancestors that were totally unlike.

Convergence in deserts. The arid deserts have engendered many characteristic adaptations which demonstrate convergence. Most people know what a cactus looks like. It is a thorny, succulent plant

adaptation: main product of evolution

Fig. 15-2 Some marsupials and their placental ecological equivalents. (From *Life: an introduction to biology* by George Gaylord Simpson and William S. Beck, copyright, 1965, by Harcourt Brace Jovanovich, Inc., and reproduced with their permission.)

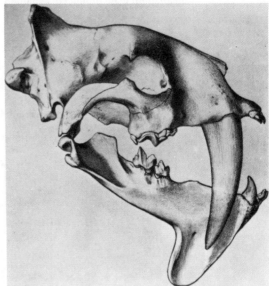

(a)

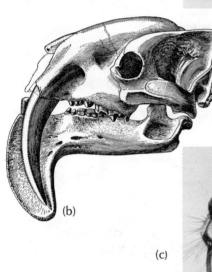

(b)

(c)

Fig. 15-3 Skulls of marsupial (a) and placental (b) saber-tooth. The marsupial saber-tooth is also shown restored (c). (From Scott.)

especially adapted to conserve moisture. It lacks leaves (except for one genus) and carries on photosynthesis in its stems. The trouble with leaves is the great surface area that they have to transpire, and thus lose water. All cacti are native to the New World and are closely related to roses. Ever see a cactus flower? In Old World deserts, similar environmental pressures have caused an entirely different family, the Euphorbiaceae, to evolve the same set of adaptations as the Cactaceae (Fig. 15-4). However, their flowers remain like regular euphorbias, and so we can easily tell them from cacti.

One of the sophisticated convergences of cacti and other arid-zone plants has occurred in a biochemical system. In order to carry on photosynthesis, plants require CO_2. To get it, their stomates must be open to the atmosphere. But in addition to collecting CO_2, open stomates lose water. (This can be a serious loss of water, for CO_2 is required when there is also sunlight and the desert heat that goes with sunlight.) Cacti and Crassulaceae (thick-leaved plants like jade plant and *Kalanchoe*) have solved this problem the same way. Their stomates open *at night* when desert humidity is high, heat is very low, and water loss is minimal. The CO_2 is stored at this time on special molecules—probably the same in both families. When daylight and heat return, the plants close their stomates and use the CO_2 they have stored during the night.

Of course, deserts have influenced the animals, as well. The sparsely vegetated deserts of North America harbor the kangaroo rat (many species), but the deserts of Africa and the Near East have jerboas (Fig. 15-5). We know these to be different because, for one thing, all members of the kangaroo rat's superfamily (including pocket gophers and some rather ordinary ratlike rodents) have fur-lined external pockets in their cheeks. Jerboas do not.

In addition to their many obvious external morphological adaptations, desert rodents have adapted physiologically to the general absence of drinking water in the desert by having very concentrated urine—little water, much nitrogenous waste is excreted. This requires them to have long Henle's loops in the nephrons of their kidneys. In this way, both forms—kangaroo rats and jerboas—achieve similarly concentrated urine. The concentration of urine is measured by the ratio of salt concentration in urine to that in the blood plasma. This ratio is often called the urine-plasma ratio, or U/P. The following data (from Schmidt-Nielsen) will serve to exemplify U/P values and show you just how superior desert rodents are at avoiding water loss in their urine.

Species	U/P
Man	4.2
Pack rat	7.0
Sheep	7.6
Lab rat	8.9
Cat	9.9
Kangaroo rat	14.0
Jerboa	16.0

(a) *Astrophytum asterias*

(b) *Euphorbia symmetrica*

(c) *Cereus validus*

(d) *Euphorbia heptagona*

Fig. 15-4 Cacti and similar-looking *Euphorbia*. (a, d, e, and f from Dr. A. B. Graf, author of cyclopedia *Exotica*. b from *The succulent Euphorbieae,* by A. White, R. A. Dyer, and B. L. Sloane; Abbey Garden Press, Pasadena, 1941. c from *The Cactaceae,* by N. L. Britton, and J. N. Rose, 1923.)

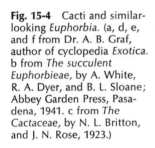

(e) *Cleistocactus buchtienii*

(f) *Euphorbia morinii*

(a)

(b)

Fig. 15-5 A bannertail kangaroo rat (a) and a jerboa (b). (*Dipodomys* courtesy Prof. K. Schmidt-Nielsen. Jerboa from Brehm's *Tierleben*, Bibliographisches Institut, Leipzig and Vienna, 1914.)

Carnivorous plants. Boggy places often have acidic soil. Such soil is harmful to bacteria. But bacteria are the organisms which cause the breakdown of the protein components of dead material. Without bacteria, such decay is extremely slow, and living plants can't obtain enough nitrogen. Many unrelated plants have solved this nutrient problem by becoming insectivorous. A trap of some kind collects raw meat and the plant's own enzymes break it down for nitrogen. (See Fig. 15-6.)

Woodland mice. Temperate woodlands grow on each side of the Atlantic Ocean. A common resident of such European forests is *Apodemus sylvaticus*, the wood mouse (Fig. 15-7a). *Apodemus* is a member of the Muridae, the same family as the house mouse and sewer rat (both

(a)

Fig. 15-6 These plants trap and digest insects to supply themselves with nitrogen: Venus flytrap (a), pitcher plant (b), and sundew (c). (Photographs by Hugh Spencer.)

of these are recent "imports" to America). In an American forest, we will find a member of the hamster family, Cricetidae. Its name is *Peromyscus maniculatus,* the deer mouse (Fig. 15-7b). Saying these two aren't in the same family is saying they are no more closely related than a skunk to a lion, or a cow to a deer. Yet, students of vertebrate biology gawk in disbelief at their first sight of the mouse from the other side of the Atlantic. The two species appear almost identical. The only way to distinguish them quickly is to examine their molar teeth: *Apodemus* has three rows of cusps on its molars; *Peromyscus* only two.

More cases could be brought out of the closet. Notice the large number of examples I have drawn from the mammal world. That's because I am most interested in mammals. An ornithologist would have regaled you with bird stories, an entomologist with examples of insects. Convergence and parallelism have been long known in many areas. How could they occur if evolution were a random or nonadaptive phenomenon?

(b)

(c)

(a)

(b)

Fig. 15-7 The wood mouse of the Old World (a) and the deer mouse of the New World (b). These rodents are in different families. (Wood mouse photograph by John Markham. Deer mouse photograph by Jack Dermid.)

MIMICRY ALSO SHOWS
THE PREDICTABLE CHARACTER OF EVOLUTION

Another set of situations is known in which we can say in advance that we know what a fit phenotype will be like. These situations are collectively called mimicry. In mimicry, organisms must somehow appear like other organisms. Hence, only those organisms that resemble certain others are fit; only these can be successful mimics.

Batesian mimicry. One kind of mimicry is called Batesian mimicry, after the famous nineteenth-century naturalist H. W. Bates, its describer. Batesian mimicry requires at least three and perhaps four kinds of organisms. There must be a consumer who is capable of learning the patterns or colors (or odors, etc.) of his favorite foods, as well as obnoxious foods. There must be an obnoxious food species (perhaps it tastes bitter or is poisonous), and a tasty species which resembles the distasteful one. Probably there must also be another tasty food which is dissimilar to the distasteful one. The distasteful species is called the model; the one that resembles it is the mimic.

Clearly the tasty mimic relies on the consumer's ability to remember the distasteful model. But also the mimic relies on its resemblance to the model. The advantage to the mimic is that since it resembles an unpalatable form, it is consumed less often. Its death rate is reduced and so its fitness is improved.

In the past decade or two, evidence that Batesian mimicry is real has been accumulating. Because people see colors and depend to a great extent on vision to collect sensory information, it is understandable that mimicry of color pattern has been most often noticed. Because birds also use their eyes to gather most of their information about the world and because they see color, too, we think they often are the teachable consumers responsible for this kind of mimicry.

One of the most famous cases of Batesian mimicry occurs in butterflies. The monarch butterfly (Fig. 15-8c) feeds on milkweed which contains cardiac glycosides. Apparently, having fed on milkweed as a larva, the adult butterfly is rendered extremely bad tasting. The viceroy butterfly (vice, meaning "instead of"; roy, meaning "the king") looks much like the monarch (see Fig. 15-8b), but it cannot tolerate milkweed. As a larva it feeds on nontoxic plants. When the viceroy emerges, it is a delectable potential morsel for any bird that can tell it from the monarch. But by mimicking the monarch, it has made that distinction a formidable problem for the bird. Few humans can do it without training. The bird is forced to look elsewhere for its food.

Jane van Zandt Brower showed the importance of distasteful models to the tasty mimic. She actually fed viceroys to caged, inexperienced scrub jays. The birds ate them readily. When fed monarchs, they sampled a few and then wouldn't eat any more. Once a jay had learned just how ob-

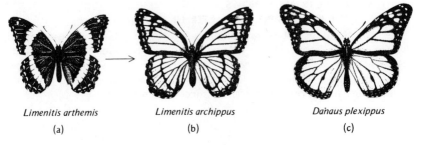

Limenitis arthemis	*Limenitis archippus*	*Daṅaus plexippus*
(a)	(b)	(c)

Fig. 15-8 A Batesian mimic, model, and the more primitive pattern of the mimic's close relative. The monarch butterfly, *Danaus plexippus* (c) is the model and is distasteful. Its tasty mimic is the viceroy, *Limenitis archippus* (b). *L. arthemis* (a) is thought to resemble the pattern from which *L. archippus* evolved. (From L. P. Brower, *Ecological chemistry.* Copyright © by Scientific American, Inc. All rights reserved.)

noxious monarchs are, it refused both monarchs and viceroys—even if, in its naive state, it had previously feasted on viceroys.

Lincoln Brower has shown that milkweed is the cause of the monarch's distastefulness. He succeeded (after much effort) at raising monarchs on cabbage. Naive captive birds gobbled up these good-tasting items, even though, as we have seen, other birds quickly learned to avoid monarchs reared on milkweed.

Recently, Cook and Brower and their colleagues tried a beautifully simple technique for investigating mimicry in the field. They painted some North American day-flying moths, *Hyalophora promethea*, to be brightly colored mimics; they camouflaged others. The ones painted as mimics were colored to resemble the color and pattern of the distasteful tropical butterfly, *Parides anchises*. The camouflage pattern was merely dark paint.

These two types of paint-jobs were released simultaneously in the tropics on the Island of Trinidad. Then they were collected in a way similar to that used by Kettlewell (Chapter 10).

In three years of work, moths were released and recaptured the next day at 26 places not previously visited by the team of workers. Results were as follows:

	Mimics	Camouflaged
Released	315	319
Recaptured	93	72
Recaptured (%)	29.5	22.6

These data show an approximate 30% advantage for the mimics in the first day. Soon, as the researchers continued releasing moths in the same places, the advantage disappeared. Presumably the predators learned what was happening.

Furthermore, when the team returned to Trinidad and investigated 32 new sites in a period of extreme insect scarcity a year later, they could find no advantage to mimicry. Surely, the birds that remained in the face of the insect decline could not afford to be as fussy in trying food. This clearly demonstrates that mimics depend for their advantage on predators with an abundance of alternate, nonmimetic, good-tasting victims.

Mullerian mimicry. There are other kinds of mimicry, too. In one, Mullerian mimicry, two species converge in appearance. Both species are somehow obnoxious, and it is reasonable to suppose they each suffer less if they can combine to teach the consumer to avoid one pattern. Evolutionists think this explains the common black and yellow striped pattern of stinging hymenopterans (hornets, bees, and so forth.) But count the wings on that next yellow-and-black bee. If there are two, it is a fly! Some such flies are Batesian mimics. Others actually eat the bees they mimic; they use the mimicry as a form of concealment from their prey. (See Fig. 15-9.)

Mimicking flax. Another unnamed but very interesting kind of mimicry has been discovered. In this case, the mimic is a plant, as is the model. The consumer is man.

Humans have been cultivating various plants for thousands of years. Our relationship with them is mutually beneficial since we benefit and in return save some of the seeds and replant our fields with them over and over. Most everyone realizes that the range and abundance of useful plants has increased markedly under agricultural practice. Thus we actually have increased the fitness of our food and fiber plants.

One weedy species, *Camelina sativa*, a kind of mustard, has taken advantage of these facts. Normally, it grows in open fields or along roadsides. It

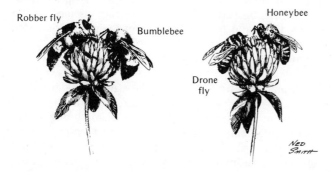

Fig. 15-9 Fly mimics of bees. The robber fly eats bumblebees. It is known, therefore, as an aggressive mimic. The drone fly is probably a Batesian mimic of the honeybee. (From R. L. Smith, *Ecology and field biology,* illustrated by Ned Smith, Harper & Row, 1966.)

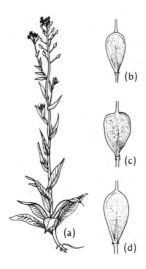

Fig. 15-10 Forms of *Camelina sativa* seeds. The two larger seeds are found in plants growing in flax fields. (From G. Ledyard Stebbins, *Processes of organic evolution,* © 1966. By permission of Prentice-Hall, Inc. Englewood Cliffs, N.J.)

is a bushy plant and fairly short. Varieties of *Camelina sativa* have evolved, however, to invade fields of flax. These are tall, as is flax, and they don't branch much. The most astonishing change has occurred to their seeds: They are larger than usual. In fact, they are about flax-sized. (See Fig. 15-10.)

Why have they mimicked flax seeds in size? The farmer winnows his impure batches of seeds in order to try to obtain nearly pure batches of flax seed. To do this, he casts his seeds in front of a wind machine. The machine blows them a variable distance away depending on their size and aerodynamic properties. The flax seeds, being of one species, all tend to be blown the same distance. Seeds of other plants—except those of the mimic form of *C. sativa*—fall nearer or farther from the machine. These members of *C. sativa* have evolved various larger sizes and shapes—all of which tend to cause them to be carried the same distance as flax. So the farmer is forced to carry them into his field and plant them with his crop. Since this weed is useless to man, its mimicry of flax results in some inevitable decline in agricultural productivity.

Chemical mimicry in trees. In 1964, the Czech biologist Karel Slama came to Harvard University for a period of research with the noted American insect-development biologist Caroll Williams. Slama brought with him his favorite experimental animal, a bug, *Pyrrhocoris apterus*. They wanted to study the development of this bug, but although Slama had not had any previous difficulty in raising it, the bugs refused to metamorphose at Cambridge, Massachusetts. As far as anyone could see, they were just being ornery; conditions were perfect.

Slama and Williams reviewed the procedure for raising the bugs and discovered only one difference between the methods in the two places. In

Cambridge, the bugs were given a piece of Scott paper towel on which to walk. Scott paper products are not used in Czechoslovakia. That trivial difference turned out to be exactly the cause of Slama's failure to raise the bugs in America. Not only Scott products, but many other American paper products prevented bug metamorphosis. All tested American newspapers did, too. But European and Japanese papers were usually fine.

One of the things Williams has done much work with is an insect hormone called juvenile hormone. This hormone prevents an insect from undergoing metamorphosis. It maintains "larvahood." But how could juvenile hormone get into American paper products?

Paper products come from trees and the trees put the hormone there. Many American needle-leaf trees—including balsam fir, eastern hemlock, American larch (tamarack), and Pacific yew—synthesize a chemical which has been named juvabione. The merest touch of juvabione prevents phyrrhocorid bugs' eggs from hatching and their larvae from developing into reproductive adults. Juvabione mimics chemically the juvenile hormone normally found in the bugs, but with one major difference. In the bugs, the substance is controlled by the bugs; it can be destroyed when it becomes harmful. But the bugs have no control over the trees, and so they simply cannot live on them. Other trees—such as European larch, short-leaf pine, and red spruce—show little or no juvabione activity and are therefore not protected from pyrrhocorids.

In all the many instances of mimicry, it is clear that the phenotype has emerged in an adaptive form. We can always put our finger on the precise best phenotype for the mimicry to be advantageous. And evolution seems to have been able to produce such adaptation quite often.

Since evolution seems so potentially, precisely predictable, judging from mimicry and from convergence and parallelism, I personally am constrained to dismiss as unreasonable the view that phenotypes have been determined at random by drift or mutation. Surely the results of evolution suggest these forces have been unimportant. Adaptation has been evolution's major product. So far, all that scientists have needed in order to account for adaptation is natural selection.

16 group selection and the evolution of survival

THE THEORY

Imagine that a species is subdivided into separate populations. Each population has a certain probability of disappearing, which probability is in part caused by the heritable phenotypes of its members. Populations with higher tendencies toward extinction, then, will tend to be replaced by populations with lower chances of extinction. Such substitutions constitute the process of group selection. *Group selection is the gradual replacement of tenuous populations by more tenacious ones.* It is, therefore, a mechanism of evolution and different from any discussed so far. In this chapter, we examine its reality and importance because an understanding of group selection is crucial to our evaluation of some of the suggested methods of population control.

There is only one case in which group selection is known to be a necessary part of the explanation of evolution. It is the odd and beautifully analyzed case of *t*, the allele for taillessness in house mice, *Mus musculus*. The evolutionary forces affecting this allele's frequency also include genetic drift and an altogether mystifying phenomenon called sperm selection.

The normal allele, *T*, can be replaced by any one of a vast number of mutations which we may simply call *t*, although they may differ in important respects. The phenotype of a male who is *tt* is variable. Often this male is an anomaly; he may lack kidneys or his entire mesoderm. If the *tt* male doesn't die, he is totally sterile. Therefore, his fitness is always zero.

The heterozygous male does not have impaired fitness with the very serious exception that some of his progeny will be *tt* males. Otherwise he is robust and fertile.

For some unknown physiological reason, when a *Tt* male produces sperm, they are almost all *t*-bearing. A normal meiosis would, of course, yield 50% *t*-bearing sperm. But this does not happen. Instead, either in the meiosis itself, the *t*-bearing chromosome destroys its normal-bearing match; or in the semen, the *t*-bearing sperm render the others dead, weak, or ineffectual. In any case about 95% of the *Tt* male's progeny receive a *t* from their father.

Lewontin has found that 19 new mutations to *t* were not all like this. He compared *t*-sperm production by heterozygotes possessing a new mutation with *t*-sperm production by wild heterozygotes.

t produced (%)	New mutations	Wild heterozygotes
99–90	3	16
89–80	1	3
79–60	0	0
59–55	2	0
54–45	8	0
44–40	3	0
39–30	2	0

As you see, some new mutations to *t* yielded only 30% *t*-sperm; many were near the normal 50%; and some were as high as 99%. Thus, there is nothing physiologically necessary about an effective minimum *t*-sperm production value of about 80%. But that is what was found in naturally occurring heterozygote males. Why are no wild mice known with values less than 80%?

In order to explain these values and also to explain the frequency of the *t*-allele in mouse populations, Lewontin had to build a complicated statistical computer program which simulated nature. He used a method which, because it contains an important element of chance, is called a *Monte Carlo* method.

We shall not go into the method here, but we can look at the natural elements of the model. Across the interior of the continent, mice are divided up into small populations living in barns. Lewontin estimates from his work that these populations are quite small: about six females and two males in each population. A colony free of *t* is in good genetic health and has a high probability of surviving. But once a colony receives any immigrant with a *t*, its future is jeopardized. In fact, the population is doomed. Heterozygous males flood the population with *t*-alleles. Eventually, by genetic drift, both males are bound to be sterile *tt* homozygotes. These males occupy the females sexually, but with no result. The adults die off without issue and the colony becomes extinct.

Since recolonization of the area will tend to occur by mice from *t*-free populations, group selection is minimizing the frequency of *t*. Drift, by increasing the extinction rate, is maximizing the power of the group selection. Furthermore, natural selection also works against *t*, because *tt* males have zero fitness and the *Tt* has many inviable or infertile offspring. Only sperm selection keeps t from disappearing. Thus, only t-alleles with a high value of sperm selection remain.

In order to arrive at a quantitative prediction of sperm selection and t frequency, Lewontin found it absolutely necessary to build group selection into his model. Natural selection alone simply did not give an accurate prediction.

Group selection works effectively to depress the t frequency because the mouse population is subdivided into many very, very small subpopulations, each with a good chance of extinction. Otherwise, it would be most unimportant that an extinct colony is likely to be replaced by immigrants from t-free colonies. That sort of subdivision seems to be the best way to produce strong, effective group selection. A paradox: Lewontin noted that group selection, the process which minimizes extinction, is important only in situations where extinction probability is very, very high.

Having faced the problem of mutation versus natural selection, you can easily understand why this should be so. Mutation does not effectively counter natural selection because mutation occurs so infrequently. Only after natural selection's work is almost complete, only when there are but a very few of the less fit phenotypes left to replace, is selective replacement a rare enough event that mutation can balance it. Similarly, only if group extinction occurs very often will it be competent to override the effects of natural selection or even to contribute significantly to the composition of a population.

Moreover, in order to benefit from group selection, a population must be subdivided into many, many groups like the mice, so that while each group faces a very high chance of extinction, there is little likelihood that all groups and thus the whole species will disappear. A population organized into only one or a few large groups will probably disappear when faced by strong group selection because the high group-extinction rates necessary for group selection will no doubt exterminate the species before it can be helped.

DO ANIMALS HUSBAND
THEIR FOOD SUPPLIES?

The individual versus the group. In the case of the t-locus, as in most cases, group selection and natural selection tend to produce the same result. But the thing that makes group selection so tantalizing is that it may oppose natural selection. When it does, group selection must not be thought of as anti-adaptive—it is, after all, promoting survival.

In the past decade, a controversy has raged over which of these two forces is superior in power when they are at loggerheads. V. C. Wynne-Edwards has produced a thick and influential book full of situations in which animal populations appear to be regulated well below the levels at which they might consume all their resources. They seem not to allow themselves to grow large enough to endanger the future of the things they eat. He feels these situations can only be explained by invoking group selection: individuals limit their own reproduction to maximize the chance their group will survive.

G. C. Williams has retaliated with a slim, closely reasoned volume showing that so far it has always been possible to explain the known facts with a hypothesis based only on natural selection, that is, on the maximization of individual reproduction.

How is it possible for natural selection to work against group survival? The key to this question is the realization that fitness pertains to individuals. We *must* speak not of the fitness of a species, but of the *average fitness* of its individual members. It is often said that natural selection works for the good of the species, but this is wrong. Sometimes the best reproducers are those that act selfishly. Whenever this occurs, selection acts in favor of these selfish individuals and against the good of the group.

Extinction from overexploitation. The best understood case of antagonism between natural and group selection concerns species which must kill food to survive. Clearly such a species will become extinct if it can hunt down every last morsel. It will have destroyed its own food supply. Furthermore, Robert MacArthur and I have shown that the predator need not be even that proficient; a species that can hunt well enough to reproduce successfully on a fairly low population of its resource species may also be in danger of extinction.

Yet, that is precisely the direction in which natural selection is pushing the exploiter. Any phenotype which can hunt more successfully or kill more successfully will tend to have a higher fitness than one less successful. So group selection and natural selection are opposed.

Does group selection stave off some or all extinctions of exploiters? Do exploiters tend to husband their resources because this avoids extinction? Perhaps you will realize from the case of the *t*-allele that this evolutionary outcome is unlikely. If what we see around us are species that are prudent (for whatever reason), then group selection cannot be the cause of their prudence. Group selection will be weak because the extinction rate is low. If group selection were responsible, we should expect to see a variety of situations running from the prudent to the dangerously proficient. And we should expect extinction from overly intense harvesting to be a relatively common affair—with natural selection constantly producing overexploitation and group selection constantly picking off the culprits. In showing the predominance of prudence among exploiters, Wynne-Edwards himself has produced the most cogent argument against prudence having evolved for its survival value!

Pseudo-prudence. A favorite example of the prudent consumer is a rodent, the lemming. Lemmings live peacefully in the northern tundras, where they eat a diet of grasses and sedges. Their population grows, and then one year there is an irruption. Lemmings are all over—but dying. In Scandinavia lemmings are known to march aimlessly, sometimes right into the ocean, sometimes off a cliff. Food *appears* to be abundant, so the explanation has been that the lemmings are committing suicide to prevent destruction of their food supply. "They are doing it for the good of the species."

However, things are not as they first appear to be. Working in Alaska, Schultz has found that although food is indeed calorically abundant, it is poor in minerals, especially phosphorous.[1] Without such nutritional value, the food cannot support life, let alone reproduction. The marching lemmings are indeed starving to death, starving for minerals. Their wandering is an attempt to find themselves a better place to live. Presumably a few find an isolated patch of grass here or there and survive. If so, natural selection does indeed explain the migration. Suicides are just a consequence of the tumult and the fact that Scandinavia has a lot of water and numerous cliffs. In Alaska, with its more uniform environment, lemming irruptions occur every three or four years, but they are unaccompanied by marches.

Miller, Watson, and Jenkins have discovered that a similar situation exists in the red grouse of Scotland. You may recall from Chapter 2 that grouse eat the shrub, heather. During irruptions, the heather is nitrogen-poor, and the grouse die without much reproduction. Their bodies, which had tied up so much of the nutrient, now rot into the soil and return the nitrogen to the heather. The stage is set for another round of grouse population growth.

The grouse investigators took their analysis one step further by adding ammonium (a nitrogen compound) to the heather fields. Sure enough, the grouse population did not crash but kept on growing.

Neither lemming nor grouse appear to be maintaining low populations for the sake of husbanding their food supplies.

EVOLUTION OF INCIDENTAL PRUDENCE

If exploiters do not husband the population that they victimize, what prevents natural selection from obliterating them by making them perfect engines of destruction? Broadly speaking, two things. First, their victims can evolve protection. And second, the exploiters themselves are a phenotypic compromise; they have many other functions to perform well in order to be fit. Some of these functions will be performed sufficiently well only at the expense of predatory perfection.

Naturally, evolutionary pressure on the victim forces the predator to be prudent in spite of itself. Furthermore, when the predator is really good at his task, the selective pressure on it to improve is slight, but the selective

---

[1] Schultz' interpretation is still controversial. But there is no evidence that lemmings die for the good of their species and some day an explanation like Schultz' (in individualistic spirit if not in detail) will no doubt be settled upon.

pressure on its victim is great. On the other hand, suppose the predator is relatively unproficient; then it is the victim which should evolve very slowly, and the predator which should evolve very rapidly. This leads us to a prediction of another evolutionary standoff as in mutation versus selection or in allele versus allele in heterosis. At some intermediate proficiency, a steady state is reached. At that proficiency, the predator cannot ever become much more or much less proficient.

It is possible to show that because both species are phenotypic compromises, the actual rate of evolution at the steady state is usually zero. Were this not true, the compromises would be violated. So both species have phenotypes that are relatively stable. Only rarely will a new allele come along to produce change. If, at the steady state of proficiency, the predator is prudent enough not to overexploit its food, it is so by accident. The prudence has evolved incidentally to the factors determining the steady state.

And a species whose selective steady state is imprudent will, of course, disappear. Group selection seems almost powerless to save it. Therefore, whenever we observe a population which appears to practice prudent population control on itself, we should suspect we are observing an illusion. Further examination should produce sound reasons for the illusion—reasons that emphasize how the individuals of that population, by acting as they do, have maximized their own individual fitness.

WASPS VERSUS FLIES

Though exploiters and victims in nature evolve at a rate near zero, if they are brought into the laboratory we should expect them to begin evolving rapidly. The laboratory is a radically different environment, and we would hardly expect them to begin at equilibrium in it. In fact, because a laboratory cage is so simple and so confining, we should expect to have conferred a large advantage on the predator. The victim should rapidly evolve better defenses. The predator on the other hand, is at such an advantage that it might even be able to sacrifice some predatory proficiency in order to improve other parts of its phenotype for other tasks.

David Pimentel and his coworkers have actually tamed such an exploitation for laboratory study and followed its evolution. Their predator is a parasitic wasp which lays its eggs in the bodies of larval flies. The eggs hatch inside and destroy the flies from within.

If Pimentel puts a population of wasps and flies together in a cage, the flies are soon extinct from imprudent exploitation. The wasps quickly follow. But he designed a clever maze of 30 population cages in which this doesn't happen. His cages are interconnected by little tubes designed so that flies can easily go through them, but the wasps have some trouble. (See Fig. 16-1.) Thus some of the time the flies can flee effectively and be hidden from the wasps. In this complex system, the wasps and flies do not

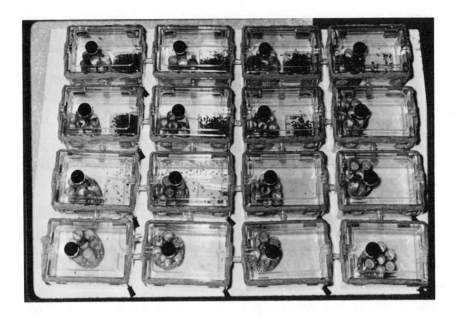

Fig. 16-1 Pimentel's cage-maze. Note the tubes through which wasps and flies can travel from cell to cell. This is the 16-cell maze and differs only in numbers from the 30-cell maze. (From D. Pimentel, *The American Naturalist* 97:144, and used with permission of The University of Chicago Press.)

become extinct. They are allowed the time it takes to evolve in their new environment.

To be able to observe evolutionary changes, Pimentel kept control wasps and flies for comparison. The control flies were not subjected to victimization by wasps; control wasps were fed an abundance of flies in a simple environment.

After only 10 to 15 generations, Pimentel was able to measure a marked change in the populations. Most of it was due to the flies which had become much more resistant to parasitization. But in addition, the experimental wasps were a bit less proficient than the control wasps (Table 16-1).

The decline of wasp proficiency is very interesting. There are two possible explanations for it. Either group selection had decreased wasp proficiency, or, in the lab environment where host flies were relatively easy to come by, the wasps were forced by natural selection to improve some other aspect of their phenotype at the expense of parasitic proficiency. From the careful way in which Pimentel did his experiment, we must believe, at least tentatively, that group selection and not natural selection was the key to the wasps' change. Why?

First, look at the cage-maze. (See Fig. 16-2.) It has all the elements required for rapid group selection. The populations are subdivided into

TABLE 16-1 THE EVOLUTION OF PARASITIC WASPS AND THEIR HOST
FLIES WHEN SUBJECT TO A SIMPLIFIED ENVIRONMENT[a]

	Results	
Populations tested	Number of young wasps per mother wasp[b]	Percentage of flies successfully parasitized by wasps[b]
Control[c] wasps, Control flies	140	52
Control wasps, Evolved flies	68	46
Evolved wasps, Control flies	123	53
Evolved wasps, Evolved flies	46	40

Source: Pimentel.
[a] The environment is simplified in that wasps find it easier to discover flies
than in nature.
[b] When tested under standard conditions outside the simplified environment.
[c] Controls were never exposed to the simplified environment.

many small subpopulations. Within each cell, the chance of extinction of
the subpopulation is very high. Therefore, wasps that parasitize flies less
proficiently will last a bit longer and colonize cells that are free of wasps
with a bit higher probability. All of this is reminiscent of the t-allele in mice!

Second, we must realize that the control wasps had an even easier time
getting hosts than the experimentals. If natural selection were solely responsible for the decrease in wasp proficiency, we should have expected the
control wasps to have decreased even more than the experimentals!

There is but one small reservation. Controls and experimentals are not
being kept in identical environments with respect to nonfly variables. To
be completely sure of our conclusion, we need to house controls in a cage-
maze under identical light, humidity, and temperature conditions as
experimentals. Then, we could pump in a continual superabundance of
flies to the control wasps to guard them from the threat of extinction and
force of group selection.

Though we can't be sure of group selection until that control experiment
is performed, the evidence definitely favors it. Yet it is also possible that
natural selection was simultaneously at work. What would you add to the
experimental tests to measure it?

RABBIT FEVER

No one ever imagined that the European rabbit, *Oryctolagus
cuniculus*, would become a pest when introduced to Australia. But that is
precisely what happened. Rabbits bred like same until the tortured land

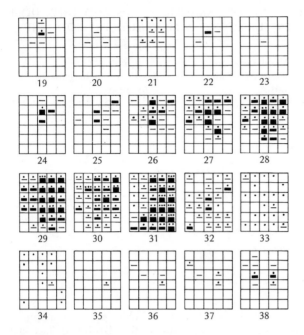

Fig. 16-2 Wasp and housefly densities throughout the 30-cell cage-maze illustrated from weeks 19 through 38. Adult wasp densities (·) are indicated by the following: (·), 1–100 wasps; (· ·), 101–200 wasps; and (· · ·), 200+ wasps. Housefly pupal densities (—) are indicated by a similar scheme. Notice the many extinctions of local wasp populations. (From D. Pimentel, *The American Naturalist* 97:160, and and used with permission of The University of Chicago Press.)

overflowed with them, and sheep pasture became severely damaged. There was no hope of controlling the bunny population by any means other than a virulent, disastrous disease. (See Fig. 16-3.)

In a South American cottontail population, researchers discovered a viral disease called myxomatosis. The myxoma virus (a pox virus) didn't harm the cottontail *(Sylvilagus)* much, but it was 100% lethal to *Oryctolagus*. Introduction of the disease into Australia has brought the rabbit population down to about 1% of its previous level.

Frank Fenner has done some marvelous work in following and explaining the evolution of the rabbit and virus in the past two decades. He has determined that the rabbits have now developed considerable genetic resistance to the disease—though it is still fatal in 40% of all cases. Fenner, of course, kept the original strain of the virus in the deep freeze as a control. With this strain as a reference disease, from time to time he compared the natural resistance of wild rabbits with the resistance of the original population of wild rabbits.

Originally, there was also a control colony of rabbits. Unfortunately this colony died out. But before it did, it seemed to yield evidence that the virus which Fenner recovered from wild rabbits had diminished in virulence. Tests to determine if the virus had lost virulence continued on lab rabbits (they are also *Oryctolagus cuniculus*). In 1970, wild myxoma killed only three-fourths of the lab rabbits it infected. (See Table 16-2.)

Fenner's explanation for this relies on natural selection, not group selection. He notes that the virus is transmitted by mosquitos which do not bite

TABLE 16-2 LETHALITY CHANGES IN MYXOMATOSIS

Time and strain	Percentage of wild rabbits killed[a]	Percentage of lab rabbits killed[a]
Ca. 1950, by control (SLS) virus	99+	99+
Ca. 1970, by control (SLS) virus	~40	99+
Ca. 1970, by recaptured virus	~25	~75

Source: Fenner and Ratcliffe, and a conversation with Dr. Fenner.
[a] Percentages are approximate.

Fig. 16-3 The devastation by rabbits in New South Wales, Australia is splendidly depicted in this photo. This is *one* picture, not two! The difference between the denuded left half and the grassy right half is due to the rabbit-excluding fence at which the three men are looking. (Courtesy of the Australian Information Service and *Country Life* (NSW) Newspaper Pty. Ltd.)

dead rabbits. Transmission does not occur until the virus reaches a very high concentration in the rabbit's blood. Too benign a strain of myxoma never reaches a high enough concentration. Too lethal a strain reaches concentration too quickly and kills the rabbit only five days after reaching it. A moderately strong virus, however, pumps progeny out into mosquitos for 15 days or more. The key to a myxoma's fitness is its transmissibility, *not* its lethality.

COEVOLUTION

A rat race to end all rat races is locked up in the evolution of exploiter and victim. Since both species are evolving against each other but at precisely the same low rate, they should adapt to each other continually and for eons. Each species should develop more sophisticated means of dealing with the other. But neither should ever get ahead.

When species are tied to each other through eons of evolutionary time, their continuing mutual adaptation is called coevolution. Many examples of coevolution have been discovered in various exploitational relationships. H. H. Ross hypothesized that some marine mollusks and the microorganisms on which they feed have been tied to each other and have been changing continuously for hundreds of millions of years.

To me, the most impressive cases of exploitational coevolution exist in chemical adaptations of herbivores and plants. For example, Paul Ehrlich and Peter Raven have cataloged both the toxins produced by plants and the detoxification powers of the butterflies that feed on them as caterpillars. They have found that when a butterfly has a good detoxification mechanism, it is a very restricted feeder. It feeds almost exclusively on the plant or plants that produce the poison which it finds harmless. (See Fig. 16-4.) It does seem that butterfly and plant are tied together and have been evolving together for eons. Butterflies which lack the ability to resist poisons are much more general in their feeding habits.

We have already examined one case of coevolution: the monarch butterfly and the cardiac glycosides that are found in the milkweed they eat. Not only is this poison benign to the butterfly larvae, but they actually take advantage of it, storing it up and using it to repel their own potential predators.

A similar situation obtains with the cinnabar moth, *Callimorpha jacobaeae* and its food, plants of the genus *Senecio* (a member of the sunflower family). *Senecio* contains a poisonous alkaloid called senecionine and other poisons, as well. These protect it from most herbivores. But *Callimorpha* is immune. As it feeds, it actually accumulates the poison in its body, thereby protecting itself from vertebrate predators of every sort (Aplin, Benn, and Rothschild).

When two species are brought together in nature, despite the fact that they have not previously been associated, there can be great trouble. Various tree pests, like the spruce budworm, when first introduced to an

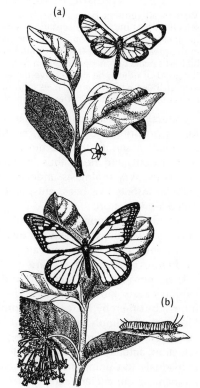

Fig. 16-4 Examples of coadapted plants and butterflies. (a) *Thridia themisto* and a nightshade. Nightshades contain the poisonous alkaloid solanin. *T. themisto* tolerates it. (b) *Danaus plexippus* and milkweed. Milkweed has cardiac glycoside, which is poisonous to other butterflies. The common name of *D. plexippus* is the monarch butterfly. (From P. R. Ehrlich and P. H. Raven, butterflies and plants. Copyright © 1967 by Scientific American, Inc. All rights reserved.)

area, ravish the trees and, flying in the face of their own survival interests, threaten to destroy their own food supply. American elms have been greatly damaged by dutch elm disease. And the American chestnut, once master of huge tracts of northeastern forest (so I am told), appears to be in its death throes under the onslaught of a totally imprudent fungus, the chestnut blight.

This emphasizes not only the great mutual adjustments that must be made by species which are successful members of an association, but also that sometimes such adjustments may not occur. Some associations of species are doomed. They do not get the chance to coevolve. Furthermore, even when species *have* coevolved there is no evidence that this has occurred because of any force pushing the predator to husband its resources. For example, Voûte reports that the cinnabar moth often entirely defoliates its food plant, *Senecio jacobea*. Coevolution occurs *as a result of the fact* that two species manage to interact without destroying each other. The opposite hypothesis, that two species don't destroy each other because they have coevolved, appears to me to be untenable.

ALTRUISTIC HUMAN BEHAVIOR

Most or all sentient beings have been developed in such a manner through natural selection, that pleasurable sensations serve as their habitual guides. We see this in the pleasure from exertion . . . , in the pleasure of our daily meals, and especially in the pleasure derived from sociability and from loving our families. . . . The highest satisfaction is derived from following . . . the social instincts. If [one] acts for the good of others, he will receive the approbation of his fellow men and gain the love of those with whom he lives; and this latter gain undoubtedly is the highest pleasure on this earth. Charles Darwin, *Autobiography*

Natural selection readily explains why a parent should risk its own life for its offspring: no offspring, no fitness. Similarly, selection explains why any relative should trouble himself for kin: his kin share his phenotype to some extent, and he is thus increasing the fitness of his own phenotype. This is the way biologists understand the sacrificial behavior of mothers, of colonial insects like bees, ants, and termites, and of rich uncles. It is often called kin selection.

But suppose a nonswimming stranger falls into deep water? If you jump in to try a rescue, you risk your own life; but you don't increase your fitness if you succeed. People who are heroes ought to be selected against. And yet heroics persist. Why? There are three general types of answers.

First, heroism and such are truly unselfish. They are produced by a natural cause, group selection. The individual actually diminishes his own fitness, but thereby increases the probability that his population will survive. Most people simply don't believe this is true today. Perhaps, they say, in eons past when human populations were numerous and small, such group selection actually occurred. But today our populations are too large, our individuals too unimportant to society as a whole. If altruism exists as the remnant of the ancient activity of group selection, it ought to be disappearing.

But even within ancient small populations, anyone not altruistic had a higher fitness than his fellows. So selfishness would take over, and the population lived or perished on the strength of selfishness. A balance between selfishness and altruism evolved. Do you believe any human population would become extinct if heroism died out? Suppose all degrees of unselfishness and charity disappeared?

Second, most or all apparently altruistic behavior is really not altruistic, but increases the fitness of the individual who performs it. If this were so, of course, natural selection would explain heroism. There are many possible arguments for this answer.

Proponents point out that primitive human societies were little more than large families in which the life you saved would usually be your cousin's. If this is the reason for altruism, it cannot be maintained in today's world and should disappear by natural selection.

Another way in which selection for altruism could proceed would be by social pact, formal or informal. Suppose his culture yields the hero (or his survivors) a lifetime of freedom from want, of social protection. Then, the hero might well be increasing his fitness by risking his life. However, I have the feeling that if this behavior ever existed, it must have lived an un-recorded life and died an unrecorded death. Do you think people reward surviving heroes? Do they tend to support in luxury (or even poverty) their widows and orphans?

I think there is an alternate way to explain selection for altruism. Sup-pose, instead of rewarding the hero, we merely diminish the fitness of the poor soul who is unlucky enough to have the chance to be "unselfish" and doesn't take it. We ostracize him, boycott him, run him out of town. Now this is getting to sound more like human behavior. Maybe unselfishness is illusory?

Robert Trivers has developed this theme into a highly interesting theory which he calls reciprocal altruism. Essentially, reciprocal altruism means, "You scratch my back, and you can expect that I'll scratch yours whenever it starts to itch." That is not as colloquial and frivolous as it might sound, because the mutual grooming of primates is one of the behaviors Trivers attributes to reciprocal altruism. In reciprocal altruism, the altruist gets his reward not from society at large, but from his beneficiary or that bene-ficiary's kin.

Trivers would probably object to my emphasis on the example of the drowning man. Too heroic. Too risky. Not common enough to be recipro-cated. No, in addition to altruism in times of danger, we should examine food sharing, tending the sick and wounded, aiding the young and old, sharing tools, and sharing information. For reciprocal selection to be effec-tive, situations leading to altruistic acts must occur often. Furthermore, the individuals must be long-lived and members of a fairly small, coherent group. Otherwise the chance for reciprocation is too small.

All this does not eliminate the tendency to "cheat." It would still be favored by natural selection. So the altruist must learn to discriminate the reciprocator from the selfish cheater and disassociate himself from the latter. In fact, it helps the fitness of reciprocal altruists to share the infor-mation with other known altruists that so-and-so is "untrustworthy" or "lazy." Thus: the evolution of gossip.

Yet it is necessary within this system that subtle cheating, or gypping, evolve and be maintained. Sutble cheaters do not fail entirely to recipro-cate, they just shortchange their benefactors. Since it is very difficult in practice to evaluate the relative merits of reciprocal favors, subtle cheaters survive. But since it is important to try to do so, people should spend a great deal of time evaluating their acquaintances and their favors and discriminating their true friends from their fair-weather friends. "A friend in need is a friend indeed." Thus: the evolution of the emotions of friend-ship. But subtle cheaters should still survive, because after all, they are somewhat useful in some situations and are not to be ostracized entirely. "Half a loaf is better than none."

Trivers, mustering the support of many anthropological and psychological studies, argues effectively that reciprocal altruism is the explanation for the foregoing, as well as for other human behavior and emotions. These include guilt, moral indignation, aggression, and systems of justice. For example, altruism and friendship do go hand in hand even in experimental situations. Moreover, arguments among primitive people like African bushmen usually do concern matters of gift-giving, stinginess, and laziness. Furthermore, no American need be told about the modern furor and indignation about "the welfare mess." When politicians talk to us about it, are they being true friends?

Could all this human altruism have evolved because of kin selection? If so, says Trivers, how can one explain the minute attention people give to reciprocity? Helping one's kin is helping one's own genes directly; no reciprocity is needed, nor should it be missed. It would indeed appear that Trivers has made his point.

The late, eminent evolutionist David Lack at one time believed that neither of the scientific mechanisms proposed above is able to account for the amount of altruism present in human society. Realizing that no other natural mechanism is known, he invoked a supernatural one. In fact, he believed that the presence of altruism in human society is the chief scientific evidence for the continuous intervention of the Divine. According to Lack, there is more goodness in the world than can be explained by science.

To ask your opinion is perhaps interesting. But it is quite extraneous. The job of the scientist is now to devise some measure of altruism and then a theory which predicts how much there should be and what its characteristics should be. Trivers has already accomplished some of this. Finally, the scientist should go and check the prediction. Perhaps Lack was correct; perhaps Divine intervention is required to produce altruism. But if this is so, unfortunately science cannot prove it. All we can do is keep trying out reasonable explanations. If one fails, we must try another. All we can say is we've failed or succeeded. If Lack's faith was accurate, we shall not succeed. But we shall no more have proved the Divine here, than we have by not devising a rational explanation of the persistence of rh factor in blood. Science is simply not suited to proof, only to tests.

17 the evolution of diversity

He who does not increase his knowledge, decreases it.
Pirke Avot i:13

In previous chapters, you should have acquired a real understanding of why a population follows its particular evolutionary pathway. But that does not help to solve the riddle of diversity. Why have there been so many pathways? Why do we find—even at the same place in space and time—such a great variety of living things?

The earlier parts of this book have given you only a few clues. Within one species, heterosis maintains much variability and mutation maintains a little. And from environment to environment, the problems of adaptation differ. Des ʿ, for example, present a plexus of problems different from bogs.

The task remaining is to expand your comprehension of diversity. However, I can give you only an inkling of the processes that have produced the wealth of nature. If you are left with a lot of unresolved questions, I will have done my job honestly. The problem of diversity is still being worked on intensively by evolutionists around the world.

Actually this chapter is one that has little bearing on the major topic (learning enough about evolution to deal with population problems). But if you are reasonably curious, you will welcome a brief introduction to the evolution of diversity, and if you are not, consider yourself forewarned.

233

VARIATION
WITHIN A SPECIES

You will remember that fitnesses are environment-specific. In other words, a phenotype has one relative fitness in a cold forest, another in a grassy plain, yet another in some third environment. The fitness of sickle-cell heterozygotes is much better in malarial regions than in malaria-free ones. In a humid climate, barley with stiff stems resists the tendency to droop to the ground under the weight of its developing grain; in the windy, arid plains of the western United States, however, the same stiff stems are harmful—the barley's fruit is blown off the stiff stems and lost.

Environmentally caused variation in fitness leads one to predict that the equilibria which natural selection will achieve will be different in different places. A widespread species will, on the average, look quite different from environment to environment. This is known as ecogeographical variation.

CLINES

When a species varies from place to place, it usually does so almost imperceptibly. The lizards of one valley are almost the same as those of the next. And those of the next are quite like those of the third, and so on. But when we come to the thirtieth and compare its lizards to those of the first, we often see noticeable differences. Such a gradual change of a species' average appearance over space is called a cline.

Clines are quite common. Furthermore, in the same species there may be clines of more than one characteristic; body size may be larger at higher latitudes, blackness may intensify with increasing humidity, brownness with increasing temperature, and so on. Thus, a species varies in almost an infinity of ways. In one characteristic, its members at place (A) may appear like those at (B). But in another, those at (A) resemble those at place (C).

SUBSPECIES

It takes a huge amount of study even to describe such complexity. But of course early workers hadn't yet done much sophisticated research. To begin with, they often considered themselves lucky to have specimens from a very few places. And their observations were usually limited to two or three superficial characteristics. Often these were size and color.

When these early students got into a place 1000 miles or more from home, things looked different. Perhaps a mouse was several shades lighter than the ones at home they knew so well. Or maybe a bird's wings were longer. Or a wolf was darker and smaller. Because the organisms were so obviously different, they were given different species names.

Soon, scientific description progressed. Intermediate places were examined and turned out to have intermediate organisms. Dividing lines became more and more difficult to draw.

Northeast

Southwest

Fig. 17-1 Longtailed weasels, with and without the facial "bridle." (From Burt and Grossenheider, *Field guide to the mammals*, Houghton-Mifflin.)

People still tried, however. Instead of giving different forms full species names, they added a third name. For example, the long-tailed weasel lacks prominent facial markings in the northeastern United States. Here it is called *Mustela frenata noveboracensis.* In Texas, members of the same species have a white "bridle," making them look masked. Texas weasels are *Mustela frenata frenata.* (See Fig. 17-1.) The only trouble is that the bridle is not an "off or on" thing. Many long-tailed weasels have only part of it. In fact all intermediates can be found. Where do you draw the line?

The answer is, you draw it on a map, more or less arbitrarily. And you draw it there because an authoritative taxonomist has told you it belongs there. (A taxonomist is a biologist who studies the kinship of populations to each other and tries to figure out reasonable ways to name the populations.) There is, most often, no really good place to draw the line at all. In the past 10 or 15 years, many fine taxonomists have attacked these lines. "Draw them only when they actually exist," they advise. I think their opinion will gradually be accepted.

The third Latin name of a population is its subspecies name. The population which owns it is a subspecies. Unless it's human. Then it's a race.

THE CASE
OF THE SPOTTED SKUNK

A graphic example of the history of increasing knowledge of a species is available for the spotted skunk, *Spilogale putorius* (Fig. 17-2). This species was described by Linnaeus himself. (Linnaeus was the Swedish naturalist who invented the system of naming species with two names, genus and species.) Linnaeus' description was published in 1758 in the 10th edition of his *Systema Naturae.* It was based on a specimen from somewhere in South Carolina.

Fig. 17-2 A spotted skunk from California. (Courtesy of Dr. D. Wake. Originally published by the University of California Press; reprinted by permission of the Regents of the University of California.)

Knowledge of spotted skunks increased very slowly. In 1820, a second "species" was described. Finally, around the turn of the century, naturalists began to grasp the widespread range of this form, and many new names were proposed. In 1906 the then-current knowledge about the genus *Spilogale* was summarized by A. H. Howell in a kind of technical taxonomic publication called a revision.

The map from this work is in Fig. 17-3. It lists 10 species and shows their range. Two species are already composed of subspecies which had been originally described as separate species, but afterwards found to merge together. Notice the geographical gaps between the ranges of the "separate species."

Howell's revision stood for almost 30 years as knowledge increased. Minor changes were made in 1933 and extensive changes were made in the early 1950s. By 1958 the map of the genus lacked almost any geographical gaps. The recognized number of species was diminished (despite the much greater area in which the skunks were known). And Hall and Kelson, the authors of the map, wonder in print if indeed there is only one species of spotted skunk. It is quite possible that there is.

RACE

All biologists recognize that human beings form one very variable species. Generally people are divided into four races: mongoloid (including Amerindians), negroid, caucasoid, and australoid (the black inhabitants of Australia sometimes known as aborigines). But I could give

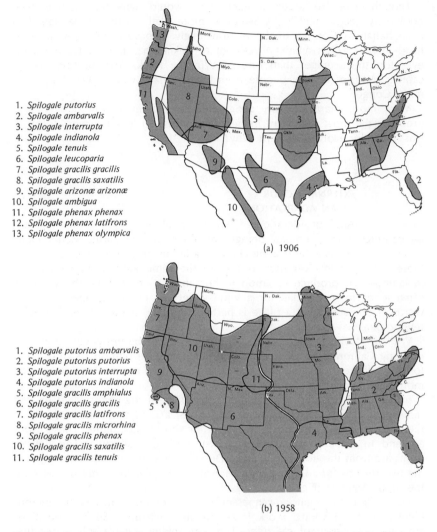

1. *Spilogale putorius*
2. *Spilogale ambarvalis*
3. *Spilogale interrupta*
4. *Spilogale indianola*
5. *Spilogale tenuis*
6. *Spilogale leucoparia*
7. *Spilogale gracilis gracilis*
8. *Spilogale gracilis saxatilis*
9. *Spilogale arizonæ arizonæ*
10. *Spilogale ambigua*
11. *Spilogale phenax phenax*
12. *Spilogale phenax latifrons*
13. *Spilogale phenax olympica*

(a) 1906

1. *Spilogale putorius ambarvalis*
2. *Spilogale putorius putorius*
3. *Spilogale putorius interrupta*
4. *Spilogale putorius indianola*
5. *Spilogale gracilis amphialus*
6. *Spilogale gracilis gracilis*
7. *Spilogale gracilis latifrons*
8. *Spilogale gracilis microrhina*
9. *Spilogale gracilis phenax*
10. *Spilogale gracilis saxatilis*
11. *Spilogale gracilis tenuis*

(b) 1958

Fig. 17-3 Knowledge of the range and forms of spotted skunks of the United States. (1906 from Howell. 1958 from Hall and Kelson, *Mammals of North America*. Vol. 2. Copyright © 1959. The Ronald Press Company, New York.)

you just as good a set of arguments for 60 races as for four. So I won't give you any arguments for any. Human races fade into each other. There is no pure Aryan race nor any other pure race. A race is a large gene pool that is part of the even larger gene pool of all humans, but around which someone compulsive has drawn a neat little line.

Though races are largely artifacts, who would deny that human gene pools vary geographically? A Swede is more likely to be six-feet tall than is an Italian. A German (male) is more likely to have a low, sloping forehead than is a Tanzanian. A resident of Peking has more fat around his eyes (on the average) than one of Window Rock, Arizona (the Navajo capital). And, of course, people from Norway have whiter skin than those in the Congo.

Many more characters vary geographically in humans, but skin color is probably the most important in people's minds. So let's concentrate on it. Has skin color evolved? When? Why?

EXTERNAL COLOR
AS AN ADAPTATION

Any consideration of human variation in skin color must not be conducted as if human beings are alone on the Earth. Many, many species of animals exhibit geographical variation in external color. Furthermore, much of this variation is due to the same kind of pigments—the melanins—that produce variation in human skin color. Last, the variation often tends to be parallel for a wide variety of related species. In other words, if one species at a place is particularly dark, many others there also tend to be.

William Hovanitz has made a detailed study of butterfly-wing pigments in many California species. He has found parallel evolution of wing color for most of them. The melanic pigments are usually more intense in cooler, more humid environments.

In Fig. 17-4, Hovanitz has arranged butterflies of the genus *Melitaea* (the same genus as the checkerspot of Chapter 3) according to the intensity of their color. Heavily melanic forms are at the top of each figure. These forms all tend to come from the cool, moist north of California. The lightest forms are from the hot, dry Mohave Desert. Clines of melanic intensity join the two regions for all the species. Hovanitz obtained the same results from the genus *Argynnis* (Fig. 17-5).

Very often investigators can associate phenotypic clines with environmental clines. Hovanitz' work is an excellent example. Such associations are called ecogeographical rules. There are many. Allen's rule states that protruding parts of birds and mammals tend to be shorter in colder climates. Bergmann's rule maintains that birds and mammals of greater latitudes are likely to be larger than members of their species nearer the equator. Rapoport's rule notes that species of springtails (collembola: primitive, wingless insects found mostly in the soil) are more often dark-colored in colder climates.

Because ecogeographical rules tend to be followed by so many species in parallel, we believe the variation is adaptive. Undoubtedly, the most convincing evidence for these clines being adaptive comes from certain

Cool
Humid

Warm
Dry

M. chalcedona   M. editha   M. leanira   M. palla

Fig. 17-4 Forms of four species of the genus *Melitaea* in California. Butterflies in each column are members of the species named at the base of the column. In addition to the black being most intense in specimens at the top of their column, red-brown and yellow are also most intense at the top and weaken progressively toward the bottom. (Courtesy Prof. W. Hovanitz.)

species with long breeding seasons. For example, the mustard-white butterfly, *Pieris napi*, has two generations per year. One set of adults flies about during the springtime. In California that is the post-rainy season. The air has not yet gotten very hot, and the soil has not yet dried up. Later this species rears a second generation. These adults are out in the summer when things *are* hot and dry. Sure enough, the summer forms are much paler than the spring ones. (See Fig. 17-6.) It is clear here that the species has adapted to the varying environment. Blacker butterflies must be more fit in cool, humid climates. Light ones must be more fit in warm, dry ones.

Cool
Humid

Warm
Dry

A. callipe   A. monticola   A. montivaga   A. adiaste   A. zerene

Fig. 17-5 Forms of five species of the genus *Argynnis* in California. Butterflies in each column are members of the species named at the base of the column. (Courtesy Prof. W. Hovanitz.)

However, we do not know the reason for the changes in fitness. To find out would take experiments like Kettlewell's on peppered moths.

Of course, where there is a problem, inventive minds propose possible solutions. Ecogeographical rules are replete with hypothetical explanations. But the answers conflict and none have been adequately tested. This is especially true for Gloger's rule. C. L. Gloger was a nineteenth-century German biologist. In 1833 he proposed the first ecogeographical rule. Populations of birds in warm, humid climates tend to be composed of intensely black individuals; in warm, dry climates, of browner ones; in cool, dry climates, of very pale ones; and in cool, humid climates, of less intensely black—but still dark—forms.

	Gloger's Rule	
Environment	Cool	Warm
Humid	Weakly black	Intensely black
Arid	Pale	Brown

Spring   Summer

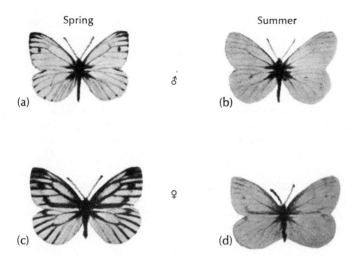

(a)   (b)

♂

(c)   (d)

♀

Fig. 17-6 Adults of *Pieris napi* in two seasons, but from the same place (central (California). The darker form is from the spring, the lighter from summer. Males are at the top. (Courtesy Prof. W. Hovanitz.)

Since 1833, people have found that not only birds, but also mammals follow Gloger's rule. In fact, people follow it, too. More than 80% of the species of birds and mammals that have been examined follow Gloger's rule. Butterflies, however, only partly follow Gloger's rule. Also, some insects exhibit precisely the reverse of Gloger's rule in their clines of body cuticle color.

Although we aren't sure why following Gloger's rule benefits fitness, it is interesting that it does. Or at least that it has enhanced fitness in the past. However, now that humans have so radically altered their environments, the geographical, racial patterns of the past are unlikely to be the optimal ones for the future. What will these future patterns be? How will changes in our environments create them? Will natural selection's pace be able to match the speed at which we change our environments? I cannot answer these questions, but the fact that human beings have evolved according to Gloger's rule may help us make sense of some things of great interest and importance.

Since we became mammals long, long before we became men (roughly 100 million years before) and since mammals usually follow Gloger's rule, it is quite likely our prehuman ancestors followed it, too. If prehumans lived in a cold northern climate, they probably were "white." Those who inhabited tropical rain forests were probably "black."

Thus, the wide distribution of *Homo erectus* around the warmer parts of the Old World indicates that our skin-color varieties are even older than our species, man. The pressures that transformed our pelvises, jaws, and brains and thus made us *Homo sapiens* were not skin-color pressures. Perhaps one of these "man-making" alleles arose in Malaysia, another in Pakistan, another in Guinea, yet a fourth in China. No one knows exactly how many alleles there were, but it is unlikely they all arose in only one population at one place. Instead, each new step arose "never mind where." And then it gradually spread by natural selection throughout the vast gene pool of the population of hominines around the world. Each new allele brought our ancestors a bit closer to that exalted and advanced stage of existence where they would have the power to declare nuclear war on themselves. But why change what was already well-adapted? Why change skin color?

A few racial varieties may not be very old. In order to live successfully in "white" climates, man probably needed much of the important cultural baggage of the stone age: good tools, fire, and knowledge of clothing and sheltering himself. Could only culturally sophisticated members of the genus *Homo* have succeeded in such climates?

Indeed, I know of no confirmed cases of a fossil Australopithecine ever found in the "whitest" parts of Europe. And the earliest indications of real progress toward the human species are all in warm countries. The best finds have been in Africa where blacks are native.

Perhaps prehumanity actually did also live in the northland, but we know that it inhabited the tropics. Surely the black race goes way back to the very origins of mankind. It may well be that the colored peoples bore the brunt of making the evolutionary progress that resulted in *H. sapiens*. If there was an "Adam and Eve" population, it would seem to have been a black one. Only after men had made considerable progress toward civilization could they have successfully colonized colder Europe and subjected themselves to the climate that caused the evolution of transparent epidermis.

VARIATION AND NONRANDOM MATING

It is not wild speculation to imagine that humans have mating preferences. Such mating preferences—together with the fact that people of a certain color are (or were) most fit in certain environments—has had tremendous impact on the evolution of human behavior and, thereby, on the history of the world. A person maximizes his fitness by producing vigorous children. And this is best done by being fit oneself and by seeking a mate who is fit.

To illustrate, I shall use a neutral example. Suppose there is an environment in which purple is the best color. People who prefer and marry purple people will tend to have more purple children. Purple children have higher fitnesses. Let us assume that these mating preferences are somewhat inherited either by genes, by tradition, or by any complex learning process. It makes no difference how. Then a preference for purple people will evolve at the same time as nonpurple skin is disappearing.

Often, since those people who remain are most fit, the evolution of mating preference tends to mean the evolution of a sense of deep appreciation for people who look like oneself. Any wise old grandmother type who has remarked on a boy marrying a wife like his mother has noted this phenomenon. Anyone who has sung (with feeling) "I want a girl just like the girl who married dear old dad," has felt it. (Anyone who has ever studied *Oedipus Rex* has thought about it in its extreme.)

Can you now guess how different standards of personal beauty have evolved in different parts of the world? Maybe you can even begin to construct a theory of the evolution of racial prejudice and chauvinism.

If prejudice and chauvinism derive from our more animalistic past, should we not supplant them with ethically based standards of conduct? Not that you shouldn't marry the spitting image of your mother if you choose; just understand the emotion of prejudice against people who are different. Do your ethical standards tell you such prejudice is wrong if it hurts someone innocent of all but the blame of being phenotypically unlike you?

SPECIATION

Darwin entitled his book on evolution *The Origin of Species.* Yet what he really described and explained was the alteration of species. Today, alteration of one species is called phyletic evolution.

The problem of how two species arise from one is different and obviously important, because there are about two million living species. Until we can figure out how life can produce more species than it begins with, we cannot hope to understand the evolution of diversity.

The process of adding to the number of species is called true speciation. Workers have proposed at least three radically different mechanisms for speciation, and at least two of these are known to have been important.

DEFINITIONS OF SPECIES

We have limped along for some hundred pages without a definition of species. Clearly, now that we want to discuss their origin, we will need to know precisely what we are talking about. Unfortunately, there appear to be two necessary definitions of species.

1. The *phenospecies* is the oldest concept of species. It is the population of organisms whose two most dissimilar phenotypes resemble each other more closely than either resembles any member of any other living species. Imagine a vatful of unsorted organisms. We take each one and examine all aspects of its phenotype closely. Then we group similar phenotypes. Each group is a phenospecies.

2. The *biospecies* is the group of naturally interbreeding organisms. The virtues of using the concept of biospecies are many. Taxonomists can actually observe interbreeding in the field, thereby making the classification

of organisms into species an objective affair. Members of the same bio-species are an evolutionary unit. Thus, the biospecies is a natural unit of classification. (See Fig. 17-7.)

Most (if not all) other units of classification are arbitrary—designed primarily for the convenience of biologists. For instance, birds and croco-diles are quite closely related. Crocodiles, in fact, are more closely related to birds than to turtles. Turtle ancestors separated from the crocodile-bird ancestor some 280 million years ago; birds and crocodiles did not diverge until about 230 million years ago. Yet, biologists agree that it is much more convenient to group crocodiles and turtles as members of the class Reptilia (along with lizards, snakes, and sphenodons) and to create a separate class, Aves, for birds.

With biospecies, no such criterion of convenience is possible. An individ-ual can either breed with another or it can't. If, through interbreeding, the genes of A can become part of the genes of B's descendants (and vice versa), then A and B are in the same biospecies. Yet, since sexual reproduc-tion is absent or at least very rare in some organisms, we cannot abandon the phenospecies altogether.

Let us concentrate on the biospecies. How does a sexually reproducing population give rise to another population which is reproductively isolated from the first? There are at least two important answers to this question: by geographical isolation and by polyploidy.

SPECIATION BY GEOGRAPHICAL ISOLATION

We already know that organisms tend to adapt to their own particular environments. So we might suspect that if some barrier were to split a biospecies into two parts, each part would begin to evolve in a

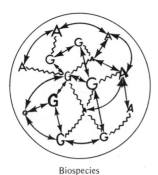

Biospecies

Elements labeled A are one
species, those of G are another.
Arrows indicate successful
mating occurs, whereas
zigzags indicate it doesn't.

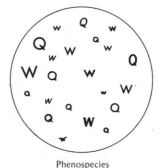

Phenospecies

Each W is more like all others
than it is like any Q.

Fig. 17-7
Two definitions of species.

Fig. 17-8 Tassel-eared squirrels north and south of the Grand Canyon. This is a photograph of four study skins prepared in standard museum fashion for easy storage. (The display skins that one sees in museum exhibits take large amounts of space, so only a small number of specimens can be prepared for display.) The two squirrels at the top of the figure are Kaibab squirrels (from the north rim of the Grand Canyon). Notice their all-white tails and black sides and bellies. (Specimens from the Museum of Southwestern Biology, University of New Mexico.)

more or less unique manner. Imagine a squirrel population on two sides of the Grand Canyon. Squirrels on each side live in a pine forest, but they are separated by the ecologically inappropriate desert of the Colorado River bottom. The altitude of the north rim of the canyon is about a thousand feet higher than the south rim, so the pressures on the two populations might be somewhat different.

In fact, these populations exist. The tassel-eared squirrel of the north rim has an all-white tail and a black belly; the squirrel of the south rim usually has a gray-white belly and a tail with a dark dorsal surface (Fig. 17-8). Occasionally one finds a southern-type squirrel in the northern population and vice versa; so we know that selection is maintaining the phenotypes as they are—different on the two rims. (We still don't know why, though.)

If these populations were to go on evolving apart for perhaps one or two hundred thousand years, great differences between them might arise. Each population might find its own solution to its own evolutionary pressures. Perhaps there will be a change in chromosome number in one.

Perhaps a new enzyme system will evolve in one, incompatible with that in the other.

In any case, there is a chance that when we allow them to interbreed (by filling up the Grand Canyon), they will not be able to, or their hybrid offspring (like the mule, offspring of jackass and mare) will be sterile or inviable. If and when this happens, we shall know that two species have evolved from one. Until then, the question of whether they are one or two species is moot and biologically unimportant.

The sequence of events in geographical speciation is then:

1. One biospecies is split into more than one isolated population by some geographical barrier.

2. Each population evolves independently in its own environment.

3. Rejoining the populations results in the opportunity for resumed interbreeding, but the populations do not or cannot successfully engage in it. They have become separate biospecies. (See Fig. 17-9.)

There is much evidence to suggest that this sequence has been the major mechanism of true speciation. I have space for only the tip of the iceberg.

Kingfishers of New Guinea. Ernst Mayr's eloquent volumes deserve much of the credit for convincing the world of the importance of geographic speciation. One case that he uncovered concerns the kingfishers of the genus *Tanysiptera* on New Guinea and the nearby Aru Islands.

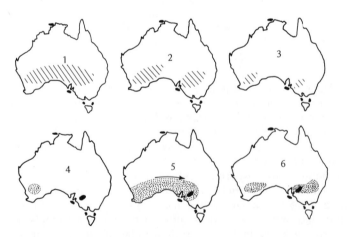

Fig. 17-9 How geographical speciation is thought to work. On outline maps of Australia, the range of a bird called thickhead is plotted. Map 1 depicts the oldest situation and shows one species. Range changes are postulated on long-term changes in vegetation and climate. In map 5 the western population has reinvaded the east and turned out to be a different species from the easterner. Map 6 shows today's distribution. (From Keast.)

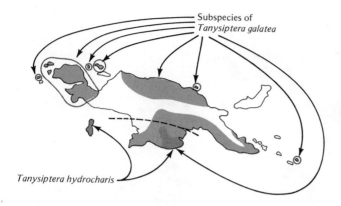

Subspecies of
Tanysiptera galatea

Tanysiptera hydrocharis

Fig. 17-10 Geographical ranges of the Papuan kingfishers of New Guinea and out-lying islands. The dashed line shows where New Guinea was once divided by a shallow sea. Populations on isolated outlying islands are very different, but the three mainland races of *T. galatea* are very similar. In one case they overlap geographically with the formerly isolated *T. hydrocharis*. There, the two do not interbreed. (Redrawn from Mayr, 1942, *Systematics and the origin of species,* Columbia University Press.)

Kingfishers are birds that, as their name implies, hunt for fish on the margins of bodies of water. They are quite sedentary compared to many other birds, and they don't migrate, either. So it doesn't take too large a barrier to isolate them.

Originally, New Guinea was inhabited by one species, *Tanysiptera galatea.* Three subspecies of *T. galatea* occur today on New Guinea, but they are quite similar. Occasionally a storm or some other accident would waft a kingfisher to a nearby island where it became an isolate.

Apparently, isolation occurred at least six times, for there are six well-differentiated forms on outlying islands. Often these forms live in the same habitat found on the nearby "mainland," and yet they look quite different. Mayr points out the great importance of this fact. The mainland is quite varied in habitat, and so a resident contains genes adapted to all sorts of environments; a little mainland population is not geographically isolated in its special environment. But with isolation comes the opportunity to diverge, to strike out on the specialist's path, to free the population of all alleles not particularly suited to the one environment in which it is living.

Is there any evidence that this has resulted in speciation? In one case it surely has. One of the islands is no longer an island. It was separated from New Guinea by a shallow sea which has been filled with the alluvial deposits that wash down from New Guinea's mountains. The form on this ex-island is called *T. hydrocharis.* We know it is a separate biospecies because Mayr has observed that its habitat has been invaded by its "parent" species, *T. galatea;* the two forms coexist without interbreeding. (See Fig. 17-10.)

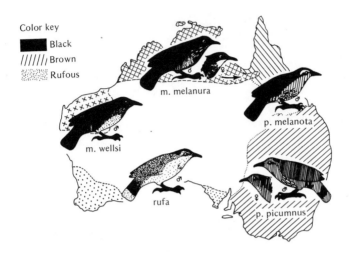

Color key

■ Black
////// Brown
▒ Rufous

m. melanura

p. melanota

m. wellsi

rufa

p. picumnus

Fig. 17-11 A superspecies: *Climacteris picumnus*. The tree creepers of the Australian savannah have been in isolated populations long enough to form a superspecies. Each form is drawn near its geographical range on an outline map of Australia. Recently *C. melanura melanura* has extended its range eastward into the range of *C.p. melanota*. In the region of overlap, no hybridization occurs. Thus, these two are surely separate biospecies. In other cases the ranges remain separated, and one cannot tell if speciation has been completed. (From Keast.)

Superspecies. Often one species appears to have been sub-divided into many isolates; the isolates look very, very different, but the geographical barriers remain. We cannot tell if there is more than one biospecies because the isolates have no natural chance to interbreed. But we don't want to call all the forms by one name—they are too dissimilar in phenotype. In such a case, the group of isolates constitutes a super-species. Sometimes the isolates have separate specific names (in agreement with the phenospecies definition); sometimes they don't. But in each case we have caught geographical speciation at work—partly finished.

Superspecies are extremely common. For instance, Mayr has shown that among the 135 species of Solomon Islands birds, there are 17 superspecies. Keast notes that one of every three species of Australian bird is a super-species member. (See Fig. 17-11.) In European snails of the Clausiliid family, there are 10 superspecies. Rodents and fish also form superspecies readily. Geographical speciation appears to be hard at work constantly.

Sometimes by bringing members of superspecies into the lab, an investigator can show that if ever again they were to intermingle, no interbreeding could occur. For instance, the flatworm *Dugesia gonocephala* resides in a large part of Europe and Asia. In the area around Italy and the Mediterranean, however, the species has often been isolated. Though the isolates look like *D. gonocephala*, they cannot interbreed with it. The organs of copulation in the various isolates are so different that even laboratory crosses never succeed. These isolates are sometimes found on islands (in Sardinia is found, *D. benazzii*, named after the investigator who analyzed the superspecies) and sometimes in mainland pockets of habitat (in Tuscany, *D. etrusca*).

Darwin's finches. Some of the most powerful evidence for the existence and preeminence of geographical speciation has come from studies on archipelagos. Darwin was himself greatly inspired by the unusual bird species on the Galápagos Islands. David Lack, in a now classic study, analyzed these species, called Darwin's finches or Geospizidae, and showed how they probably originated. Each population, after establishing itself on an island, evolved along its own pathway. Later some returned to the islands whence came their remote ancestors. There they found a population like their ancestors. But they themselves, having responded evolutionarily to the pressures of their new island, had become very different. Often enough they were reproductively isolated and could coexist with their ancestral population as a second biospecies.

Darwin's finches include species with large, medium, and small beaks. Also there are species that no longer eat seeds but have adapted to the role of insect eaters and changed accordingly in appearance. Most astonishingly, one finch, the woodpecker finch, performs like a woodpecker; in lieu of the woodpecker's long, probing beak, it breaks off cactus spines or twigs and uses them to dig insects out of woody tissue.

Six hundred miles from the Galápagos (and 300 from Panama) is Cocos Island, one of the world's most isolated. Here we find the only other living species of geospizid. (See Fig. 17-12.)

Cocos Island is the size of one of the smaller islands of the Galápagos. In addition, it is a tropical forest island, and tropical forests usually contain more bird species than any other kind of habitat. So we might expect to find several species on Cocos. But there is only one. Why?

It appears likely that there is no place for an isolate of the Cocos finch to form. How, on this tiny outpost, can nature develop the geographical barriers that would permit speciation? And so, though it appears that Cocos could provide for more than one geospizid, it is likely that it will never get the opportunity. Here is the most powerful evidence that geographical barriers may be absolutely essential as the first step in gradual speciation for many animals.

POLYPLOIDY: INSTANT SPECIATION

Suppose there were a way to double the number of chromosomes in each cell of an organism. Or suppose there were a way to combine the chromosomes of one species with those of another to form a new organism. In either case, if the resulting organism does not need a mate

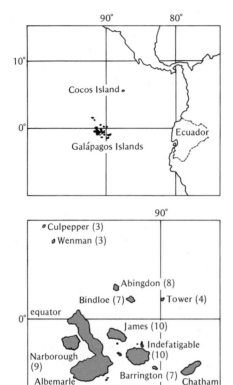

Fig. 17-12 Pacific Ocean maps showing the Galápagos and Cocos Island, their isolation, and the number of species of Darwin's finches on each island. Cocos has only one. (From maps in *Darwin's finches* by D. L. Lack. Published by Cambridge University Press. Reprinted from *Biological science* by W. T. Keeton. Illustrated by Paula Di Santo Bensadoun. By permission of W. W. Norton and Co., Inc. Copyright 1967 by W. W. Norton and Co., Inc.)

to reproduce (if it is parthenogenetic or hermaphroditic), it also would be a new biospecies.

What would isolate this new organism from its parent species? It would be reproductively incompatible with them because it would have more chromosomes than they. Imagine that the parents of the new species each have two sets of chromosomes and that each set has seven members. Thus the number of chromosomes in a parent cell is 14. But in a cell of the new species, there would be 28 chromosomes.

When an organism produces a gamete (sperm and egg), it does so by meiosis. One of the crucial steps in this process is synapsis, the pairing-up of like chromosomes. Pairing ensures that each gamete will receive one of each type of chromosome. An unpaired chromosome will not appear in each and every gamete.

If a seven-chromosome sperm of a member of the parent species fertilizes a 14-chromosome egg of a member of the new species, they produce a 21-chromosome offspring. This progeny is sterile because when it undergoes meiosis, it has seven unpaired chromosomes. Its meiosis is a disorderly disaster. Each unpaired chromosome may or may not occur in a gamete. If it does occur, that is no assurance any of the others will. And the occurrence of two does not guarantee a third or a fourth, and so on.

Doubling the number of chromosomes or combining the chromosomes of two different species can actually occur. Either event is called polyploidy. Doubling is autopolyploidy. Combining is allopolyploidy. The new species is called a polyploid.

Polyploidy requires an anomalous meiosis. The gametes which will form the polyploid are produced when, by accident, *all* the chromosomes of synapsis move to one of the daughter cells. The other daughter cell is empty. The full daughter cell goes on to produce two diploid gametes by means of a normal cell division.

Autopolyploidy. Suppose two such diploid gametes fuse to form a zygote (fertilized egg). The result is a tetraploid zygote, founder of a new biospecies (Fig. 17-13). This new species might later do the same thing, resulting in an octaploid species.

Sometimes autopolyploids are formed of a diploid gamete and a normal haploid one. These are, of course, triploid; but they are sexually sterile for their third set of chromosomes has no match in synapsis, so they can't produce normal gametes. Bananas, for instance, are triploid and must propagate vegetatively. Bananas do not yield viable seeds.

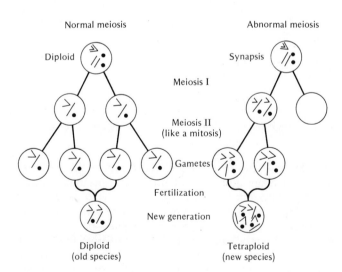

Fig. 17-13 Speciation by autopolyploidy—doubling of the chromosomes of one species.

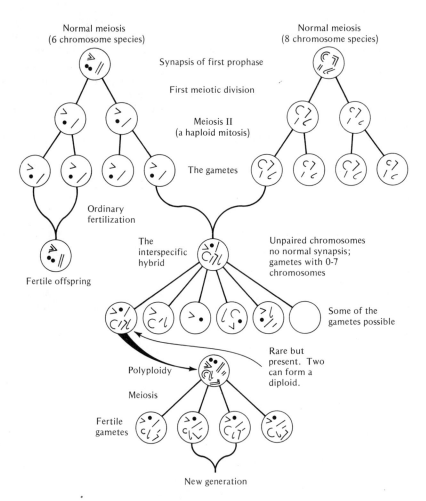

Fig. 17-14 Speciation by allopolyploidy—hybridization of two species followed by doubling.

Allopolyploidy. If the new species is a result of the union of two old species, we say it is an allopolyploid (from *allo*, meaning "different"). This occurs in a slightly different way from autopolyploidy. The first step in obtaining an allopolyploid is the hybridization of two unlike but normal haploid gametes. The product is a haploid zygote—part of its one set of chromosomes comes from one parent, the other part from the second.

Such a hybrid is virtually sterile because none of its chromosomes can pair in synapsis when (and if) the hybrid matures and undergoes meiosis. Each of its chromosomes gravitates to one of the daughter cells independently of what the others do. (See Fig. 17-14.)

Sometimes, purely by chance, all the chromosomes go to only one daughter cell. This yields a functional haploid gamete, a gamete with the same number of chromosomes as the hybrid adult. If two such gametes fuse, a diploid zygote results. When it begins to undergo meiosis as an adult, the diploid has no problem. Each of its chromosomes is paired. It is therefore a reproductively competent adult and, if it is viable, represents a new hybrid biospecies.

Evidence for polyploidy. Has instantaneous speciation via polyploidy ever occurred? Absolutely and for sure! It has been performed right in the laboratory. Allopolyploids of radishes *(Raphanus sativus)* and cabbages *(Brassica oleracea)* have formed the laboratory species, *Raphanobrassicus*. *Raphanobrassicus* has 18 pairs of chromosomes; each of its parents has nine (Fig. 17-15). Two species of primrose have formed an allopolyploid in the lab: *Primula verticillata* and *P. floribunda* formed *P. kewensis*. With modern techniques of manipulating cell division using the chemical colchicine, it is rather easy to get laboratory polyploids.

But has polyploidy in nature ever yielded a new species? Apparently it has in plants, over and over again. And also it has occurred frequently in appropriate animals. G. L. Stebbins, one of the two or three most respected botanical evolutionists in the world, estimates that between one-fourth and one-third of the world's plant species were formed by polyploidy.

To discover polyploidy in nature, researchers have simply examined the chromosomes of organisms and looked for cases of doubling and trebling. For instance, the various species of wheat have chromosome numbers of either 14, 28, or 42. The 28 could be an autopolyploid or an allopolyploid of two 14-chromosome species, and the 42 could be an allopolyploid between a 28 and a 14. Wild cotton species have 26 chromosomes; cultivated ones, 52. The flatworm, *Dendrocoelum lacteum*, has 16; its quite similar relative, *D. infernale*, has 32. Many, many cases could be cited.

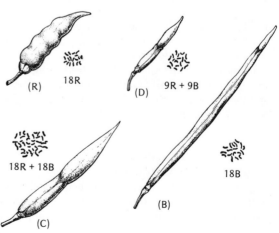

Fig. 17-15 Pods of the radish (R), cabbage (B), and *Raphanobrassica*. (D) is the haploid hybrid; (C) is the allopolyploid. The chromosomes appear as short, thick, sausage-shaped structures near the pods. (From *Principles of genetics,* 5th edition. Sinnott, Dunn, and Dobzhansky. Copyright 1958 by and used with permission of McGraw-Hill Book Co.)

(R) 18R

(D) 9R + 9B

18R + 18B

18B

(C)

(B)

There is something about all this that deserves mention. Autopolyploidy does result in the addition of whole chromosome sets of the same haploid number. So we can understand why there should be a progression from 2n (diploid) to 4n (tetraploid) to 8n (octoploid). But why should this be the case with allopolyploidy?

If a 5-chromosome gamete of species B joins a 9-chromosome gamete of species C, a 14-chromosome hybrid results. The allopolyploid will have 28 chromosomes. This is neither twice 10, nor twice 18. How is it that known allopolyploids usually do have twice the number of either of their parent species?

Perhaps evolutionists haven't found many allopolyploids that don't have exactly twice their parents' chromosome number because these are more difficult to discover. Maybe, on the other hand, allopolyploids really are ordinarily formed of unlike species which share the same haploid number. If so, that would be a pattern and a problem of possible interest to cellular biologists as they attempt to understand the processes of cell division and zygote formation.

Recreating polyploid species. Because of the ease with which polyploids are produced in the lab, one can readily test hypotheses about the origin of species via polyploidy. If you think that species A is an allopolyploid of species B and C, then get some B and C, obtain the hybrid, and make the allopolyploid. If it is like A, your hypothesis is confirmed.

The most famous case of such a laboratory confirmation concerns bread wheats. These have 42 chromosomes. Percival long ago hypothesized that bread wheat was the allopolyploid of a hybrid whose parents had been one of the 28-chromosome wheats (for example, durum wheat) and goat grass, a common weed of Mediterranean wheat fields.

Investigators in this country produced the hybrid and then the polyploid. Sure enough, it looked just like bread wheat. What is more, its chromosomes were just like those of bread wheat, for when it was crossed with *Triticum spelta* (spelt, a 42-chromosome bread wheat), it produced perfectly fertile offspring. This showed that a set of its chromosomes could pair with a set of spelt's in synapsis, which is possible only if the two sets of chromosomes are essentially alike.

Hitoshi Kihara produced the hybrid in his lab too, but instead of producing the polyploid artificially, he waited to see if the hybrid could do it spontaneously. It did, proving that bread wheat could have evolved in nature without the help of colchicine.

HOW CAN SO MANY SPECIES PERSIST?

When species have ecological roles that are similar, one of them may become extinct as a result of interspecific competition. The one that disappears is said to have suffered *competitive exclusion*. Species avoid competitive exclusion if they are each specialized in some different way. Were it not for specialization, only one species at a time could persist at any one place.

There are only a few categories of specialization that can preserve the richness produced by speciation.

1. A species can adapt to a special habitat and stay in it much of the time or even all of the time. The barnacles in Scotland (Chapter 2) are a good example of this. One requires a wetter environment than the other.

2. A species can adapt to a certain time of the day or year and become inactive in the off-season. For instance, the desert pocket mouse retreats in the winter (hibernates). Its competitor, the cactus mouse, sleeps in the hot, dry season (estivates).

3. A species can belong to a certain trophic level. Plants can persist with their consumers, the herbivores. Herbivores and carnivores can share an environment. Their specializations lie in adaptation to each other as well as to their habitat. Only the carnivore is adapted to consuming herbivores. Only herbivores are adapted to consuming plants.

4. A species might be fit only if it adapts by restricting its feeding behavior. This is the most complex sort of specialization. It is called resource allocation because it results in a sharing out of the food resources within a community. A wolf, for example, hunts mostly large-hoofed mammals; it is too big to be fit if it wasted its time on mice or even rabbits. On the other hand, the coyote hunts mostly rabbits and rats; it is too small for moose, elk, and deer. The gray fox, even smaller than the coyote, hunts mostly mice. (See Figs. 17-16 and 17-17.)

Not only can such specializations prevent competitive exclusion of the hunters, they can prevent it in the hunted, as well. The mouse must adapt to the fox, the deer to the wolf.

WHY ARE THERE
JUST SO MANY SPECIES?

What is happening to the number of species? We know from our examination of speciation that both geographical speciation and polyploidy are at work producing new species. So perhaps the number of species is increasing.

But species can become extinct too. In fact, the fossil record suggests that almost all species that have existed exist no more. Over 99% are extinct. So we have two things to balance: a positive term from speciation and a negative one from extinction.

The available evidence indicates that these two terms tend to cancel each other out. Figure 17-18 shows an enumeration of the number of families in the fossil record during each epoch of life. Except for the marked

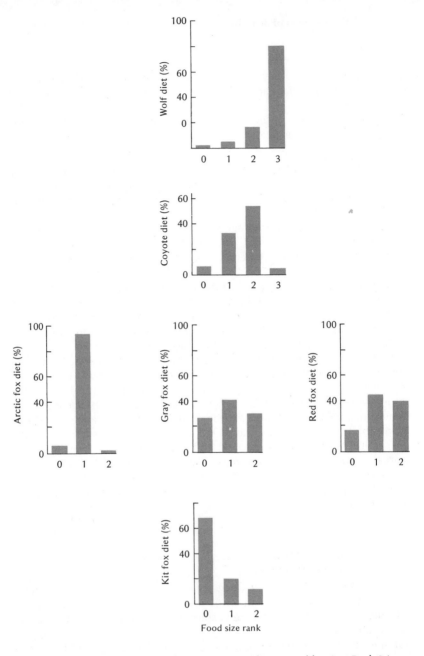

Fig. 17-16 Animal foods of North American canids arranged by size. Rank 0 is insects and other arthropods. Rank 1 contains animals to 1.5 pounds (mice, rats, smaller squirrels). Rank 2 contains mammals from 1.5 to 25 pounds (larger squirrels, rabbits). Rank 3 has beaver and hoofed mammals. The approximate weights of the canids are: wolf, 80 pounds; coyote, 30; kit fox, 4.5; other foxes 9–10. Thus, the larger the canid, the larger its victims. (Data from Rosenzweig, 1966 and MacPherson, in litt.)

Fig. 17-17 Cats. Marion Seawell's conception of the size diversity of cats illustrates how carnivores of various sizes (but smaller body plans) are really acting as a harmonious unit to exploit various sizes of prey. (Copyright 1971 by Marion Seawell, 3491 Sacramento St., San Francisco. All rights reserved.)

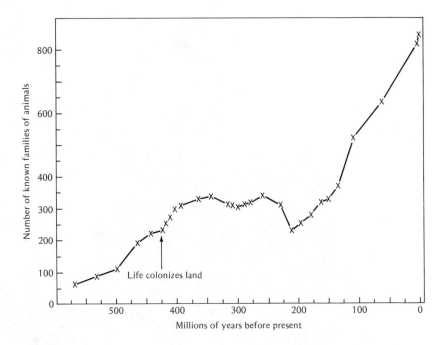

Fig. 17-18 The number of known families of fossils during different geological epochs. (Data from Newell, 1963.)

increase when organisms were first adapting to terrestrial environments, these data suggest that the number of families alive in the ocean at one time hasn't changed much for some 700 million years, and hasn't changed on land in about 350 million years. Notice especially that from about 350 million years ago to about 125 million years ago, the number of families seems to have hovered around 325. The marked rises at other times are easily interpreted as resulting from the fact that we know more about the fauna and flora of the more recent past than the distant past. Now, if we admit that taxonomists are reasonable, then the average number of species per family should be about constant. Hence, the number of species appears to have been remarkably stable.

Such long-lasting stability suggests the existence of a steady state. As species increase in number beyond the stable point, extinction rates should get larger than speciation rates; if they are less, speciation should exceed extinction. There is some evidence that this is true.

EVIDENCE FOR EQUILIBRIUM
IN THE NUMBER OF SPECIES

Previous to the last several million years, South America was a huge island (like Australia is today). In North and South America, many

(a)

(b)

Fig. 17-19 Restorations of two ungulates of the old, native taxa of South America. These forms belong to orders which have become extinct. They date from the Santa Cruz fauna, late Miocene, about 15 million years ago, long before the great transmigrations began. They are not at all closely related to modern ungulates, which they may remind you of. For instance, *Diadiaphorus* (a) and *Theosodon* (b) are both litopterns, despite the fact that the first looks much like a horse, the second like a llama. The horse and llama groups invaded South America much later, though it seems reasonable to suppose that their way of life had been led by *Diadiaphorus* and *Theosodon* before them. (Restored by C. R. Knight for Scott.)

TABLE 17-1   GENERA OF LAND MAMMALS IN NORTH AMERICA

Age	Approximate time (in millions of years ago)	Approximate duration (in millions of years)	Approximate average number of genera alive
Clarendonian	11.7–9.9	1.8	64
Hemphillian	10.0–4.1	5.9	57
Blancan	4.1–1.5	2.6	60
Irvingtonian and Rancholabrean	1.36–0.01	1.35	79
Recent	0.01–0	0.01	78

Source: Webb.

identical environments existed. So, many North American forms and South American forms converged. Different species that fill similar ecoroles in different places are called ecological *vicars*. Remember the sabertooths? These were vicars. North and South America also had their own individual brands of rodents and hoofed herbivores (Fig. 17-19).

When the North and South American continents were joined by the volcanic activity that completed Central America, there were unprecedented migrations; Yankee species moved south, Latin species north. This migration gave us the opposum and the armadillo, among others. It gave South America the deer and the puma, as well as other animals. It brought many ecological vicars into contact and greatly increased the number of species in one place.

If there is a stable number of species, then, the rate of extinction should have been much higher than the rate of speciation at this new higher number of species. A net reduction in species should have ensued. Indeed, there was a wave of extinction, and it brought the number of species very near what it had been (we cannot tell exactly because Simpson, who performed this research, enumerated families, not species).

Recently, Webb enumerated the North American land-mammal genera of several geological ages. A careful count was also made of extinctions and of originations of genera. Furthermore, the originations could be separated into those caused by evolution and those caused by immigration from other continents. As we shall see, these data tend to add evidence that extinction and evolution are dynamically balanced. (In Table 17-1, the names of the geological ages are peculiar to the North American continent; they are given other names elsewhere.)

Notice that for the first 10 million years or so of this record, the number of genera was virtually constant. Yet there were 118 generic extinctions and 121 originations! This was hardly a static fauna. In the past two million years there may have been an increase. But two million years is hardly enough time to make conclusions about such slow-moving events. Still, let

Extinctions	Originations	
	Evolution	Immigration
36	28	
55	37	13
27	25	18
36	24	31
0	0	8

us examine the record more closely to see whether we can explain or understand this apparent change.

During the last two million years there has been significant geological unrest. We have already mentioned the volcanic activity that joined North and South America. In addition to that, the ice ages brought a physical union of Siberia and Alaska. This occurred because so much of the Earth's water was tied up in the glaciers that sea level dropped hundreds of feet and left a large corridor of dry land joining Asia to North America (by the way, through this corridor the first humans almost certainly moved into the New World). Both of these events caused a marked influence in the immigration of new genera to North America. In the recent past, man has exerted the same effect. We have brought in *Rattus* (rats), *Mus* (house mice), *Sus* (pigs), *Equus* (horses), *Bos* (cattle), *Capra* (goats), and *Herpestes* (mongeese). All but goats and cows have formed successful wild populations in at least some of North America.

Such an increase in the immigration rate of new genera should not affect the rate at which extinction occurs. A fauna or set of animals in a region with 56 genera will have a fixed rate of generic extinction regardless of high or low immigration rate. And there is no reason to believe immigration affects the rate of origination by evolution. Therefore, if at 60 genera, the old rate of origination was equal to the old rate of extinction, then when immigration increases, the new rate of origination should be higher than extinction. At 60 genera, the fauna grows. As it grows, extinction increases and origination is soon overtaken. Finally, at some new and richer fauna (78 genera?), the two come back into balance. (See Fig. 17-20.)

Perhaps then there has been a real increase in the stable number of genera in the past two million years. Perhaps we are at a new and higher plateau. Except by waiting around for another 10 million years, no one yet knows how to find out.

Judging from the evidence from mammals, as well as from birds (which I have not presented here), the world may have reached a point where new species originate about as fast as old ones disappear. Probably only man has the power to change such an equilibrium much. He could do it

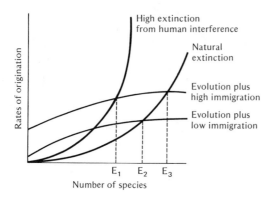

Fig. 17-20 A model of land-mammal flux through the ages. Where extinction and origination lines cross, an equilibrium number of species is achieved. Extinction rates increase in more diverse communities because of increased likelihood of competitive exclusion, decreased resistance to catastrophe, and increased genetic drift. Speciation rates climb toward a ceiling because in more diverse communities each species tends to occupy a smaller geographical range and will thus form fewer isolates. E_3 is higher than E_2 solely because of higher immigration; such an increase has presumably occurred in the past two million years. If humans increase extinction rates, a smaller number of species, E_1, is to be expected.

by greatly increasing extinction rates. Let us hope he conscientiously refrains from exercising that power. Since man is so intense and successful a competitor, refraining from causing a high extinction rate will not be a negative act. It will require positive acts of self-restraint. Perhaps the most important of all of these is self-control of our population's size. A human species which lives on every square foot of available land does not leave much room for its competitors.

EVOLUTION:
A CONTINUOUS PROCESS

No one hopes to prevent all extinctions. Extinction is a natural process and it will continue. Moreover, as long as extinctions take their toll, as long as the Earth's environments continue to change, and as long as victims continue to be selected for increased ability to avoid disease and depredation, so long will phyletic evolution and speciation continue. There is no end in sight. As long as there is life, there will be change. Perhaps Heraclitus was right when he long ago maintained that the only constant in the world is change. In fact, if I were asked to characterize life, to pick the great unifying factor that defines it, to discriminate it finally from physics and chemistry, I would have to insist that it is evolution directed by natural selection. That which is alive is that which is subject to it. Everything else follows naturally from the environment in which life happens to exist.

V methods of population control

A . . . precondition for solving our problems is a realization that all of them are interlocked, with the result that they cannot be solved piecemeal. They must be approached as a set of problems, each of which interacts with the other. Sometimes it is easier to solve ten interlocking problems simultaneously than to solve one by itself.

Harrison Brown

The day is short, the work is great . . . and so is the reward.

Pirke Avot ii:20

18 a method that won't work and another that should not be allowed to

The "fittest" which survives in the struggle for existence
may be, and often is, the ethically worst.

T. H. Huxley

PURE VOLUNTARISM
The most popular idea for remedying our population problem
is telling people what the world can expect if we don't, and then asking
them to limit their own personal production of babies. This has been called
pure voluntarism by Garrett Hardin. Hardin is the most articulate biologist
pointing out why pure voluntarism is not going to produce population
control, and you ought to read him in the original, especially if you find
this meager translation wanting.

The difficulty with pure voluntarism is natural selection. Natural selection
is also the ultimate cause of a growing population. To make this plain, let
us outline what we know about selection and relate that to both population
growth rate and population size.

The theory of natural selection is summarized as follows:

1. If different behavioral and physical traits cause people to tend to
produce different numbers of fertile offspring (if different phenotypes
have different fitnesses), and

2. if offspring tend to inherit the behavior and physical appearance of
their parents (if phenotypes are partly heritable),

3. then those traits that result in above-average production of young
will become more and more frequent in the population.

Although that theory (like all other scientific statements) will never be proved, it has been tested thoroughly, tested as well or better than any other scientific conclusion. And it has *not* been found wanting. It is the only known successful explanation for life as we know it today. In the preceding section, we watched natural selection handle many mysteries of the real world: Fossils were explained by it. Because of it, American Negroes lost much of their susceptibility to sickle-cell anemia, mosquitos developed resistance to DDT and *Streptococcus* to penicillin, and moths blackened to blend with the soot of factories. Our farmers harnessed it and made it work for us. We have even mimicked natural selection in our laboratories.

Medical science has minimized human mortality early in life. In a modern civilization almost everyone lives to reproduce. Thus, virtually all differences in susceptibility to early demise have been eliminated. Only one major component of human fitness remains: family size. The bigger a parent's family size, the larger is that parent's fitness. This makes human fitness in a developed country rather easy to measure.

Is human fitness at all heritable? We have seen the evidence that it surely is. Return to Chapter 13 and reread the study of British peeresses. Can you imagine a modern society *more* governed by voluntary compliance with social norms than upper-class Victorian England? Yet, even in this group of unliberated women, there were significant differences in fitness. And those differences were partly inherited.

The fact that we have heritable fitnesses should come as no surprise. After all, humans have evolved adaptively. And it takes heritable fitness to do that.

Since we have heritable fitnesses, we are still subject to natural selection. Any man and wife tending to have a large family who can transmit that tendency to their children have a high fitness. I don't know exactly what such people look like or act like. I don't know how beautiful or intelligent they are. But whoever they are, they are the future. Natural selection will ensure that in the long run, birth rates will climb until our population is so dense that its members are living limited, marginal lives and, on the average, raising only two children per couple.

That should not surprise you either. By maximizing reproduction, natural selection always works to increase population size until a species is at its natural limit. If we can keep our population below this size, we shall be the first species to refuse to capitulate to this life-shaping force. It is by defeating selection, not by ignoring it, that man can achieve permanent humanity.

One must realize that reproduction is the only biological good. Natural selection does not select for comfort, education, culture, or civilization. Selection in a low-death-rate society cares only for larger families. Personally, I find this a rather shallow, totally unsatisfying standard.

However, it does help us to understand ourselves. We can understand why we love and want babies. Those who didn't, didn't raise large enough families, and natural selection weeded them out. Every time a sociologist interviews people and asks them, "How many children make an ideal family?" he gets an average answer that is too large to prevent population growth. Old people and young, those planning families, those building families, those with completed families—all answer with a number that would result in population growth. Hindu and Moslem, Christian and Jew, biologist and ad man, rich and poor—all are products of eons of natural selection; all want more children than is good for their world or their children.

Blake has presented some of the data for U.S. women. Women past their 21st birthday were asked how many children make an ideal family. Here are the average answers of non-Catholic women in 1968 (a year more or less typical of the decades of the 1950s and 1960s):

Education

College	High school	Grade school	
3.2	3.3	3.7	

Economic status

High	Upper middle	Lower middle	Lower
3.2	3.0	3.4	3.6

All classes
3.3

As I write this, the U.S. Census Bureau is releasing figures to suggest that the average size of completed U.S. families has been very low for a year or two. Families are so small, it seems we are approaching the day when our population will stop growing. Don't you believe it! Natural selection will keep that from happening until people are suffering massive deprivation. A year or two of data is just a blip on the chart. And even in this low year—one of many years of data—birth rates have not fallen much below replacement. How can we achieve an average birth rate which equals the rate needed for replacement of our deaths, if one year in 10 (say) the birth rate is as low as that needed for replacement, and the rest of the years it is higher than that needed for replacement?

How is family size inherited? We don't know. Perhaps different people feel their emotions in different ways, ways that are heritable. Perhaps a mother's pelvic structure subjects her to different degrees of discomfort in childbirth—influencing her decision to bear again. Perhaps. But this is immaterial to selection. Selection cares only that something is partially inherited, not how. And family size is partly heritable.

Now suppose we do plead for reproductive sanity on a voluntary basis. We entreat each individual family to decide to limit its children to two. What would happen? People would react differently. They always do. Some would still not know the name of the President of the United States—can we expect them to become educated to the world's problems? Some would be selfish, some remain dubious (requiring, no doubt, that their own children be cut down by overpopulation before they believe in population control). And some would exercise self-control. Suppose there were enough of the latter to achieve an average completed family size of two (a few couples will remain sterile; some will want only one child). We have learned that to reach steady state would then take about 70 years, or two generations.

Yet, while all this time is passing, natural selection will also be at work. It will be increasing the proportion of couples who pay no attention to the rest of society, who reproduce regardless of the damage they do. Gradually it will destroy our no-growth status, and we'll be growing all over again. Using today's Americans as its raw material, selection will have produced a race of reproductive renegades.

The situation is analogous to the case of the man with a mild strep throat. His physician, not understanding natural selection, decides to give the man small doses of antibiotic, gradually increasing the dosage as he needs to. At first, the infection responds nicely; the man feels better for a while. But the doctor has merely killed off all the susceptible germs; he has not used a strong enough dose to get the resistant ones. The resistant bacteria thrive and increase, and soon the patient is really sick—sick with a disease that medicine can cure only through long, heroic measures. The doctor has done more harm than good. Proper medical practice requires walloping those germs hard enough right away. Similarly, proper practice of population control requires **beginning** with a program that does not encourage reproductive irresponsibility.

How long would it take for selection to ruin our progress in population control? We don't know for sure, and we won't know until we try the experiment. Perhaps it will take two generations, perhaps ten. But we are dealing with a problem whose solution takes two generations. Shall we go to all that trouble only to know our gains will be dissipated soon after they are achieved. Simply asking a family to exercise restraint in producing babies is as cruel as asking a man to go grab a gun and stand off an invading army by himself. It is wrong to ask people to relinquish their right to more than two children unless they can have some reasonable hope that their sacrifice will be meaningful.

As yet, there is no such hope. We are still living in an environment in which man has not renounced the myth of infinite growth. The first step in controlling our population's size is to educate him to abandon that myth. The second is to show him that the population explosion is everyone's baby. The third is to explore *and choose* reasonable ways to damp that explosion. Then and only then can you and I as individuals participate in rational regulation of our population's size.

ECONOMIC SANCTIONS AND INCENTIVES

The second most talked about scheme for controlling reproduction proposes to put economic teeth into our pleas for reproductive sanity. We must ask a penetrating evolutionary question about such teeth: Is money more important than babies? Since you have read this text, you can agree that money (at least as far as natural selection is concerned) is of no importance compared with babies. Yet, in a modern society it takes money to rear children. So, if penalties are severe perhaps such a system could work. Indeed it can work, but I think you will soon agree that it should never be allowed to.

Schemes for economic regulation usually plan on using tax exemptions. Either people would lose money for having lots of children or gain money for not having them. Such schemes are well-motivated but are morally and evolutionarily unsatisfactory. They do recognize that regulation of our density requires discouraging the birth of too many children. But instead of straightforwardly calling for everyone's enlightened participation, they cynically assume that Americans respond only to their pocketbooks.

The penalties proposed certainly do not affect the rich, middle, and poor alike. This is a serious moral problem. But there is no way to impose a monetary penalty that affects all classes equally. Rich people shouldn't be immune from any penalties, and they would not be seriously affected by such a tax plan. Poor people do not pay much tax, so they wouldn't be hurt much either. It is the middle class—the really tax-pinched class—that would be affected. And the lower middle class would be most seriously constrained.

At first glance, that might seem desirable. The middle class is responsible for two-thirds of the country's population growth. Yet the poor and near-poor cause growth, too. In fact, their current growth rate per person is higher than the more well-to-do. To handle this, the money schemes include a system of rewards: Pay people who have zero, one, or two children. Pay people to delay birth. Some say we should deny welfare for second and third illegitimate children.

These additions, however, still do not affect the wealthy. Furthermore, they have at times also been espoused by racists for reasons that had nothing to do with population control. We cannot achieve regulation without the cooperation of all races. And we must recognize that economic sanctions have been interpreted as racist by many blacks. A little reflection on the effects of economic reward systems will show that they are not completely wrong.

Buying nonbabies from one class is a form of marketing nonlife. It is very close to buying babies, a problem that I thought the U.S. Civil War settled. Population regulation is generally championed by persons with the highest humanitarian motives. They should be especially careful not to suggest anything which, owing to inequality, would reek of unfairness and border on genocide and slavery.

Inequality is a serious problem with a sanction and reward system. But it is not the most serious. That lies in the way money would work to regulate population size. It would deprive and kill or it wouldn't work at all. "Not so," object our friends. "We propose mild policies. Our policies would not harm or deprive babies. Rewards and fines would be only strong enough to influence parents."

Such a retort is naive. It ignores the force of natural selection operating on the variable response of parents. Remember, because of selection, those now alive are those who have inherited a strong tendency to reproduce. Faced with this new environment (money for nonbabies), selection can not fail to interfere. It will increase the tribe of those who think babies more important than a piddling extra luxury or two. After a while (and I think perhaps right away, too) a mild monetary program will be nothing more than a distasteful and disliked tax on babies. It won't prevent population growth at all.

Practically speaking, one must admit that because of natural selection, monetary sanctions have to be hard and cruel to succeed. In the end they must so severely punish those who indulge in extra births that the prolific do not raise more children than the prudent. They must be brutal enough to prevent births by threatening utter penury. And they must follow through by actually enforcing terrible deprivation in the prolific—terrible enough to kill their extra children.

Who needs such laws? We are trying to avoid poverty and death. Even though despair would remain scarcer with such programs than with naturally imposed shortages, we should seek alternatives. If we can find none, we must at least be honest enough to admit that density regulation via money is going to torture some people. Money control's only possible excuses are that a few will be deliberately tortured to avoid similar torture for all, and that all will have (at least ostensibly) the freedom to choose plenty, instead of all being forced into a deprived state by nature.

Fortunately, alternatives do exist.

19 two practical, maximally moral programs

Not learning, but doing is the chief thing.

Pirke Avot i:17

We can defeat natural selection if only we recognize and understand her. She is uncomplicated enough. Her speed is proportional to the inherited variation in family size. She grinds to a halt when no variation is present. So if everyone is having the same number of babies, there is no selection for family size. It turns out that we need not even insist that each family have two, only two or less. Some will want less at first. Eventually though, any inherited tendency to want less will disappear. This chapter discusses programs that can master selection and maintain low family size if people are willing to impose birth limitations on each other by law.

I ask those who consider mandatory birth limitation repressive or dictatorial to consider whether outlawing bigamy is as important to the quality of human life as recognizing by law the necessity of population control. Yet, we do outlaw bigamy. This country has imprisoned many for having more than one wife. Isn't that just as personal a matter as the number of one's children? In fact, it is much *more* personal, since how many husbands or wives one has, has no effect on the death rates of one's neighbors. And as far as giving up the temporary freedom to have large families is concerned, is this not a worthwhile sacrifice to avoid the consequences that would otherwise result? If you truly value freedom, return to Chapter 6 and read again about the Chinese situation. Return to Chapter

7 and rediscover the meaning of subsistence in eighteenth-century Imperial Japan.

Would you rather your grandchildren raise two children in a spacious house full of whatever it is they find pleasant or raise two of the four or five they bear (the others would die) in the crowded squalor of a 200 square-foot room, amidst the despair and disease of a teeming throng of constrained rabbits like themselves?

Shall we not take advantage of our ability to see the two alternatives? Nature decrees a limit to this world and all in it; so eventually couples will raise two children, no more. Shall we not conform to life's pattern before it is too late to preserve the joy of being alive?

PUT SOMETHING IN THE WATER

One perfectly workable solution to the population problem is to turn everyone off. Put a sterilant in the drinking water. Then distribute antidotes to people so they could have babies. Antidote distribution could be done in either of two ways.

The first way would be to license individual births. People would come, hat in hand, to request a birth permit. No more permits would be issued than a country would need to replenish its deaths.

One difficulty with this is obvious. People are put in the position of having to ask for a license to exercise their rights. A benign government might execute this authority evenhandedly. But why give the government the authority in the first place? Putting the government in the life-licensing game is asking for trouble. It is asking for population control to become confused with eugenics, euthanasia, and racism. Eventually some dictatorship (of the majority or of plutocrats or of an autocrat) is bound to misuse this power. It is bound to say so-and-so may not have babies at all because she has purple eyes and purple-eyed people are unhealthy, or worse, inferior. It might begin to refuse licenses to women whose parents were in old-age homes. "Let us put your poor old father to sleep, and then we'll talk about your license. After all, he is a burden to the state."

Of course, any government that practiced eugenic monstrosities would insist it was doing so to "improve its people." But who is to judge what is good and bad in man? Certainly no one can ever eliminate his genetic diseases; because of mutations and heterosis, we each carry about five alleles that could cause death in a quarter of our children if we should accidentally marry the wrong person. The only fair and successful program of eugenics would be mass suicide. Eugenics must be excised from population control. We must not make it easy for governments to practice Hitlerian heinousness.

The second method for distributing antidotes is less unfair. Antidotes would be added to the water by a computer on a random basis. The antidote would be added just often enough to cause births to match deaths.

The computer would work automatically and impartially. Of course, no one could be allowed to know when the water was potentiating. Presumably people would still be allowed to use birth control devices so that they wouldn't *have* to have babies when antidote was floating around.

So, what is wrong with this method? Just this. The computer cannot recognize individual rights when putting the antidote in the water. A birth in one family is the same as a birth in any other. Only the population counts. Therefore, some women will be lucky. They will accidentally be allowed by the computer to have four (or even more) children. Others who want two, may not even get one. After a while, this won't be selected for because luck isn't heritable. But at first, people who spend practically their whole lives in bed will have a tremendous advantage. Eventually, all other forms of entertainment should become extinct.

The thinking reader will chuckle at this. He knows I haven't come to the all-encompassing objection to this program. We don't *have* anything to put in the water. As far as I know, no one is even testing any such substance. Yet, the problems of overpopulation are already upon us.

We may not mind producing a nation with a superpotent id, but first we must find a way to do it and do it safely. To test a new sterilant once it has been invented requires from 40 to 50 years, 4 to 10 years for animal tests, a decade for preliminary human tests to check for efficacy and for immediate side effects, and an additional 30 years in a larger human test to check for rarer, long-term effects such as cancer. Add this to the 70 years needed to stop population growth and the unknown amounts of time needed to discover the substance in the first place and install appropriate, safe machinery to add it to the water after it has been tested, and we require a minimum of over a century to do the job—the job that could stand doing tomorrow. Forget it. We can do much better.

POPULATIONAL PAREGORIC
FOR A MODERATE CASE OF CRAMPS

Density regulation can be minimally obstrusive, democratic, humane, and evolutionarily sound. In fact, it is the simplest program that has all these attributes. Since overpopulation is indeed everyone's problem, it is equally everyone's responsibility to do something about it.

Everyone has the right to reproduce. We should take steps to insure, with proper medical care, that everyone is permitted to reproduce. But no one should have the right to overreproduce, to have more than two children. It should be everyone's job to shoulder the burden of controlling natural selection and keeping human population at comfortable, life-preserving, submaximal densities. That is consonant with the nature of a democracy. Unfortunately, this requires a national decision. To get that decision requires an intensive program of education in population ecology. Who knows; perhaps the people, when informed of their opportunity, will prefer the marginal world of maximum population. I doubt it. But that will be a question of values and priorities. I would disagree, but only as a liberty-loving, religious individual. As a scientist, I could not prove such a decision wrong. It would be scientifically sound.

Assuming the people also disagree, they must press their president and legislators for a legislative program. An acquaintance, a famous conservation lawyer, is of the opinion that such a program may even require a constitutional amendment. I don't know. I can only outline the scientific elements such a set of laws must contain. The formal structure of such laws must be left to legislative experts. To minimize the burden on one congress, this set of laws could be enacted in stages.

Stage one: voluntary compliance. The American people are almost certainly unique in their willingness to sacrifice for their country. Undoubtedly to a large extent this is due to their sense of their country's being truly a *res publica*, a thing of the people. I believe that if they are honestly told the reasons for population regulation, that almost all will be happy to participate. Sure they'll gripe, just as they do in paying income tax. But they pay. And they are proud of their record of not cheating much.

The worst possible mistake a law could make is to assume that the people need to be browbeaten into compliance. They will be happier to participate if their sense of individual responsibility is acknowledged. In any event, coercing a recalcitrant population into compliance is undoubtedly impossible, except by unacceptable police-state methods—in part, just what population regulation seeks desperately to avoid. For our density to be regulated, *most* of the people will have to realize the importance of their individual acts and participate freely.

Thus, the first thing the Congress must do is declare and enable a policy of zero population growth. On behalf of future generations, Congress must ask for the gift of a stable, submaximal population size. Then, it must make sure everyone has the means to comply. Last, it must make sure everyone has a reason to comply—that none of us is being forced to live in the kind of world that overpopulation will create.

The first is fulfilled with a declaration of the absolute right of each man and each woman to be the natural parent of two children, but no more. This means that a divorced person with one child would have the right to one more in a second marriage; that a mother of two illegitimate children would have used up her rights; that a widower with two children would have used his. Obviously, any parent who had suffered the tragedy of losing a child would have the right to replace it. Adopted children would not count against their parents, but against their natural mother and father.

Giving everyone the means to comply means providing *absolutely free* all methods of birth control to anyone who asks. This includes more than the pill, diaphragms, jellies, foams, condoms, and IUDs. It means free voluntary sterilization (India actually pays her people to get sterilized) and free abortion. Some people are unable to retain the IUD. Some are unable to take pills. Different religions will prefer different methods. But with abortion and sterilization as completely effective backstops, our birth-control technology is already competent to achieve a steady state. The amount of money and misery the country will save easily justifies the costs of such a program.

Last, we must recognize that whatever the cause, many of our people are already living with the symptoms of overpopulation. They are sardined into decrepit tenements. Their diets are so inadequate that their children eat plaster from the walls. In rural areas they suffer from filthy water, from worms and insect-borne diseases. Their clothes are inadequate (there's an understatement). They are poorly educated, as much because starving children make sleepy, inattentive students as for any other reason. They have much higher death rates and shorter, more brutal lives. The city poor never even see a cow or a blade of grass, let alone a deer or a forest. They spend most (or all) of their lives within a few blocks of their birthplaces.

Is it an accident that our poorer countrymen exhibit the whole over-population syndrome—riots included? Perhaps (though I think not). Never-theless, they have nothing to gain from population regulation. We must repair their environment before we can expect their help. We must make sure that every American is guaranteed a low-density standard of living. Not a certain amount of money—that is often just a salve to rich consciences. But good food, decent shelter, adequate clothes, and sound health care should be their right. Children should be guaranteed a few summers at truly natural camps. Public transportation must provide everyone with a meaningful right to travel. That is a massive job for our country. But it is vital. We must have the enthusiastic support of all segments of our people before we can succeed at density control.

Is all this verbiage just another excuse for a welfare state? That is a jaundiced view. If we take it, you can be sure our grandchildren will wish bitterly that we had been less greedy. Their lives will be the same or worse than that of the ghetto blacks, whose help we need so desperately.

If a decent all-ages social-security system still bothers you, look at it this way. Nobody will get real luxuries. In return for each person's willing-ness to harness his prodigious reproductive power in order to maintain a healthy, free society, society will guarantee him his necessities and his environmental rights. That is fair compensation for a most essential task.

Stage two: research and planning of population densities on a local basis. Congress will create and fund a network of study institutes to develop an idea of what densities people want and what these densities will mean for their standard of living and way of life. Final answers will require much more research, an incredible program of education, and a massive infusion of public opinion. Once population control is embarked upon, however, time is *not* of the essence. We'll have all the time in the world to increase *after* we decide we want to. I'll bet we'll decide to live at lower densities in much of our country.

Stage three: coercion. It is possible that an overwhelming majority of Americans will prefer a lower than bursting-point density, but that a small percentage will not care. Perhaps the majority will become indignant and insist that their elected officials see to it that the renegade few are not allowed to run roughshod over the many—both alive and unborn. If so, our population control policy will be asked to grow teeth.

Though these reproductive renegades will be true criminals, the teeth can be much gentler than prison, much more specific and less damaging than fines. Penalties should be environmental. They should be directed only against parents of two living children who allow a third child to be born. These people will have shown no respect for the environmental rights of others. They will threaten by their actions to bring death to countless millions of babies. Such irresponsibility could justify any punishment, but in my opinion, cruel revenge is unbefitting a moral society. Fitting penalties need not kill.

For misuse of their reproductive power, such people could be required to give it up. Tubal ligation of the women *and* vasectomy of the men does not deprive them of any sexual potency (in some, potency is even enhanced). But it does deprive them of the opportunity for further antisocial behavior.

For the threat to nature, such parents can be denied hunting and fishing licenses (there will be no more in an overpopulated world). Their access to public parks and recreation areas can be rationed or denied. They can be placed on a strict gasoline ration and prohibited from buying more than the smallest necessary cars. For their attempted rape of the land, they can be denied the privilege of purchasing it or of owning more than a small house lot. They should be disqualified from service on the great boards of American corporations, whose large land holdings and all-pervasive decisions place them in a vital position and saddle them with a public trust of far-reaching proportions.

It is hoped this stage will be totally unnecessary. But if it is necessary, the suggestions above demonstrate that relevant, environmentally oriented penalties are possible and serious.

Stage four: development of an effective, temporary sterilant. Even the tiniest amount of heritable renegadism is going to ruin us in the long run if it is ignored. We must, therefore, continue our efforts to develop a totally safe, individual, temporary sterilant. When we get one, people with two children, still facing the possible loss of one, could be required to use it. Mandatory *temporary* sterilization would not punish anyone, but it would prevent everyone from committing renegade acts. In this case, prevention is the only long-term remedy. A fringe benefit of preventive, temporary sterilization is that all penalties would become unnecessary.

Probably we shall not have the means for stage four until a century has passed. Fortunately we shall probably not need it for two or three hundred years.

For reasons now obvious to the reader of this chapter, mandatory, permanent, preventive sterilization is unsatisfactory (another understatement). It deprives honest, responsible parents of the right to replace their own prematurely lost children. It is therefore a punishment. In this country, the innocent are not supposed to be punished intentionally.

Stage five: maintaining our stable densities. Since babies are alive, they run the risk of death. Man cannot hope to eliminate that risk entirely. Some people will lose babies after they are unable to replace them. Also some families will die in accidents. Some will elect to have one child or remain childless. Finally, we may never know how to ensure everyone's fertility—some couples are likely to be sterile even with the finest medical care possible. All these people create a deficit in population. To maintain a steady state, our country will have to make up for their loss. Some women with two children will need to have a third.

Extra births can come only from those who have already exercised their birth rights. In contemporary America, for example, couples must average about 2.1 or 2.2 children per family to cause, in 60 to 70 years, the attainment of a steady state. Allowing for sterile, childless, and one-child people, about three families out of ten would need to have three children. This proportion would decline if medical practice improves even more.

We must not allow these extra births to accrue to people solely by choice. If we do, natural selection will soon force everyone to choose three. We must instead distribute these extra birth rights at random, again without regard to race, creed, color, religion, physique, talent, intelligence, or any other attribute. When the time comes—and that will be in a generation or two, as soon as we decide on our optimal densities—we must erect what will be the grandest, most humanely inspired lottery the world has ever seen. One and only one ticket will be available to people with two children who would like a third. Tickets will be free and nontransferable. Enough extra birth rights would be distributed to make up that year's (or months's) deficit. Needless to say, no one could have four children until everyone who wanted three had had three.

With such a system, extra births are a function of luck. They are not inheritable. Thus, we contradict one of the two basic requirements of natural selection: heritability of differences in phenotype. Family size will not increase. Selection will not be able to defeat us in our attempt to preserve a humane, civilized environment.

Stage six: multiple births. Now we must really gaze deeply into our evolutionary crystal ball. The tendency to produce twins and triplets is also known to be inherited. So, after a few hundred years, we should begin to see an increase in the incidence of twins at second delivery and of triplets at first. No one can blame such mothers. They are innocent of intention. But just the same, their tendency will eventually scuttle our population plans. Within the next 500 years, we need to learn to control multiple births. Since medicine already has a drug to *increase* their incidence, decreasing them would seem a realistic goal.

There are probably other questions and problems which occur to the reader. This chapter is meant merely as a guide, not an encyclopedia. But it does deal with most of the important biological issues. And it hints at the all-pervasive nature of any human attempt to maintain an artificially low birth rate.

Density regulation ought not be undertaken in panic by any country. Granted we are already in a bind. But the mess we have created has crept upon us gradually. Overpopulation is not a sudden phenomenon. Granted, too, that the mess will worsen—and at an accelerating rate. Still, population regulation will take a long, long time to have its final effects. It will start to work very slowly, and only after a generation will its effects be noticeable. Speed is of the essence, but the phrase "all deliberate speed" applies. We must proceed deliberately, rationally, knowledgeably. The sooner we embark on a practical program, the faster the mess will clear and the less debilitating will be its nadir. But if we stampede into half-baked, part-way legislative guesswork, the forces pitted against us will easily withstand our unarmed attack. We shall be worse off than if we'd done nothing. Only the combined onslaught of the entire American people, using all the available knowledge of population biology, can succeed in holding the fort. Shouting slogans, hunting witches, and declaring doomsday are, however well-intentioned, polarizing, unrealistic, and defeating activities. Education; calm, rationally optimistic persistence; and a love for human life will bear, someday within this generation, informed legislative fruit containing the seeds of mankind's most important victory.

POPULATION DAY

What can we as individuals do to help? Learn and teach—in that order. Where matters of life and death are concerned, we must be intolerant of irresponsible hot air. Have no respect for the person who begins a long, emotional tirade on the superfluousness of population regulation or the absence of overpopulation problems by saying, "I don't know, but it's my opinion. . . ." Opinions don't count in this, only bloated bellies and maddened crowds. The only relevant opinion is whether a marginal existence is better or worse than giving up the temporary right to more than two children. That is exactly our choice.

Ours is one of the few nations in which the people can shape their laws. But to do it they must be patient and persistent. Their first attempts are often frustrated, but they must not tire of expressing themselves. Their legislative representatives will enact appropriate laws as soon as the people's mandate becomes clear.

Therefore, let those who understand the issues do one thing more. Let them conduct an unorganized, spontaneous, annual national referendum.

I propose that February 1 of each year be declared, by the action of concerned people, Population Day. Each person who feels he has learned
enough to make a decision should write his congressman, his senator, and
the president to express himself on this matter. The letter need not be long.
Its very existence would proclaim the individual's concern over the serious-
ness of the problem. In fact, enterprising greeting-card companies might
want to offer people a handy variety of ready-to-sign sentiments befitting
receipt by our political leaders.

From now on, each February 1, my letters will look something like this:

Dear Mr. President,
I am concerned that overpopulation in our country will do great harm to our
people. It threatens to sap us of our strength, deprive us of adequate food, clothing,
and shelter, destroy our magnificent natural wealth, and rob us of our tranquility.

Today, there is no program in the United States to achieve zero population
growth. For the sake of my children and theirs, I demand the right to participate
effectively along with my fellow Americans in such a program. Please help to grant
me this right. Please give first priority to the design of legislation that would
simultaneously ensure everyone's right to two children and declare that no American
has the right to more.

Giving up our transitory right to have large families is the greatest possible gift we
can bestow on the generations that succeed us. Only thus can we hand on to them
God's green Earth—properly husbanded, reasonably fruitful, goodly and pleasant.

bibliography

Whosoever reports a thing in the name of him that said it brings deliverance into the world.

Pirke Avot vi:6

I

ALLEN, D. L. 1962. *Our wildlife legacy.** Rev. ed. Funk & Wagnalls, New York. 422 pp.

BUSTARD, H. R. 1970. The role of behavior in the natural regulation of numbers in the gekkonid lizard *Gehyra variegata. Ecology* 51:724–728.

CAUGHLEY, G. 1970. Eruption of ungulate populations, with emphasis on Himalayan thar in New Zealand. *Ecology* 51:53–72.

CONNELL, J. H. 1961. The influence of interspecific competition and other factors on the distribution of the barnacle *Chthamalus stellatus. Ecology* 42:710–723.

CONNELL, J. H. 1970. A predator-prey system in the marine intertidal region. I. *Balanus glandula* and several predatory species of *Thais. Ecol. Monog.* 40:49–78.

COOK, E. 1971. The flow of energy in an industrial society. *Sci. Amer.* 225(3):134–144.

CROWCROFT, P. 1966. *Mice all over.** G. T. Foulis, London. 121 pp.

CROWCROFT, P., and F. P. ROWE. 1958. The growth of confined colonies of the wild house mouse: the effect of dispersal on female fecundity. *Pr. Zool. Soc. Lond.* 131:357–365.

* References appearing with an asterisk are general works written in nontechnical language.

DEL MORAL, R., and R. G. CATES. 1971. Allelopathic potential of the dominant vegetation of western Washington. *Ecology* 52:1030–1037.

DETHIER, V. G., and R. H. MacARTHUR. 1964. A field's capacity to support a butterfly population. *Nature* 201:728–729.

EINARSEN, A. S. 1945. Some factors affecting ring-necked pheasant population density. *Murrelet* 26:39–44.

EISENBERG, R. M. 1966. The regulation of density in a natural population of the pond snail, *Lymnaea elodes*. *Ecology* 47:889–906.

ELTON, C., and A. J. NICHOLSON. 1942. The ten year cycle in numbers of the lynx in Canada. *J. Animal Ecol.* 11:215–244.

FREMLIN, J. H. 1964. How many people can the world support? *New Scientist* No. 415:285–287.

GASHWILER, J. S. 1970. Plant and mammal changes on a clearcut in west-central Oregon. *Ecology* 51:1018–1026.

GATES, D. M. 1971. The flow of energy in the biosphere. *Sci. Amer.* 225(3):88–100.

GIDDINGS, J. C., and M. B. MONROE, eds. 1972. *Our chemical environment.* Canfield Press, San Francisco. 367 pp.

GILPIN, M. 1973. Do hares eat lynx? *Amer. Natur.* 107:727–730.

GOUGH, W. C., and B. J. EASTLUND. 1971. The prospects of fusion power. *Sci. Amer.* 225(3):50–64.

HAARTMAN, L. v. 1971. Population dynamics. Pp. 391–459. In Farner, King, and Parkes, eds., *Avian biology.* Vol. 1. Academic, New York. 586 pp.

HARDIN, G. 1959. Interstellar migration and the population problem. *J. Heredity* 50:68–70.

HARDIN, G. 1969. *Population, evolution, and birth control.* 2nd ed. Freeman, San Francisco. 386 pp.

HASLER, A. D. 1970. Man induced eutrophication of lakes. Pp. 110–125. In S. F. Singer, ed., *Global effects of environmental pollution.* Springer, New York.

HENSLEY, M. M., and J. B. COPE. 1951. Further data on removal and repopulation of breeding birds in a spruce–fir forest community. *Auk* 68:483–493.

HUBBERT, M. K. 1971. The energy resources of the earth. *Sci. Amer.* 225(3):60–70.

KEMP, W. B. 1971. The flow of energy in a hunting society. *Sci. Amer.* 225(3):104–115.

KESSLER, A. 1968. Social behavior and population dynamics: evolutionary relationships. Pp. 169–177. In D. C. Glass, ed., *Genetics.* Rockefeller University Press and Russell Sage, New York. 260 pp.

KEYFITZ, N. 1971. On the momentum of population growth. *Demography* 8:71–80.

KLEIN, D. R. 1968. The introduction, increase, and crash of reindeer of St. Matthew Island. *J. Wildl. Mgmt.* 32:350–367.

KLUIJVER, H. N. 1951. The population ecology of the great tit, *Parus m. major* L. *Ardea* 39:1–135.

KOZLOVSKY, D. G. 1968. A critical evaluation of the trophic level concept. I. Ecological efficiencies. *Ecology* 49:48–60.

LACK, D. L. 1964. A long-term study of the great tit *(Parus major).* Pp. 159–173. In A. MacFadyen and P. J. Newbould, eds., *British ecological society jubilee symposium.* Blackwell Scientific, Oxford. 244 pp.

LACK, D. L. 1966. *Population studies of birds.** Clarendon, Oxford. 341 pp.

LAO TZU. 1958. *Tao teh king: the book of nature and intelligence.* Interpreted by A. J. Bahm. Ungar, New York. 126 pp.

LINDEMANN, R. 1941. Seasonal food-cycle dynamics in a senescent lake. *Amer. Midl. Natur.* 26:636–673.

MILLER, G. R. 1968. Evidence for selective feeding on fertilized plots by red grouse, hares and rabbits. *J. Wildl. Mgmt.* 32:849–853.

MILLER, G. R.; A. WATSON; and D. JENKINS. 1970. Responses of red grouse populations to experimental improvement of their food. Pp. 323–335. In A. Watson, ed., *Animal populations in relation to their food resources.* Blackwell Scientific, Oxford. 477 pp.

MILLS, G. A.; H. R. JOHNSON; and H. PERRY. 1971. Fuels management in an environmental age. *Env. Sci. Tech.* 5:30–38.

PALMBLAD, I. G. 1968. Competition in experimental populations of weeds with emphasis on the regulation of population size. *Ecology* 49:26–34.

PARK, T.; P. H. LESLIE; and D. B. MERTZ. 1964. Genetic strains and competition in populations of *Tribolium. Physiol. Zool.* 37:97–162.

PETIPA, T. S.; E. V. PAVLOVA; and G. N. MIRONOV. 1970. The food web structure, utilization and transport of energy by trophic levels in the planktonic communities. Pp. 142–167. In J. H. Steele, ed., *Marine food chains.* University of California Press, Berkeley. 552 pp.

RAPPAPORT, R. A. 1971. The flow of energy in an agricultural society. *Sci. Amer.* 225(3):116–132.

REYNOLDSON, T. B. 1961. A quantitative study of the population biology of *Dugesia lugubris. Oikos* 12:111–125.

SCHEFFER, V. B. 1951. The rise and fall of a reindeer herd. *Sci. Monthly* 73:356–362.

SELYE, H. 1956. *The stress of life.** McGraw-Hill, New York. 324 pp.

SLOBODKIN, L. B. 1961. *Growth and regulation of animal populations.** Holt, Rinehart & Winston, New York. 184 pp.

SOUTHWICK, C. H. 1955. The population dynamics of confined house mice supplied with unlimited food. *Ecology* 36:212–225.

STEWART, R. E., and J. W. ALDRICH. 1951. Removal and repopulation of breeding birds in a spruce-fir forest community. *Auk* 68:471–482.

STIMSON, J. 1970. Territorial behavior of the owl limpet, *Lottia gigantea. Ecology* 51:113–118.

SUMMERS, C. M. 1971. The conversion of energy. *Sci. Amer.* 225(3):148–160.

WATT, K. E. F. 1973. *Principles of environmental science.** McGraw-Hill, New York. 384 pp.

WILSON, R. E., and E. L. RICE. 1968. Allelopathy as expressed by *Helianthus annus* and its role in old field succession. *Bull. Torrey Bot. Club* 95:432–448.

WOODGERD, W. 1964. Population dynamics of bighorn sheep on Wildhorse Island. *J. Wildl. Mgmt.* 28:381–391.

WOODWELL, G. M. 1970. The energy cycle of the biosphere. *Sci. Amer.* 223(3):64–74.

WYNNE-EDWARDS, V. C. 1968. Population control and social selection in animals. Pp. 143–163. In D. C. Glass, ed., *Genetics.* Rockefeller University Press and Russell Sage, New York. 260 pp.

II

AIRD, J. S. 1960. The present and prospective population of mainland China. Pp. 93–133. In *Population trends in eastern Europe, the U.S.S.R. and mainland China.* Milbank Memorial Fund, New York.

BAYSAL, A. 1968. Present situation in Turkey regarding malnutrition in infants and preschool children—types of problems, magnitude of problems, location. Pp. 45–60. In Shields.

BENGOA, J. M. 1966. The prevention of malnutrition in young children. Pp. 36–43. In Western Hemisphere Nutrition Congress—1965.

BERG, A. 1971. Priority of nutrition in national development. Pp. 12–25. In N. S. Scrimshaw and A. M. Altschul, eds., *Amino acid fortification of protein foods.* MIT Press, Cambridge, Mass. 664 pp.

BLIX, G., ed. 1963. *Mild-moderate forms of protein calorie malnutrition.* Swedish Nutrition Foundation, Bastad, Sweden. 159 pp.

BOFFEY, P. M. 1970. Japan: a crowded nation wants to boost its birthrate. *Science* 167:960–962.

BORGSTROM, H. 1969. *Too many.** Macmillan, New York. 368 pp.

BOULDING, K. E. 1956. *The image.* University of Michigan Press, Ann Arbor, Mich.

BRINTON, C. C. 1952. *The anatomy of revolution.* Rev. ed. Prentice-Hall, Englewood Cliffs, N.J. 324 pp.

BRONFENBRENNER, M., and J. A. BUTTRICK. 1961. Population control in Japan: an economic theory and its application. Pp. 160–181. In M. G. Shimm and R. O. Everett, eds., *Population control.* Oceana, Dobbs Ferry, N.Y.

BROWN, L. R. 1970. *Seeds of change.** Praeger, New York.

BROWN, L. R. 1970. Human food production as a process in the biosphere. *Sci. Amer.* 223(3):160–170.

BRYCE-SMITH, D. 1972. Lead pollution—a growing hazard to public health. Pp. 140–145. In Giddings and Monroe.

CHISOLM, J. J., Jr. 1971. Lead poisoning. *Sci. Amer.* 224(2):15–23.

CHOW, T. J., and J. L. EARL. 1970. Lead aerosols in the atmosphere: increasing concentrations. *Science* 169:577–580.

CRAIG, P. P. 1972. Lead, the inexcusable pollutant. Pp. 134–136. In Giddings and Monroe.

CRAVIOTO, J., and E. R. DeLICARDIE. 1968. Nutrition and mental subnormality. Pp. 132–144. In Third Far East Symposium.

CRAVIOTO, J., and B. ROBLES. 1963. The influence of protein-calorie malnutrition on psychological test behavior. Pp. 115–126. In Blix.

DASMANN, R. F. 1963. *The last horizon.** Macmillan, New York.

DLAMINI, V. M. 1969. Report on nutrition in Swaziland. Pp. 96–106. In Eastern African Conference.

DROPPERS, G. 1894. The population of Japan in the Tokugawa period. *Trans. Asiatic Soc. Japan,* 22:253–284.

DUMONT, R., and B. ROSIER. 1969. *The hungry future.** Praeger, New York.

EASTERN AFRICAN CONFERENCE ON NUTRITION AND CHILD FEEDING (Proc.). 1969. Agency for International Development, U.S. Department of State, Washington, D.C. 311 pp.

EHRLICH, P. R. and A. H. 1970. *Population, resources, environment: issues in human ecology.** Freeman, San Francisco.

EHRLICH, P. R., and J. HOLDREN. 1971. Impact of population growth. *Science* 171:1212–1216.

EICHENWALD, H. F., and P. C. FRY. 1969. Nutrition and learning. *Science* 163:644–648.

FISHER, J. 1969. The easy chair—the Minnesota experiment: How to make a big city fit to live in. *Harper's Magazine* 238(1427, April):12–32.

FLAHERTY, D. L., and C. B. HUFFAKER. 1970. Biological control of Pacific mites and Willamette mites in San Joaquin Valley vineyards. *Hilgardia* 40:267–330.

FRIEND, M. O., and D. O. TRAINER. 1970. Polychorinated biphenyl: interaction with duck hepatitis virus. *Science* 170:1314–1316.

GIBBON, E. 1776–1788. *The history of the decline and fall of the Roman empire.* Many editions.

GOLDSMITH, J. R., and A. C. HEXTER. 1967. Respiratory exposure to lead: epidemiological and experimental dose-response relationships. *Science* 158:132–134.

HABTE, D. 1969. Report on nutrition in Ethiopia. Pp. 32–40. In Eastern African Conference.

HARDIN, G. 1971. Nobody ever dies of overpopulation. *Science* 171:527.

HEMPHILL, F. E.; M. L. KAEBERLE; and W. B. BUCK. 1971. Lead suppression of mouse resistance to *Salmonella typhimurium*. *Science* 172:1031–1032.

HEYDAYAT, H. 1968. The present situation in Iran. Pp. 75–80. In Shields.

HOROWITZ, A. 1966. The physician's view of nutritional needs in the western hemisphere. Pp. 3–7. In Western Hemisphere Nutrition Congress.

HUANG, Y. C. 1971. Birth control education campaigns. P. 27. In Piotrow.

HUNTINGTON, E. 1911. *Palestine and its transformation.* Houghton Mifflin, Boston.

INTENGAN, C. 1968. Progress report of nutrition in the Philippines. Pp. 71–77. In Third Far East Symposium on Nutrition.

JELIFFE, D. B. 1969. *Child nutrition in developing countries.* Agency for International Development, U.S. Department of State, Washington, D.C. 200 pp.

KEVANY, J. 1966. Nutritional problems in Latin America. Pp. 50–57. In Western Hemisphere Nutritional Congress.

LADEJINSKY, W. 1970. Ironies of India's green revolution. *Foreign Affairs* 48:758–768.

LANGER, W. L. 1972. Checks on population growth. *Sci. Amer.* 226(6):92–99.

LAZRUS, A. L.; E. LORANGE; and J. P. LODGE, Jr. 1970. Lead and other metal ions in United States precipitation. *Env. Sci. Tech.* 4:55–58.

LINTON, R. M. 1970. *Terracide.** Little, Brown, Boston, Mass. 376 pp.

LOCHRIE, G. 1969. Report on nutrition in Botswana. Pp. 12–31. In Eastern African Conference.

MEEK, R. 1954. *Marx and Engels on Malthus.* International Publishers, New York.

MEIJER, M. J. 1971. *Marriage law and policy in the Chinese People's Republic.* Hong Kong University Press, Hong Kong, B.C.C. 369 pp.

MILES, R. E., Jr. 1971. *Man's population predicament. Pop. Bull.* 27(2), 40 pp.

MISOMALI, Y. H. 1969. Report on nutrition in Malawi. Pp. 69–79. In Eastern African Conference.

MOWAT, F. 1952. *People of the deer.** Little, Brown, Boston, Mass. 344 pp.

MUYANGA, S. L. D. 1969. Report on nutrition in Uganda. Pp. 128–135. In Eastern African Conference.

OISO, T. 1968. Supplementary foods for infants and school children. Pp. 145–152. In Third Far Eastern Symposium on Nutrition.

PATWARDHAN, V. N., and W. J. DARBY. 1972. *The state of nutrition in the Arab Middle East.* Vanderbilt University Press, Nashville. 308 pp.

PIOTROW, P. T., ed. 1971. *Population and family planning in the People's Republic of China.* Victor-Bostrum Fund and Population Crisis Committee, Washington, D.C. 35 pp.

RAHMAN, M. H. 1968. Present situation of nutritional status of infants and pre-school children in Pakistan. Pp. 61–74. In Shields.

ROSENZWEIG, M. L. 1971. Paradox of enrichment: destabilization of exploitation ecosystems in ecological time. *Science* 171:385–387.

ROSENZWEIG, M. L. 1972. *Reply to* Stability of enriched aquatic ecosystems. *Science* 175:564–565.

SAUVY, A. 1961. *Fertility and survival.** Chatto & Windus, London. 232 pp.

SEMITI, G. A. 1969. Report on nutrition in Tanzania. Pp. 107–127. In Eastern African Conference.

SERENI, E., and R. E. ASHERY, eds. 1936. *Jews and Arabs in Palestine.* Hechalutz, New York.

SHETRONE, H. C. 1945. A unique prehistoric irrigation project. *Annual Rep. Smithsonian Inst.* 379–386.

SHIELDS, L. L., ed. 1968. *CENTO conference on combating malnutrition in pre-school children.* CENTO, Ankara.

SIMPSON, D. 1968. The dimensions of world poverty. *Sci. Amer.* 219(5):27–35.

SNOW, E. 1971. Population care and control. Pp. 6–11. In Piotrow.

STERLING, C. 1972. The Aswan disaster. Pp. 84–90. In Giddings and Monroe.

THIENES, C. H., and T. J. HALEY. 1972. *Clinical toxicology.* 5th ed. Lea and Febiger, Philadelphia. 459 pp.

THIRD FAR EAST SYMPOSIUM ON NUTRITION. 1968. Republic of the Philippines and National Institute of Health, Washington, D.C. 317 pp.

TURK, A.; J. TURK; and J. T. WITTES. 1972. *Ecology, pollution, environment.* Saunders, Philadelphia. 217 pp.

VAMOER, A. P. 1969. Report on nutrition in Zambia. Pp. 152–173. In Eastern African Conference.

WEBB, G. 1959. *A Pima remembers.* University of Arizona Press, Tucson. 126 pp.

WESTERN HEMISPHERE NUTRITION CONGRESS—1965. 1966. American Medical Association, Chicago. 255 pp.

WILLIAMS, C. D. 1966. Factors in the ecology of malnutrition. Pp. 20–24. In Western Hemisphere Nutrition Congress.

III

PADDOCK, W. and P. 1967. *Famine—1975!* Little, Brown, Boston, Mass.

IV

ALLISON, A. C. 1955. Aspects of polymorphism in man. *Cold Spring Harbor Symp. Quant. Biol.* 20:239–255.

ALLISON, A. C. 1956. Sickle cells and evolution. *Sci. Amer.* 195(2):87–94.

ALLISON, A. C. 1964. Polymorphism and natural selection in human populations. *Cold Spring Harbor Symp. Quant. Biol.* 29:137–149.

APLIN, R. T.; M. H. BENN; and M. ROTHSCHILD. 1968. Poisonous alkaloids in the body tissues of the cinnabar moth (*Callimorpha jacobaeae* L.). *Nature* 219:747–748.

ARDITTI, J. 1966. Orchids. *Sci. Amer.* 214(1):70–78.

BAJEMA, C. T., ed. 1971. *Natural selection in human populations.* Wiley, New York. 406 pp.

BARGHOORN, E. S. 1971. The oldest fossils. *Sci. Amer.* 224(5):30–42.

BARGHOORN, E. S., and S. A. TYLER. 1965. Microorganisms from the Gunflint Chert. *Science* 147:563–577.

BRAIDWOOD, R. J. 1960. The agricultural revolution. *Sci. Amer.* 203(3):131–148.

BRIGGS, D., and S. M. WALTERS. 1969. *Plant variation and evolution.** World University Library. McGraw-Hill, New York. 256 pp.

BRONOWSKI, J. 1963. The clock paradox. *Sci. Amer.* 208(2):134–144.

BROWER, J. V. Z. 1958. Experimental studies of mimicry in some North American butterflies. Part II. *Evolution* 12:123–136.

BROWER, L. P. 1969. Ecological chemistry. *Sci. Amer.* 220(2):22–29.

BROWER, L. P.; J. V. Z. BROWER; and J. M. CORVINO. 1967. Plant poisons in a terrestrial food chain. *Pr. Nat. Acad. Sci. (U.S.A.)* 57:893–898.

BROWN, J. H. 1971. The desert pupfish. *Sci. Amer.* 225(5):104–110.

BRUES, C. T. 1951. Insects in amber. *Sci. Amer.* 185(5):56–61.

CHAMBERS, K. L., ed. 1970. *Biochemical coevolution.* Oregon State University Press, Corvallis.

CHUBB, S. H. 1913. The horse under domestication. *Amer. Mus. Natur. Hist., Guide Leaflet* 36(2):36–60.

CLARK, W. E. L. 1955. *The fossil evidence for human evolution.* University of Chicago Press. 181 pp.

COLBERT, E. H. 1965. *The age of reptiles.** Norton, New York. 228 pp.

COOK, L. M.; L. P. BROWER; and J. ALCOCK. 1969. An attempt to verify mimetic advantage in a neotropical environment. *Evolution* 23:339–345.

COOPER, C. F. 1961. The ecology of fire. *Sci. Amer.* 204(4):150–160.

CROW, J. F. 1959. Ionizing radiation and evolution. *Sci. Amer.* 201(3):138–160.

DART, R. A. 1949. Innominate fragments of *Australopithecus prometheus. Amer. J. Phys. Anthropol.* (n.s.) 7:301–333.

DARWIN, C. 1845. *The voyage of the Beagle.** Many editions.

DARWIN, C. 1859. *The origin of species by means of natural selection.* Many editions.

DARWIN, C. 1958. *Autobiography.** Edited by N. Barlow. Harcourt, New York. 253 pp.

DEEVEY, E. S., Jr. 1952. Radiocarbon dating. *Sci. Amer.* 186(2):24–28.

DIAMOND, J. 1969. Avifaunal equilibria and species turnover rates on the channel islands of California. *Pr. Nat. Acad. Sci. (U.S.A.).* 64:57–63.

DOBZHANSKY, T. 1948. Genetics of natural populations XVIII. Experiments on chromosomes of *Drosophila pseudoobscura* from different geographic regions. *Genetics* 33:588–602.

DOBZHANSKY, T. 1950. The genetic basis of evolution. *Sci. Amer.* 182(1):32–41.

DOBZHANSKY, T. 1960. The present evolution of man. *Sci. Amer.* 203(3):206–217.

DOBZHANSKY, T., and A. H. STURTEVANT. 1938. Inversions in the chromosomes of *Drosophila pseudoobscura. Genetics* 23:28–64.

EHRLICH, P. R., and P. H. RAVEN. 1965. Butterflies and plants: a study in coevolution. *Evolution* 18:586–608.

EHRLICH, P. R., and P. H. RAVEN. 1967. Butterflies and plants. *Sci. Amer.* 216(6): 104–113.

EISELEY, L. 1959. Charles Lyell. *Sci. Amer.* 201(2):98–106.

FALCONER, D. S. 1960. *Introduction to quantitative genetics.* Oliver & Boyd, Edinburgh. 365 pp.

FENNER, F. J., and F. N. RATCLIFFE. 1965. *Myxomatosis.* Cambridge University Press, London. 379 pp.

FISHER, R. A. 1958. *The genetical theory of natural selection.* 2nd rev. ed. Dover, New York. 291 pp.

FORD, E. B. 1965. *Ecological genetics.** 2nd ed. Methuen, London. 335 pp.

GAUSE, G. F. 1934. *The struggle for existence.* Williams & Wilkins, Baltimore, Md.

GLAESSNER, M. F. 1961. Pre-cambrian animals. *Sci. Amer.* 204(3):72–78.

GLASS, H. B. 1953. The genetics of Dunkers. *Sci. Amer.* 189(2):76–81.

GRAF, A. B. 1963. *Exotica third.* Roehrs, Rutherford, N.J. 1828 pp.

GRANT, V. 1951. The fertilization of flowers. *Sci. Amer.* 184(6):52–56.

GREGORY, W. K. 1920. On the structure and relations of *Notharctus,* an American eocene primate. *Mem. Amer. Mus. Natur. Hist.* (n.s.) 3(2):45–243.

GREGORY, W. K., and M. HELLMAN. 1926. The dentition of *Dryopithecus* and the origin of man. *Anthrop. Papers Amer. Mus. Natur. Hist.* 28:1–123.

HALDANE, J. B. S. 1932. *The causes of evolution.** Longmans, Green, London.

HALDANE, J. B. S. 1949. The rate of mutation of human genes. *Pr. Int. Congr. Genet.* 8:267–273.

HALL, E. R., and K. R. KELSON. 1959. *The mammals of North America.* 2 vols. Ronald Press, New York. 1083 pp.

HOCKETT, C. F. 1960. The origin of speech. *Sci. Amer.* 203(3):89–96.

HOVANITZ, W. 1941. Parallel ecogenotypical color variation in butterflies. *Ecology* 22:259–284.

HOWELL, A. H. 1906. Revision of the skunks of the genus *Spilogale*. *N. Amer. Fauna* 26:1–55.

HOWELLS, W. W. 1959. *Mankind in the making.** Doubleday, Garden City, N.Y. 382 pp.

HOWELLS, W. W. 1966. *Homo erectus*. *Sci. Amer.* 215(5):46–53.

HURLEY, P. M. 1949. Radioactivity and time. *Sci. Amer.* 181(2):48–51.

JUSTER, N. 1961. *The phantom tollbooth*. Random House, New York. 256 pp.

KEAST, A. 1961. Bird speciation on the Australian continent. *Bull. Mus. Comp. Zool. (Harvard U.)* 123:305–495.

KEETON, W. T. 1967. *Biological science*. Norton, New York. 955 pp.

KETTLEWELL, H. B. D. 1959. Darwin's missing evidence. *Sci. Amer.* 200(3):48–53.

KETTLEWELL, H. B. D. 1961. The phenomenon of industrial melanism in Lepidoptera. *Ann. Rev. Entom.* 1961:245–262.

KIHARA, H. 1940. Verwandtschaft der *Aegilops*-Arten im Lichte der Genomanalyse. Ein Uberlick. *Der Zuchter* 12:49–62.

KROGMAN, W. M. 1951. The scars of human evolution. *Sci. Amer.* 186(6):54–57.

KURTEN, B. 1969. Continental drift and evolution. *Sci. Amer.* 220(3):54–63.

LACK, D. L. 1947. *Darwin's finches.** Cambridge University Press, London.

LACK, D. L. 1953. Darwin's finches. *Sci. Amer.* 188(4):66–72.

LACK, D. L. 1961. *Evolutionary theory and Christian belief*. Rev. ed. Methuen, London. 141 pp.

LEDERBERG, J., and E. M. 1952. Replica plating and indirect selection of bacterial mutants. *J. Bacter.* 63:399–406.

LEIGH, E. G., Jr. 1971. *Adaptation and diversity.** Freeman, Cooper, San Francisco. 288 pp.

LERNER, I. M. 1968. *Heredity, evolution and society.** Freeman, San Francisco. 307 pp.

LEWONTIN, R. C. 1961. Evolution and the theory of games. *J. Theor. Biol.* 1:382–403.

LEWONTIN, R. C. 1970. The units of selection. *Ann. Rev. Ecol. and Systematics* 1:1–18.

LEWONTIN, R. C., and L. DUNN. 1960. The evolutionary dynamics of a polymorphism in the house mouse. *Genetics* 45:705–722.

LOTKA, A. J. 1925. *Principles of physical biology*. Dover, New York.

LURIA, S. E., and M. DELBRUCK. 1943. Mutation of bacteria from virus sensitivity to virus resistance. *Genetics* 28:491–511.

MacARTHUR, R. H. 1972. *Ecological biogeography.** Harper & Row, New York.

MacARTHUR, R. H., and J. H. CONNELL. 1966. *The biology of populations.** Wiley, New York. 200 pp.

MAJOR, R. H. 1955. *Physical diagnosis*. Saunders, Philadelphia.

MANGELSDORF, P. C. 1953. Wheat. *Sci. Amer.* 189(1):50–59.

MAYR, E. 1954. Change of genetic environment and evolution. Pp. 157–180. In *Evolution as a process*. Allen and Unwin, London. 367 pp.

MAYR, E. 1963. *Animal species and evolution*. Belknap Press of Harvard University Press, Cambridge, Mass. 797 pp.

McDANIEL, R. G., and I. V. SARKISSIAN. 1968. Mitochondrial heterosis in maize. *Genetics* 59:465–475.

McFADDEN, E. S., and E. R. SEARS. 1946. The origin of *Triticum spelta* and its free-threshing hexaploid relatives. *J. Hered.* 37:81–89, 107–116.

MEDAWAR, P. B. 1959. *The future of man.** Basic Books, New York.

MEDAWAR, P. B. 1965. Do advances in medicine lead to genetic deterioration? *Mayo Clinic Pr.* 40:23–33.

MEDAWAR, P. B. 1967. *The art of the soluble.** Methuen, London. 160 pp.

MILKMAN, R. D. 1967. Heterosis as a major cause of heterozygosity in nature. *Genetics* 55:493–495.

MILLOT, J. 1955. The coelacanth. *Sci. Amer.* 193(6):34–39.

MONTAGU, M. F. A. 1960. *An introduction to physical anthropology.* 3rd ed. Thomas, Springfield, Ill. 771 pp.

MORCH, E. T. 1941. Chondrodystrophic dwarfs in Denmark. *Operat ex Domo Biologiae Hereditariae Humanae* 3:1–200. Munksgaard, Copenhagen.

NAPIER, J. 1962. The evolution of the hand. *Sci. Amer.* 207(6):56–62.

NAPIER, J. 1967. The antiquity of human walking. *Sci. Amer.* 216(4):56–66.

NEWELL, N. D. 1963. Crises in the history of life. *Sci. Amer.* 208(2):76–92.

NEWELL, N. D. 1972. The evolution of reefs. *Sci. Amer.* 226(6):54–65.

OSBORN, H. F. 1918. Equidae of the Oligocene, Miocene, and Pliocene of North America. *Mem. Amer. Mus. Natur. Hist.* (n.s.) 2:1–217.

PFEIFFER, J. E. 1969. *The emergence of man.** Harper & Row, New York. 447 pp.

PILBEAM, D. R. 1970. *The evolution of man.** Funk & Wagnalls, New York. 216 pp.

PIMENTEL, D.; W. P. NAGEL; and J. L. MADDEN. 1963. Space-time structure of the environment and the survival of parasite-host systems. *Amer. Natur.* 97:141–167.

RANSON, S. L., and M. THOMAS. 1960. Crassulacean acid metabolism. *Ann. Rev. Plant. Physiol.* 11:81–110.

RAPOPORT, E. H. 1969. Gloger's rule and pigmentation of Collembola. *Evolution* 23:622–626.

RICHARDS, H. G. 1953. *Record of the rocks.* Ronald, New York. 413 pp.

ROBINSON, A. E. 1954. *Basketweavers of Arizona.* University of New Mexico Press, Albuquerque.

ROMER, A. S. 1959. *The vertebrate story.** 4th ed. University of Chicago Press, Chicago. 437 pp.

ROSENZWEIG, M. L. 1966. Community structure in sympatric carnivora. *J. Mamm.* 47:602–612.

ROSENZWEIG, M. L. 1968. Strategy of body size in mammalian carnivores. *Amer. Midl. Natur.* 80:299–315.

ROSENZWEIG, M. L. 1973. Evolution of the predator isocline. *Evolution* 27:84–94.

ROSENZWEIG, M. L., and R. H. MacARTHUR. 1963. Graphical representation and stability conditions of predator-prey interactions. *Amer. Natur.* 97:209–223.

ROSS, H. H. 1962. *A synthesis of evolutionary theory.* Prentice-Hall, Englewood Cliffs, N.J. 387 pp.

ROTHSCHILD, M. 1965. Fleas. *Sci. Amer.* 213(6):44–53.

SAHLINS, M. D. 1960. The origin of society. *Sci. Amer.* 203(3):76–87.

SARICH, V. M. 1968. The origin of the hominids: an immunological approach. Pp. 94–121. In S. L. Washburn and P. C. Jay, eds., *Perspectives on human evolution, 1.* Holt, Rinehart & Winston, New York. 287 pp.

SARKISSIAN, I. V., and H. K. SRIVASTAVA. 1969. High efficiency, heterosis, and homeostasis in mitochondria of wheat. *Pr. Nat. Acad. Sci. (U.S.A.)* 63:302–309.

SCHMIDT-NEILSEN, K. 1964. *Desert animals.* Clarendon, Oxford.

SCHMIDT-NEILSEN, K. and B. 1953. The desert rat. *Sci. Amer.* 189(1):73–78.

SCHOLANDER, P. F. 1955. Evolution of climatic adaptation in homeotherms. *Evolution* 9:15–26.

SCHULTZ, A. H. 1944. Age changes and variability in gibbons. *Amer. J. Phys. Anthrop.* (n.s.) 2:1–129.

SCHULTZ, A. H. 1969. *The life of primates.* Universe Books, New York. 281 pp.

SCHULTZ, A. M. 1964. The nutrient-recovery hypothesis for arctic microtine cycles. II. Ecosystem variables in relation to arctic microtine cycles. Pp. 57–68. In D. J. Crisp, ed., *Grazing in terrestrial and marine environments.* Blackwell, Oxford. 322 pp.

SCOTT, W. B. 1937. *A history of land mammals in the western hemisphere.* 2nd ed. Macmillan, New York. 786 pp.

SEILACHER, A. 1967. Fossil behavior. *Sci. Amer.* 217(2):72–80.

SIEGEL, S. M.; K. ROBERTS; H. NATHAN; and O. DALY. 1967. Living relative of the microfossil *Kakabekia. Science* 156:1231–1234.

SIMONS, E. L. 1964. The early relatives of man. *Sci. Amer.* 211(1):50–62.

SIMONS, E. L. 1967. The earliest apes. *Sci. Amer.* 217(6):28–35.

SIMONS, E. L. 1972. *Primate evolution.* Macmillan, New York. 322 pp.

SIMPSON, G. G. 1950. History of the fauna of Latin America. *Amer. Sci.* 38:361–389.

SIMPSON, G. G. 1951. *Horses.** Oxford University Press, New York. 247 pp.

SIMPSON, G. G. 1953. *The major features of evolution.** Columbia University Press, New York. 434 pp.

SIMPSON, G. G., and W. S. BECK. 1965. *Life: an introduction to biology.* 2nd ed. Harcourt, New York. 869 pp.

SINNOTT, E. W., and L. C. DUNN. 1925. *Principles of genetics.* McGraw-Hill, New York. 431 pp.

SINNOTT, E. W.; L. C. DUNN; and T. DOBZHANSKY. 1958. *Principles of genetics.* 5th ed. McGraw-Hill, New York. 459 pp.

SMITH, H. W. 1953. *From fish to philosopher.** Little, Brown, Boston, Mass. 264 pp.

SMITH, R. L. 1966. *Ecology and field biology.* Harper & Row, New York. 686 pp.

SONNEBORN, T. M. 1950. Partner of the genes. *Sci. Amer.* 183(5):30–39.

SONNEBORN, T. M. 1963. Does preformed cell structure play an essential role in cell heredity? Chapter 7. In J. M. Allen, ed., *The nature of biological diversity.* McGraw-Hill, New York.

SPENCER, H. 1897. *The principles of biology.* Appleton, New York.

STEBBINS, G. L. 1966. *Processes of organic evolution.** Prentice-Hall, Englewood Cliffs, N.J. 191 pp.

STIRTON, R. A. 1941. Phylogeny of North American Equidae. *Univ. Calif. Publ., Bull. Dept. Geol. Sci.* 25:165–198.

TRIVERS, R. L. 1971. The evolution of reciprocal altruism. *Quart. Rev. Biol.* 46:35–57.

VOGEL, F., and M. R. CHAKRAVARTII. 1966. ABO blood groups and smallpox in a rural population of West Bengal and Bihar (India). *Humangenetik* 3:166–180.

VOLPE, E. P. 1967. *Understanding evolution.** Brown, Dubuque, Iowa. 160 pp.

VOLTERRA, V. 1926. Variazione e fluttuazioni del numero d'individui in specie animali conviventi. Mem. Accad. Naz. Lincei. 2:31–113. *Partly translated in* Chapman, R. N. 1931. *Animal ecology.* McGraw-Hill, New York.

VON KOENIGSWALD, G. H. R. 1958. L'hominisation de l'appareil masticateur et les modifications du regime alimentaire. English translation in W. W. Howells, ed., *Ideas on human evolution.* Harvard University Press, Cambridge, Mass.; and Atheneum, New York.

VOUTE, A. D. 1946. Regulation of the density of the insect populations in virgin forests and cultivated woods. *Arch. Neerl. Zool.* 7:435–470.

WADDINGTON, C. H. 1957. *The strategy of the genes.** Allen and Unwin, London. 262 pp.

WADE, N. 1969. Two genetic detective stories. P. B-3. *Washington Post,* Sunday, 8 June. Washington, D.C.

WALLACE, A. R. 1859. On the tendency of varieties to depart indefinitely from the original type. *J. Proc. Linnean Soc. (London)* 3:53–62.

WALLACE, B. 1968. *Topics in population genetics.* Norton, New York. 481 pp.

WASHBURN, S. L. 1960. Tools and human evolution. *Sci. Amer.* 203(3):63–75.

WEBB, S. D. 1969. Extinction-origination equilibria in late Cenozoic land mammals of North America. *Evolution* 23:688–702.

WECKER, S. C. 1964. Habitat selection. *Sci. Amer.* 211(4):109–116.

WICKLER, W. 1968. *Mimicry in plants and animals.** McGraw-Hill, New York.

WILLIAMS, C. M. 1970. Hormonal interactions between plants and animals. Pp. 103–132. In E. Sondheimer and J. B. Simeone, eds., *Chemical ecology.* Academic, New York. 336 pp.

WILLIAMS, G. C. 1966. *Adaptation and natural selection.** Princeton University Press, Princeton, N.J. 307 pp.

WILLS, C. 1970. Genetic load. *Sci. Amer.* 222(3):98–107.

WORTMAN, J. L. 1896. Species of *Hyracotherium.* . . . *Bull. Amer. Mus. Natur. Hist.* 8:81–110.

WRIGHT, S. 1931. Evolution in Mendelian populations. *Genetics* 16:96–159.

WYNNE-EDWARDS, V. C. 1962. *Animal dispersion in relation to social behavior.** Oliver & Boyd, Edinburgh. 653 pp.

WYNNE-EDWARDS, V. C. 1964. Population control in animals. *Sci. Amer.* 211(2): 68–74.

V

BLAKE, J. 1969. Population policy for Americans: Is the government being misled? *Science* 164:522–529.

BROWN, H. 1971. Scenario for an American renaissance. *Saturday Review* 54(52): 18–19.

DARWIN, C. 1958. *The problems of world population.** Cambridge University Press, London. 42 pp.

HARDIN, G. 1968. The tragedy of the commons. *Science* 162:1243–1248.

answers to problems

11-5. If A is 10%, I eliminates V. If A is 70%, V eliminates I.

11-6. About 111 males will sound like pickerel frogs and 889 like normal green frogs.

12-1. All will be black.

12-2a. All will be flat.

12-2b. Half will be flat; half, round.

12-3. Half will be white; half, roan.

12-4a. Half will be pink; one-quarter, white; one-quarter, red.

12-4b. Half will be red; half, pink.

12-4c. Half will be white; half, pink.

12-4d. All will be pink.

12-5. Two-thirds.

13-1. $+ = 0.311$; $vg = 0.689$

13-2. $F = 0.235$; $f = 0.765$

13-3a. 40

13-3b. 0.300

13-4a. 0.800

13-4b. 350

13-5a. $(1 - \sqrt{.96})$

13-5b. $2\sqrt{.96}\,(1 - \sqrt{.96}) \cong 0.039$

13-6. $(1 - \sqrt{.185}) = 0.570$

13-7a. Tasters

13-7b. 0.49

13-8. About 11.1%

13-9. 1.97

13-10. 0.273

13-11. 1-egg phenotype is 0.416; 2-egg, 0.75; 3-egg, 1.00; 4-egg, 1.00.

13-12a. Absolute fitnesses: *MX*, 2.27; *ST*, 2.25; *CH*, 1.00

13-12b. Relative fitness: *MX*, 1.00; *ST*, 0.99; *CH*, 0.44

13-13. Resistant, 1.50; Heterozygote, 1.00; Nonresistant, 0.133. Nonresistant will disappear.

13-14a. $\Delta p = +0.138$; should have been $+0.083$; Discrepancy probably due to random sampling accidents because population is so small (see "Genetic Drift," Chapter 15).

13-14b. $+0.11$; -0.000043.

13-14c. Both *ST* and *CH* should remain in a large enough population. But the equilibrium of *CH* is only about 0.02.

13-15a. The *s*-allele should disappear.

13-15b. $+0.119$

13-15c. Before, 0.873; after, 0.976; $\Delta F = +0.103$

13-16. 0.242; ebony disappears; 1.00; 0.97

14-1a. 14.5; 145

14-1b. 11.6 per 100,000

14-2. 1000; 2.5 billion babies must be born before one can be expected to have the genotype *RR*.

14-3. 15 per 100,000

14-4a. -11 per million

14-4b. 0.00332

14-4c. 0.00661 (that is, 66 people per 10,000, or one person in 151)

index

Adaptive evolution, 179, 200
Aegyptopithecus, 107, 110
Age of marriage, 65
Age structure, 36
Agricultural revolution, 72, 73, 107. *See also* Green revolution
Ahmed, A. A., 51
Albinism, 185
Albumins, 110, 111
Algae, 11, 16, 17
Allele frequency, 151
Alleles, 137
    selectively neutral, 147
Allelopathy, 14, 15
Allen, D. L., 11
Allen's rule, 238
Allison, A. C., 163, 165
Allopolyploidy, 251–254
Altruism, evolution of, 230–232
Anemones, 17
Aneuploid, 143
Antibiosis, 14, 15
Antibodies as indicators of kinship, 110, 111
Apes
    differences from men, 102–105
    similarities to men, 103, 110–112
Aplin, R. T., 228
Archaeopteryx, 93
Artificial selection, 183
Aswan high dam, 50, 51
Atomic disaster, evolution afterwards, 189, 190

Australopithecus, 112–117
Autopolyploidy, 251, 254
Average fitness, change because of natural selection, 171–173
Averages, 171, 172

Baby battering, 57
Bajema, C. T., 147
Balance of nature. *See* Steady state
Balanced polymorphism. *See* Heterosis
Barberry, 24
Barghoorn, E. S., 96
Barley, 234
Barnacles, 12, 15, 16, 18, 19
Bass, 33
Bateman, G., 192–194
Bates, H. W., 213
Baysal, A., 47
Bengoa, J. M., 48, 75
Berg, A., 47
Bergmann's rule, 131, 238
Bigamy, 271
Bighorn sheep, 34
Bilharziasis, 50, 51
Biological control, 18, 51, 226–228
Biospecies, 243, 244
Bipedalism, 103
Birth control
    in China, 65, 66
    in Japan, 70
    need for free supply, 274
Birth limitation in spaceships, 8
Birth rates, 28, 30

Birth rates *(Continued)*
  resources and, 24
  response to population density, 25
  significance of current U.S., 267
Blair, W. F., 176
Blake, J., 267
Blood types, 147
Boffey, P. M., 60
Borgstrom, G., 49, 50, 52, 53, 59, 60, 72, 73
Botswana, malnutrition in, 48
Boulding, K. E., 71
Brachiopod, 94
Brain size. *See* Cranial capacity
Brinton, C. C., 64
British Thermal Unit, 5
Bronfenbrenner, M., 68
Bronowski, J., 132
Broom, R. B., 113
Brower, J. van Z., 213
Brower, L. P., 214
Brown, H., 263
Brown, L. R., 49
Bryce-Smith, D., 56
Buffalo, 16
Butterflies, 30, 31, 137, 213–215
  coevolution, 228, 229
  parallel evolution, 238–241

Cacti, 204, 207, 208
Calcutta mandible, 109
Calories, 4
Camelina, 215, 216
Camouflage, 121–124, 133
Canids, foods of, 256
Canine teeth, 107
Cannabalism, 19, 20, 70, 114
Carnivorous plants, 209–211
Cats, 257
Caughley, G., 18
Chile, infant mortality, 48
Chipmunks, 25
Chisolm, J. J., 55
Chondrodystrophy, 197, 198
Chou En-Lai, 65
Chow, T. J., 55, 56
Chromosomes, 138
  inversion, 167
  patterns of replication, 139–143
Cistrons, 136
Classification, reasons for, 244
Clines, 234, 235, 238–240
Coccyx, 146
Coelacanths, 95
Coevolution, 228, 229

Communist doctrine
  overpopulation and, 66, 67
Competition, 15–18
Competitive exclusion, 16, 254
  avoidance of, 255–257
Connell, J. H., 12, 16, 18, 19
Convergence, 202–212, 259, 260
Cook, L. M., 214
Cooper, C. F., 148
Cotton, 253
Craig, P. P., 56
Cranial capacity, 113–117
Crassulacean acid metabolism, 207
Cravioto, J., 44, 45, 46
Creation, story of, 124, 125
Crime and population size, 58
Crinoid, 94
Crossveinlessness, 192–194
Crowcroft, P., 20, 21

Dart, R. A., 112, 113
Darwin, C., 79, 91, 126, 129, 135, 145, 146, 150, 162, 171, 230, 243
Darwin, E., 145
Darwin's finches, 249, 250
Dasmann, R. F., 51
Death rates, 28, 30
  effect of economic sanctions on, 269, 270
  maternal, 74
  resources and, 24
  response to population density, 25
Deer, 16, 18, 21, 33, 34, 63
del Moral, R., 15
Delta *p*, 154–157
Dethier, V. G., 30
Deuterium, 6
Diploid, 143
Disease
  exacerbation by malnutrition, 46, 47
  lead pollution and, 62
  pesticides and, 61, 62
  population density and, 24, 58, 59, 61
Disease virulence, evolution of, 49, 225–228
Dlamini, V. M., 48
Dobzhansky, T., 166–168, 176
Dominance, 137, 138
Droppers, G., 69, 70
Drosophila, 166–168, 185–190, 192, 193, 198
Dryopithecus Y-5 molar, 107, 108
Dryopithecine fossils, 103, 107–110
DuBois, E., 113
Ducks, resistance to disease when subjected to pesticides, 61, 62

Dumont, R., 44
Dwarfism, 197

Ecogeographical rules, 131, 238, 240
Ecogeographical variation, 234–242
Ecological vicars, 260
Economic sanctions, 268–270
Efficiency, 7, 54, 168–171
Egypt
  Aswan dam, 50, 51
  infant mortality, 76
  malnutrition in, 48
Ehrlich, P. R., 228, 229
Eichenwald, H. F., 47
Einarsen, A. S., 33
Einstein, A., 132
Eisenberg, R. M., 10, 29, 30
Elton, C., 32
Energy, 4–7, 9, 54, 168
Energy-rich molecules, 5
Engels, F., 66
England, decline in infant mortality, 75
Environmental rights, 79, 81, 275, 276
Eohippus, 119–120
Equilibrium, 28–30. See also Steady state
  of alleles influenced only by muta-
    tion, 195
  of gene pools, 159, 161
  between mutation and natural selec-
    tion, 196
  unstable, 159
Erythroblastosis foetalis, 159–161
Ethiopia, malnutrition in, 48
Eugenics, 87, 88, 272
Euphorbia, 207, 208
Europe at steady state, 70, 71
Eutrophication, 11, 52
Evolution, 92, 93
  adaptiveness of, 217
  of altruism, 230–232
  of antibiotic-resistant bacteria, 124,
    181–184
  of beauty, 243
  of cheating, 231
  of disease virulence, 49, 225–228
  of family size, 266
  of friendship, 231
  by genetic drift, 201, 218
  of gossip, 231
  by group selection, 218–221, 224, 225
  of horse teeth, 117–120
  of human tools, 106
  of insect resistance to pesticides, 124,
    176
  by kin selection, 230
  Lamarckian, 180, 181, 191
  of mating preference, 242, 243
  by natural selection, 128
  observed today, 120–124
  predictability of, 202–217
  of prudence, 221–228
  of race, 238–242
  by random mutation, 194, 195
  rate of, 115, 117–120
  relationship to overpopulation, 88, 89
  religion and, 82, 124, 125
  of skin color, 238–242
  by sperm selection, 218–220
Exploitation, 18, 24, 130, 131
  evolution of, 222–228
  as a limit to victim population, 18,
    19, 225–228
Extinction, 218, 219, 255, 258, 260–262

Family size
  inheritance of, 148, 149, 266, 267
  preferred, 267
Famine. See also Starvation
  in Ireland, 71, 72
  in Japan, 69, 70
  in New Mexico, 61
Fecundity. See Birth rates
Fenner, F. J., 226–228
Fern, 94
Fertility. See Birth rates
Fertilizer, 10, 49, 52
  effect on human population, 73
  world supply and distribution, 50
First law of thermodynamics, 3, 7
Fisher, J., 54
Fisher, R. A., 148–150, 178, 179
Fitness, 127
  absolute, 127
  change in average, 171–175
  of chondrodystrophic dwarfs, 197
  effect of change in environment on,
    148, 149
  heritability of, 147–149
  an individualistic trait, 221
  of moths, 122
  relative, 127, 128
  of various blood types, 147
Fitness relationships of two alleles, 157–
  162
Flaherty, D. L., 51
Flatworms, 9, 248, 249, 253
Florey, W., 181
Flour beetles, 20
Flycatchers, 12, 13
Food chains, ecological, 6, 7, 54
Foramen magnum, 103, 113

Ford, E. B., 137
Fossil fuels, 5, 6
Fossils, 92–96
    dating, 97, 98
    Dryopithecine, 103, 107–110
    names of, 117
Founder principle, 201
Free energy, 7
Freedom
    effect of overpopulation on, 85, 86
    of population density, 79, 81
Friend, M. O., 61, 62
Fremlin, J. H., 7
Fundamental theorem of natural selec-
    tion, 179
Fusion. See Heavy water

Gashwiler, J. S., 23, 24
Gasoline. See also Fossil fuels; Lead
    pollution
    as source of lead pollution, 55
Gause, G. F., 130
Geckos, 12
Gene frequency. See Allele frequency
Gene pool, 150
Gene replication patterns, 139–143
Genes, 136
    location of, 138
    locus, 143, 151
Genesis, 83–85, 124, 125
Genetic assimilation of acquired char-
    acteristics, 189, 191–194
Genetic drift, 201, 202, 218, 219
Genetics, evolution and, 135
Genius and population size, 46
Genotype, 141
Geological time, 99–101, 260
Gibb, J., 26
Gibbon, E., 70
Giddings, J. C., 7
Gilpin, M., 32
Glading's gallinaceous guzzler, 11
Glass, H. B., 201
Goldsmith, J. R., 56
Graf, A. B., 208
Green revolution, 49, 50, 168. See also
    Agricultural revolution
Gregory, W. K., 108
Group selection, 218–221, 224, 225
    requirement for strength, 220
    weakness of, 221
Grouse, 10, 11, 222

Haartman, L. von, 12, 13
Habitat specialization, 255
Habte, D., 48

Haldane, J. B. S., 150
Half-life of a radioactive isotope, 97
Hall, E. R., 236, 237
Haploid, 143
Hardin, G., 8, 265
Hardy, W., 164
Hardy-Weinberg distribution, 152, 153
Harmful alleles, fate of, 196
Hasler, A. D., 11
Heat pollution, 7
Heavy water, 6, 7. See also Deuterium
Hemophilia, 176
Hemphill, F. E., 62
Hensley, M. M., 13
Heraclitus, 262
Heritability, 126
Heterosis, 161–171, 175
Heterozygote, 137
    inferiority, 158, 174
    intermediacy, 157, 158, 173
    superiority, 161–171, 175, 186
Heydayat, H., 47
Hohokam civilization, 71
Hominidae, 102
Homo erectus, 114, 115
Homozygote, 137
Horowitz, A., 48
Horses, 117–120
Horseweed, 14, 28
Hovanitz, 238–241
Howell, A. H., 236, 237
Howells, W. W., 113
Huang, Y. C., 65
Human evolution, 98, 102–117, 241, 242
Huntington, E., 71
Huxley, T. H., 265
Hybrid vigor, 168–171, 186
Hylobatidae, 110
Hypotheses, 129

Immigration rate, effect on number of
    species, 261, 262
Impossibilities, 4, 85
India, malnutrition in, 47
Industrial melanism, 120–124
Industrial revolution, 72
Infanticide, 70
Inheritance
    of acquired characteristics, 180
    blood and, 136
Intengan, C., 47
Intelligence and nutrition, 44–46
Interaction of symptoms of overpopula-
    tion, 60–62
Iran, malnutrition in, 47
Iraq, infant mortality, 76

Ireland, potato famine, 71, 72
Israel
  decline in infant mortality, 76
  population trends, 71

Japan
  decline in infant mortality, 75
  density, 60
  recent growth of population, 37, 38
  at steady state, 68–70
Jennings, H. S., 180
Job, 84
Jonah, 83
Jordan
  infant mortality, 76
  malnutrition in, 48
  population trends, 71
Jerboa, 207, 209
Juvabione, 217

Kaibab deer, 18
Kaibab squirrel, 245
Kakabekia, 96
Kangaroo rat, 207, 209
Keast, A., 246, 248
Kessler, A., 21
Kettlewell, H. B. D., 121–124, 176
Kevany, J., 46
Keyfitz, N., 38–39
Kihara, H., 254
Kin selection, 230, 232
Kingfishers, 246, 247
Kirtland's warbler, 148
Klein, D. R., 34
Kluijver, H. N., 13
Kozlovsky, D. G., 6
Kwashiorkor, 44, 47, 48

Lack, D. L., 23, 26, 27, 82, 176, 232, 249,
    250
Ladejinsky, W., 49
Lamarck, 180–182
Land. See Space
Langer, W. L., 70
Latin America, infant mortality in, 48
Lazarus, A. L., 55
Lazarus, E., 70, 71
Lead pollution, 55, 56
  and disease, 62
  rate of increase, 56
  toxicity, 55
Leakey, L. S. B., 109
Leakey, M., 113
Lederberg, J., 182
Lemmings, 11, 221, 222
Lerner, I. M., 147, 166, 183, 201

Lewontin, R. C., 167, 219, 220
Life span, nutrition and, 191
Light year, 7
Limpets, 16, 17
Lindemann, R., 6
Linnaeus, C., 235
Litopterns, 259
Lochrie, G., 48
Locus of a gene, 143
Lotka, A. J., 130
Luria, S. E., 182
Lynx population oscillations, 31, 32

MacArthur, R. H., 131
McDaniel, R. G., 168–171
Malaria, 165
Malawi, malnutrition in, 48
Malnutrition. See Nutritional shortage
Malta, decline in infant mortality, 76
Mao Tse-tung, 64
Marasmus, 44, 47, 48
Marsupials, 203–206
Marx, K., 66
Mating preferences, evolution of, 242,
    243
Mayr, E., 246, 248
Mechanisms of evolution, 128. See also
    Evolution
Medawar, P. B., 117
Medicine, role in population growth,
    73–76
Meek, R., 66
Meijer, M. J., 65
Meiosis, 142
  in polyploidy, 250–253
Mendel, G., 136, 139, 140
Mexico, infant mortality, 48
Mice, 20, 21, 25, 132, 133
  convergence of woodland forms, 209,
    210, 212
  group selection in, 218–220
  resistance to disease when injected
    with lead, 62
Milkman, R. D., 168
Miller, G. R., 10, 11, 222
Mills, G. A., 5
Mimicry
  aggressive, 215
  Batesian, 213–215
  of flax seeds, 215, 216
  of insect hormones by trees, 216, 217
  Mullerian, 215
Misomali, Y. H., 48
Missing link, 102, 113
Mites, 51
Mitosis, 142

Monte Carlo methods, 219
Morch, E. T., 197, 198
Mortality. *See also* Death rates
  infant, 47, 48, 72, 74–76
Moths, 120–124, 228, 229
Mowat, F., 43, 46
Multiple births, 277, 278
Muramatsu, M., 60
Mutation, 178
  beneficial, 186–190
  domination by natural selection, 196
  harmfulness of, 183–189
  as a mechanism of evolution, 179, 194, 195
  rates, 198, 199
  sublethal, 185, 186, 188
  to taillessness, 219
Muyanga, S. L. D., 48
Myxomatosis, 226–228

Napier, J., 105
Natality. *See* Birth rates
Natural selection, 128, 265
  effect on economic sanction method of population control, 270
  effect on voluntary method of population control, 266–268
  fundamental theorem of, 179
  on gene pools, 151–162
  group selection dominated by, 221
  of laboratory mice, 21
  life's fundamental property, 262
  mimicking Lamarckian evolution, 191–194
  raw material for, 178
Neanderthal man, 106, 116
Neoteny, 115, 116
Nest sites, 13
Newell, N. D., 101, 258
Noah, 83, 84
Nuclear fusion, 6
Number of fossil families, 258
Number of species, 255, 258, 260–262
Nutrition
  effect on intelligence, 44–46
  life span and, 191
  limiting effect, 9
Nutritional shortage, 43–48
  combatting, 49–52

Oiso, T., 74
Oliver, M., 112
Oscillations of population, 31, 32
Ostrich callouses, 191

Overpopulation, relationship to evolution, 88, 89

Paddock, W., 85
Pakistan, malnutrition in, 47
Palmblad, I. G., 27, 28
Paper pulp
  U.S.A. share, 59
  world distribution, 59
Parallelism, 202, 203
  in butterflies, 238–240
Paramecium, 180, 181
Park, T., 20
Particulate inheritance, 135–137
Patwardhan, V. N., 48
Percival, J., 254
Père David, 63
Perrins, C. M., 26
Perturbation, resistance of population size to, 29, 30, 31
Pesticides, 51, 54, 57
  and diseases, 61, 62
Petipa, T. S., 7
Pheasants, 33
Phenospecies, 243
Phenotypes, 92
  evolution and, 128
  indeterminacy, 189
Philippine Islands, malnutrition in, 46
Photosynthesis, 5
Phyletic evolution, 243
Pimentel, D., 223–226
Pineal body, 146
Piotrow, P. T., 65
Pithecanthropus, 113
Plasmodium, 165
Pleiotropy, 137
Ploidy, 143
Poisons. *See* Lead pollution; Toxins
Police costs and population size, 58
Pollution, 54–57. *See also* Lead pollution; Salt pollution
  moth evolution and, 121–124
Polyploidy, 143
  speciation by, 249–254
Population
  heat and, 7
  of China, 66
Population control, 87
  coercion, 268–270, 276
  by economic incentives, 268–270
  by legislated birth limitation 271–279
  by mass chemical techniques, 272–273
  multiple births and, 277, 278
  by natural limits, 9–21, 82–86

Population control (Continued)
 by voluntarism, 265–268
Population day, 278, 279
Population density
 and disease, 24
 effect on birth and death, 25
 freedom of, 79, 81
Population explosions, 32–34
Population growth, 8, 10
 causes, 72–76
 explosive, 33
 pollution increase and, 56, 57
Population regulation, 22
Population size
 genius and, 46
 police protection and, 58
 proposals for control, 87
Primroses, 253
Predation. See Exploitation
Prognathism, 102
Protein-calorie malnutrition, 44–48, 60
Prudence, evolution of, 221–228
Pueblo de las Humanas, 60, 61
Pupae, 20
Pyrrhocoris, 216

Quail, 11

Rabbits, 225–228
Race, 235–238, 241–243
Radioactive clocks, 97, 98
Rahman, M. H., 47
Ramapithecus, 109, 110
Random evolution, 179
Raphanobrassicus, 253
Rapoport's rule, 238
Rats, 20
Recessive, 138
Reciprocal altruism, 231, 232
Reindeer, 33, 34
Religion
 attitude toward nature, 83–85
 evolution and, 124, 125
 role in population control, 83
Replica plating, 182–184
Resource allocation, 255–257
Resources
 distribution of, 64
 effect on birth and death rates, 24
 recyclability, 7
Reynoldson, T. B., 9
Rh factor, 159–161
Richards, H. G., 101
Right to reproduce, 274
Robinson, A. E., 107
Roosevelt, T., 18

Rosales-Ronquillo, M., 165
Rosenzweig, M. L., 52, 131, 221, 256
Ross, H. H., 228
Rubus, 24

Sabertooths, 204, 206
Salt pollution, 50, 52, 71
Sarich, V. M., 110, 111
Sarkissian, I. V., 168–171
Sauvy, A., 65, 73, 74
Scale insects, 177
Scheffer, V. B., 33
Schistosomiasis. See Bilharziasis
Scholander, P. F., 131
Schultz, A. H., 105, 117
Schultz, A. M., 222
Science and ethics, 88
Second law of thermodynamics, 3, 6,
 54, 56
Selective neutrality, 146, 147
Selye, H., 20
Semiti, G. A., 48
Senecio, 228, 229
Serendipity, 132
Sereni, E., 76
Sewage, 54
Shetrone, H. C., 71
Sickle-cell anemia, 162–166, 175
Siegel, S. M., 96
Simons, E. L., 101, 107, 109, 117
Simpson, G. G., 117, 260
Skunks, 235–237
Slama, K., 216, 217
Slobodkin, L. B., 33
Smith, H. W., 124
Snails, 10, 18, 19, 29, 30, 50, 249
Snow, E., 66
Sonneborn, T. M., 180
Southwick, C. H., 21
Space
 competition for, 17
 need per American, 59
 as a resource, 12
 shortage, 59, 60
 U.S.A. supply, 59
Space travel, 7, 8
 energy costs, 8
Specialization of species, 255–257
Speciation
 geographical, 244–249
 by polyploidy, 249–254
 rates of, 255, 258, 260, 262
Species, 243, 244
 number of, 255, 258, 260–262
Spencer, H. G., 130
Sperm selection, 218–220

Spruce budworms, 13, 228
Squirrels, 245, 246
Starvation, 43–48
Steady state, 22, 28, 29
    number of births per family needed
        for, 277
    in number of species, 258, 260–262
    of population size, 26, 34
    robustness, 28, 29, 31
Stebbins, G. L., 183, 253
Sterilization, 272–277
Sterling, C., 51
Stern, C., 138
Stewart, R. E., 13
Stimson, J., 16
Storks, 22, 23
Stress syndrome, 20, 57, 58
Subspecies, 234–237
Succession, 15
Sulfur dioxide, 55
Sunflowers, 14
Superspecies, 248, 249
Survival of the fittest, 128. See also
    Natural selection
Swaziland, malnutrition in, 48
Synapsis, role in polyploidy, 250

Tanzania, malnutrition in, 48
Tasmanian wolf, 204, 205
Taxonomist, 235
Tay-Sachs disease, 199
Technology, 3, 7
    effect of overpopulation on, 46
    green revolution and, 50
Teeth, as indicators of maturity, 109
Territoriality, 12, 13
Tetraploid, 143
Theories
    disproof, 129–131
    reasons for, 131, 132
    scientific, 129
Thermodynamics, laws of, 3, 6, 7, 54,
    56
Thickheads, 246
Thymus, 146
Tinbergen, N., 122
Tits, 13, 26, 27
Tools, 106
Toxins, 14, 15, 24. See also Lead pollu-
    tion
    improved resistance of heterozygotes
        to, 171

Transportation, 5
    requirement for as a function of pop-
        ulation, 57
    right of, 275
Tree creepers, 248
Trilobite, 94
Trivers, R. L., 231, 232
Turk, A., 50
Turkey, malnutrition in, 47
Twinflower, 24

United States
    consumption of fertilizer, 50
    supply of space, 59
Uganda, malnutrition in, 48

Vamoer, A. P., 48
Variability, maintenance of, 233, 239,
    241, 254–257. See also Balanced
    polymorphism; Equilibrium; Het-
    erosis
Variation, ecogeographical, 234, 242
Venezuela, infant mortality, 48
Vestigial organs, 146
Violets, 24
Volterra, V., 130
Voluntarism, 265
Voluntary compliance with law, 274

Waddington, C. H., 191–194
Wade, N., 185
Wallace, A. R., 145
Wallace, B., 166, 185–190
Wasps, parasitic, 223–226
Waste, 6
Water shortage, 11, 12, 52, 53
Watt, K. E. F., 57, 58, 61
Weasels, 235
Webb, G., 71
Webb, S. D., 260, 261
Weismann, A., 180
Wheat, 254
White, A., 208
Williams, C. D., 76
Williams, C. M., 216, 217
Williams, G. C., 221
Wilson, R. E., 14
Woodgerd, W., 34
Wright, S., 150, 157, 201
Wynne-Edwards, V. C., 10, 220, 221

X-rays, a cause of mutation, 185

Zambia, malnutrition in, 48

74 75 76 77 9 8 7 6 5 4 3 2 1